Political Systems

Some Sociological Approaches

Herbert Victor Wiseman

Routledge
Taylor & Francis Group

First published in 1966
by Routledge & Kegan Paul Ltd.

This edition first published in 2024 by Routledge
4 Park Square, Milton Park, Abingdon, Oxon, OX14 4RN

and by Routledge
605 Third Avenue, New York, NY 10017

Routledge is an imprint of the Taylor & Francis Group, an informa business

© H. V. Wiseman, 1966

Publisher's Note
The publisher has gone to great lengths to ensure the quality of this reprint but points
out that some imperfections in the original copies may be apparent.

Disclaimer
The publisher has made every effort to trace copyright holders and welcomes
correspondence from those they have been unable to contact.

A Library of Congress record exists under LCCN: 66070320

ISBN: 978-1-032-70030-4 (hbk)
ISBN: 978-1-032-70034-2 (ebk)
ISBN: 978-1-032-70033-5 (pbk)

Book DOI 10.4324/9781032700342

POLITICAL SYSTEMS

Some Sociological Approaches

by
H. V. WISEMAN

Professor of Government
University of Exeter

LONDON
Routledge & Kegan Paul

First published 1966
by Routledge and Kegan Paul Limited
Broadway House, 68–74 Carter Lane
London, E.C.4

Printed in Great Britain by
Blackie & Son, Ltd.
London and Glasgow

Political Systems

First published in 1966, *Political Systems* provides an examination of political systems through a sociological approach. This comprehensive survey summarizes the theories of many of the most eminent and influential political scientists- Gabriel Almond, David Easton, Edward Shils, Seymour M. Lipset, Harry M. Johnson, T.B. Bottomore, James S. Coleman, Leonard Binder, Robert K. Merton, David Apter, to name a few.

Beginning with the description of general concepts, Mr. Wiseman discusses political culture and the typologies of political systems; this is followed by a methodical examination of political systems, analyzed from a wide range of sociological aspects. An appraisal of political systems from the standpoint of economic and social development then leads to a final section devoted to a study of structural functional analysis. Authoritative, thorough, well documented and conveying complex theories with a clarity for which every reader will be grateful. This is a must read for students and scholars of political science, political sociology and sociology.

Contents

Contents

Preface

THIS book has one simple, basic, and unpretentious purpose: to provide an introduction to some sociological approaches to a study of political systems. Political sociology is becoming of increasing interest, whether as part of political science teaching or as part of general sociological teaching. Ample material is readily available and at reasonable prices on such problems as voting habits, pressure groups, political parties, bureaucracies and ideology. But when it is desired to fit these patterns of political behaviour into a broader and more generalised study of whole political systems, or of political sub-systems in the total social system or society, two difficulties arise.

Firstly, political scientists have, for the most part, not acquired the basic sociological theory; this is particularly true of undergraduates, though their senior guides and mentors are not always much more skilled in the appropriate discipline. The general sociologist is often not more helpful; even if his approach is useful to the political scientist he is not always interested in the patterns of political behaviour or the institutions of the political system. Secondly, the studies of political scientists or political sociologists in this field are not readily accessible to the average student. They are either contained in learned journals of which even the best-stocked libraries will possess only one copy, or in introductions to large and expensive books dealing with specific areas which are not included in particular courses but which must be purchased for the sake of a sixty- or seventy-page introduction at an almost prohibitive cost. The kinds of articles and introductions we have in mind are clearly indicated in the text.

We have, therefore, attempted to provide first, enough general sociological theory—admittedly, for the most part, of the structural-functional and pattern-variable analysis kind—

Preface

for undergraduate political scientists and to relate this specifically to the political system. We have also applied the general
notion of culture to the political system. Next, we examine a
number of approaches to a study of whole political systems
which are to a greater or less extent based on this kind of
sociological approach. Finally, although we have not attempted
a sophisticated critique of this approach, we have tried to
indicate some of its short-comings and to raise certain general
problems related to its application to political systems.

We have not attempted to sustain the claim that this is the
only way to examine political systems or to make comparisons
between them. We are certainly not convinced that this approach
must make possible the operationalisation of concepts and
theories and the quantification which some claim will lead to a
'real science' of politics—whatever that may mean. But we
have used the approach to obtain new insights into the working
of political systems and to make meaningful comparisons
between different systems which are not confined to a relatively
narrow group of systems bounded by geographical, historical,
cultural, or institutional similarities. More important, perhaps,
there is some evidence that our students have gained such
insights by looking afresh at political systems under the guid-
ance of this kind of sociological approach.

The book, therefore, aims to assist students who have already
studied a number of political systems to which, after mastering
the elementary and relatively unsophisticated conceptual and
theoretical approaches outlined, they may return for reappraisal
and reassessment. For graduate students, and even more for
our own colleagues in the field of political science, it is merely
a guide—or a goad!—to the literature to which only very
rough justice has been done in our own summary treatment.

One personal note must be added. Our own interest in this
approach developed only with the publication of Almond's and
Coleman's study of the *Politics of the Developing Areas*. We tried
to apply their scheme in an amateurish way for one session, and
then had the good fortune to spend a year in the United States.
Although we met few of the 'masters', and then only briefly, we
found that American political scientists in general had made
considerably more progress in the application of this kind of
sociological approach. In particular, we are grateful to a

colleague at Temple University, Philadelphia, Harry Hall, who guided us through his library of Talcott Parsons, R. K. Merton and others, and, above all, persuaded us to lunch more frequently with the sociologists than with the political scientists! The result, some two or three years later, is the present volume.

H. V. WISEMAN

Dept. of Government,
The University,
Exeter,
March, 1965.

I

Some General Concepts

THE purpose of this first chapter is to introduce political scientists who may have little knowledge of general sociology or of structural-functional analysis to some of the basic concepts which are necessary to a sociological approach to the study of political systems. Sociologists may find the analysis either simplified or superflous; they may however be interested in the application of this method specifically to political systems, since few general works of sociology devote much space to the political aspects of societies or to the political sub-system as a functional sub-system with particular if not completely special-ised structures for the performance of its functions. One further introductory explanation is necessary. This study is primarily concerned with total political systems, with macro-units; it does not deal with the literature on particular aspects of the political system which have been studied by political sociologists, such as parties, pressure groups, bureaucracies or voting habits; these are mentioned only in relation to the political system and its functions for society.

A sociological approach to a study of total political systems such as we are concerned with involves some acquaintance with the notion of social systems in general, of the total social system, or society, and of the total political system as a sub-system of society. We attempt to provide only the minimum account, at least of the first two concepts, for the full under-standing of which it is necessary to consult general works on sociology. However, since, as we have said, most of these deal very cursorily with the political system as such, the relevance of their general theories will be examined, however briefly, in such manner, hopefully, as to persuade political scientists that they can be used so as to offer insights into the political institutions and behaviour with which they are concerned.[1]

The term 'system' implies an orderly patterning in the parts of the system; i.e. a structure; the elements of the system must be specified. More exactly, 'social system' implies the existence of inter-related acts of people; 'structure' involves some degree of regularity or recurrence in these acts. Or we may express this as involving two or more persons engaged in a patterned or structured form of relationship or interaction, this pattern or structure being relatively permanent. More precisely still, Talcott Parsons describes a social system as a system of *processes of interaction* between *actors*: the *structure* of relations between actors as involved in an interactive process is the structure of the *social system*. The system is a *network of such relationships*: each actor is involved in a *plurality* of such interactive relationships, each with one or more partners in the complementary *role*. The participation of an *actor* in a patterned *interactive system* is the most significant *unit* of the social system. (Our italics.)

Social systems exist in complicated relationships to other social systems. This is true at any level, whether it be, for example, the relationships between a political system and an economic system or within the political system, a legislature and its committees, caucuses, and other sub-systems. The relationships involved may be formal (legislatures and officially appointed committees) or informal (legislatures and regional, ethnic or religious groups within the legislature). A role (which we define below) is always a role in a particular system and there are role-structures, again formal or informal, corresponding to each sub-system. The links between one system and another are through its members' other roles in another system. A minister may play a role in the executive, the legislature and the political party and will link all three sub-systems. There are, therefore, also role-structures corresponding to each overlapping or linked system. A civil servant may play different roles in the bureaucracy, in the linked system involving him and his political head, and in the linked system between him and the legislative members, The norms (which we also define below) governing his actions may be different in each case.

The participants in a social system, then, are the occupants of roles; in permanent groups these roles persist beyond their occupancy by any one person, and are therefore more stable than role-occupants. These permanent groups are organised as sub-groups within the larger system and some of them persist longer than the individuals who are members, for example parties in a political system, and as types for longer than any specific group e.g. types of famiies, or of executives or assemblies in a political system. There is thus some regularity, recurrence, and stability in social interaction. Moreover, a social system has certain boundaries which determine its members; it tends to establish an equilibrium or balance of the forces which tend either to integrate or disintegrate the system. (See further, Easton, below, pp. 221 ff.) Another way of expressing this is to say that a series of socially relevant actions is ordered into a series of sub-systems of social action; each sub-system is normally bounded and tends to maintain boundaries within which action relevant to the system occurs. Certain social institutions or 'recognised normative patterns' are the central points around which each of the boundary-maintaining action systems cluster. The constitution of the legally-established machinery of government may be such in a political system, though 'conventions' and, even more, informal usages may also help to determine recurrent patterns.

We have spoken of occupants or participants, but also of groups, which are congeries of roles. It must be emphasised that without intending in any way to personify or reify groups, we may speak of 'collectivities' as well as of individuals. Interaction is ordered about a system of roles, which, in turn, are organised into inter-related collectivities i.e. systems of interaction which involve a sense of solidarity on the part of members. In this sense we may regard collectivities as well as individuals as actors performing roles. In the political system we may thus speak of pressure groups, parties, the cabinet, and even 'the sense of the House as a whole' e.g. in the British House of Commons.

To turn from social systems in general to society, we must recognise this as a particular kind of social system, one which is comprehensive and differentiated enough to be self-sufficient with respect to the diverse functional needs of its members. A social system is a 'society' in so far as it meets the pre-requisites of 'long-term persistence' from within its own resources. This, of course, does not imply a crude economic self-sufficiency since exchange between societies is possible just as relations between political systems or states may exist without destroying their 'sovereignty' or independence.

We now examine the concept of *role* in more detail. Apter has defined a role as a functionally defined position in a social system. (For further details of Apter's approach, see below, pp. 117 ff.) It is socially conceived and while played by individuals is analytically separate from them. We may compare Almond's definition of role as that organised sector of an actor's orientation which constitutes and defines his participation in an interactive process.[4] (For further details of Almond's approach, see below, pp. 134ff.) Individuals play a variety of roles. All roles are institutionalised forms of behaviour. Rights are always associated with their performance, while action, in so far as it is structured through roles, becomes motivated by the expectations induced by the roles themselves. Another way of expressing this is to say that behaviour can be related to a position in a social structure. Actual behaviour can be related to the individual's own standards (his role cognitions—the way he 'sees' his role); to other people's ideas about what he will do (their expectations); or to other people's ideas about what he *should* do. The last two, of course, may influence the first. The action of an individual in any social setting responds to the expectations (here used generally to include all three of the above elements) peculiar to that setting. A set of norms and expectations will be applied to the incumbent of a particular position—Prime Minster, Member of Parliament (different from e.g. Congressman!), bureaucrat, party-militant, voter etc. in a political system.

The term *norm* implies obligations to other people. Norms exist between groups as well as between individuals. They may include legal prescriptions, regulations, and informal understandings. Johnson suggests that they may impose obligations, and be described as 'relational'; or they may be permissive and be called 'regulative'. It is frequently stated that action is guided by *norms* and *values*, without any attempt being made to distinguish between the two. This raises too sophisticated a problem to pursue in detail here. But we may say simply that

4

norms provide a relatively specific pattern of expected behaviour while values are more general guides to purposive behaviour. Values are derived from, or are part of 'culture', which is discussed below (pp. 21 ff).

Our own separation of social structure from culture does, in fact, beg another fundamental question. Can one, in fact, separate the two? We may say either that the social structure operates *within* a set of cultural values, and is influenced by them; or that it *includes* them. To us it seems more convenient to adopt the former approach, without, of course, ignoring inter-connections. An example of how they may be usefully considered separately may be taken from a discussion of stratification.[2] Briefly, it is argued that a people's stratification system is rooted in its *culture* and particularly in its 'culturally elaborated image of the "admirable man"'. But stratification is equally rooted in *social structure* in the sense of the 'nature of routinised relations, based upon mutual understandings and expectations about behaviour'. (Lloyd Fuller pursues the argument further by reference to *secondary culture* i.e. ideas and beliefs about stratification—about how and why persons are allocated among roles as they are, and about the justice or injustice of this process, as contrasted with the *primary* definitions of excellence; and *secondary structure* i.e. the structures and processes whereby persons are allocated among roles as distinguished from the *primary* differentiation of roles, or division of labour. loc. cit. p. 163.)

We return to this in our section on political culture. Meanwhile, the argument so far may be summed up. The general structure of a social system includes: (i) a number of subsystems or sub-groups each inter-connected by relational norms; (ii) roles of various types within either the larger system or the sub-systems; (iii) each role-system being connected with others by relational norms; (iv) regulative norms governing subsystems and roles, and (v) cultural values. More simply, any actual, i.e. empirical, social system consists of (i) individuals who are (ii) interacting with others on the basis of a minimal degree of complementary expectations by means of, and according to (iii) a shared system of beliefs, standards, and means of communication.[3]

II: FUNCTIONAL PROBLEMS OF SOCIAL SYSTEMS

Every social system has certain functional problems which must be met if the system is to persist. In this section we discuss generally the broad nature of these functional problems and make some reference to the part played by the political (sub-) system in their solution. We shall return later to a more detailed consideration of the latter. It is generally agreed among sociologists that every social system must deal with four functional problems; nor is there any significant difference between them as to the description of such problems. The problems are:

1. Pattern-maintenance and tension-management, or the maintenance of the value and normative system. Since many of the values and norms are latent rather than manifest, Hoselitz has called this the 'latency-function'.[4] Sutton uses the term 'expressive'.[5]
2. Adaptation.
3. Goal-attainment or goal-gratification, which Sutton calls 'instrumental'.
4. Integration.

It is, further, generally agreed that these four functional problems *tend* to be handled by four different sub-systems or sets of structures and processes, each sub-system becoming more differentiated as the social system becomes more complex, though this differentiation is never complete and there is no one-to-one relationship between structure and function, every structure being to a greater or lesser extent multi-functional. (For the extent to which this is alleged to lessen the validity of structural-functional analysis, see below, Chapter 7.) Nevertheless, each sub-system tends to become functionally specialised with respect to the solution or attempted solution of one of these sets of problems (and, within each sub-system certain structures tend to become functionally more specialised). It is agreed also that the social structure of every system does to some extent succeed in solving these problems or else the system ceases to exist. Action in conformity with a social norm or value makes some contribution to meeting the needs of the system. When conformity to any partial structure—sub-system, role, norm, value—makes such a contribution to the needs of the system it is said to have a *function* for the system. We now analyse the four functional problems in more detail.

Pattern-maintenance, the maintenance of cultural and normative patterns of interaction, and tension-management, are essential if the system is to persist. The values and norms of the system, 'standards' of behaviour in recurring situations, must be transmitted from generation to generation, and intern-alised, i.e. incorporated, in the personality systems of members, i.e. individuals who are born into the culture and who must learn their 'social heritage'. The units or actors, both individuals and collectivities, must learn and respect the patterns of behaviour and the norms and values behind them or embodied in them. These include political attitudes and behaviour. This is done by the mechanism of socialisation, including political socialisation, through family, school, and other institutions, and through the appropriate rituals, ceremonies, and other symbols.[6]

Adaptation to both the non-social and the social environment is necessary. For sub-systems, it should be noted, the environment consists largely of other sub-systems. For society it is, primarily, the economy which meets the need for adaptation, though, as we shall see, the polity or political system makes varying contributions to adaptation in different societies. The economy partly controls and partly adjusts to the environment. Every permanent social system has its division of labour and some degree of role-differentiation would appear to be essential. Broadly speaking, our concern with this problem will arise only in so far as the political system may be involved.

Goal-attainment is peculiarly the concern of the polity, and here the government, which is a part of the polity, may have a predominant though not an exclusive role. Goals can be achieved only by co-operative effort, and the struggle for power inherent in Hobbes's 'war of all against all' must be mitigated in the course of social interaction. The polity expresses the drive to power (or to the right to make authoritative decisions) and it is a field for its exercise. But it also regulates the struggle for power of both governors and governed. The polity also plays a part in the allocation of members to roles, which is important both for adaptation and for goal-gratification. These two, indeed, are often difficult to separate even analytically. While the economy produces goods and services for a wide variety of purposes, the polity mobilises goods and services for the attainment of the specific goods of the total society. (We enquire later in what way a 'society' may be said to have 'goals'.)

Mitchell[7] puts it thus: 'The mobilisation of societal resources for system goals centrally concerns the political action of society. The polity is the sub-system most involved in problems of goal-attainment.' Hoselitz (*op. cit.*) suggests that political institutions *mediate* goal-gratification activity. Decisions arrived at through such institutions, including governmental institutions, are generally regarded as binding.

Although Talcott Parsons has not applied his conceptual framework in detail to the political system, he has indicated his broad agreement with this association of the polity with goal-attainment. It is seen as providing generalised leadership for the larger social system in setting and attaining collective goals. This is acknowledged by interested social groups who supply generalised support in the expectation that their demands will be met satisfactorily. Within the polity a variety of social groups advocate the particular policies that eventually result in the specific decisions of public officers, which then become binding on all citizens. The competitive struggle within the elite, sometimes for generalised but usually for specific support, gives those outside the authority structure access to political power.[8]

Integration is concerned with the interaction of the units, the individuals and collectivities of the system, and the maintenance of solidarity and morale. Co-operative activities require a procedural consensus, an accepted pattern of decision-making, and a hierarchy of authority which possess legitimate power to give orders. It requires also regulative norms. There is need for social control and, if disputes arise, agreed social arrangements for meeting them. All patterns of social interaction which are institutionalised are, in a sense, integrative. But some partial structures are more clearly and more exclusively concerned with integration. Patterns of authority serve to co-ordinate or integrate the units of the system. We shall see later that Sutton (*op. cit.*) considers that the polity is of great significance in the effective performance of this function. Hoselitz (*op. cit.*) takes as a specific example of integration the determining of membership within a society as a whole (e.g. nationality and

8

immigration laws) and of the relationships between members and groups of members. This, he says, is critical on the level of nationhood, and especially in new nations. Such an approach is certainly useful in examining the reasons for the development of strong central government and of one-party systems in such nations. (That the polity or government is important but not decisive here is illustrated by the fact that integration of Negroes into the American system cannot be achieved by legal action alone but requires changes in norms of individuals and groups in their social relationships. On the other hand, in Britain the case is argued for some legislation on 'the colour problem', presumably in the hope that government action may help to produce the desired norms among those members who at present do not accept them.) Apter has pointed out the effects of economic growth and political modernisation in this respect; the need for integration may be increased just as its basis is being undermined by the development of a fragmented culture (between the 'modern' and 'traditional' sectors of society). We may also cite the linguistic problem in India, the centrifugal tendencies in Indonesia, regionalism in Nigeria, and tribalism in almost every new African state. In all such cases the role of the polity in integration may be decisive.

III: FUNCTIONAL SUB-SYSTEMS OF SOCIETY

In dealing with functional problems we have necessarily touched on functional sub-systems in passing. We must now pursue the problem of the latter in more detail. The structure of every social system can be analysed in relation to the four functional problems. If society is the system of reference, the sub-systems immediately subordinate are functional sub-systems of the society. Below this level there are, of course, sub-sub-systems or sub-groups and, as we shall see later, there are also the *structural* sub-systems of the society which cut across the *functional* sub-systems. In this section we shall be concerned primarily with the political (sub-) system.

For each of the four functional problems of society there is a corresponding sub-system. But we must recall the statement that there is no one-to-one relationship between structure (or sub-system) and function and that all structures (sub-systems)

9

are multi-functional. The four sub-systems under reference are *abstracted* or *analytical* concepts. The 'economy', for example, is not a definite number of concrete groups each of which is exclusively 'economic'. In some, if not all, societies, groups such as the family, the schools, the religious groups, the recreational groups, overlap both the adaptive and the pattern-maintenance systems—and even the goal-gratification and integrative systems. We have already mentioned various views concerning the functions of the polity, however specialised to goal-attainment it may be, Political parties straddle the boundaries between systems. Pressure groups have functions other than those which bring them into the political system. Governmental institutions have pattern-maintenance and tension-management, integrative, and adaptive as well as goal-attainment functions.

Nevertheless, each functional sub-system has special functions (crystallised out to varying degrees in different societies) in relation to one of the four functional problems. So far as goal-attainment is concerned, the polity, and within it the government, has primacy. Elections, where they occur, bring large numbers of people into 'societal goal-definition and attainment'. Various groups generate power for the attainment of system goals and help indirectly to attain them, as well as helping to define the goals themselves. Media of communication play a part in this process. Parties, legislatures, political executives, and bureaucracies are involved, and by the 'feedback' process influence electors, groups, and media of communication. If we apply Spiro's analysis of the political process[9] —the recognition of problems; the statement of issues; deliberation; the resolution of issues; and the solution of problems— a wide variety of individuals and groups participate in this process. But the greater part of such process occurs within the polity. The polity, to repeat Hoselitz's phrase, 'mediates goal-attainment'. Since the bulk of this book is concerned with the manner in which the political system performs this function we shall not pursue the argument further at this stage.

But we must refer again to the important point that each of the functional sub-systems of society can itself be analysed as a social system with its own system problems. For each sub-system the other sub-systems are the most significant part of the environment, and all have systematic exchanges with one another. We repeat that a functional sub-system of society is not composed of concrete groups but of all those aspects of the total social structure which have a bearing on the functional problem under reference. Each sub-system may itself be treated as a four-sector system, with four functional problems. Further, each institution or sub-sub-system within each of the four sub-systems may be analysed in the same way. Again, this will be pursued later in relation to the political system.

To return to the point that no one functional sub-system deals solely with one functional problem, we refer again to Hoselitz (*op. cit.*). Social actions whose predominant functions fall within one of the four sectors—as, for example, the social actions of such institutions as legislatures or bureaucracies—do not *all* fall within the goal-gratification section. They may have integrative, adaptive, and pattern-maintenance or tension-management functions for society—as well as their *own* needs or problems within each of these fields.

However, since the polity is generally regarded as having specialised functions in relation to goal-attainment, it is appropriate at this point to examine the arguments of Sutton(in La Palombara, *op. cit.*), who takes the view that the polity is pre-eminently concerned with the integrative function. He begins with consideration of a 'particular kind of representative agency' which arises from the fact that territorial relations have a special character and importance in societies: they are connected with the control of the use of force. Diverse social systems (below the level of the total system, or society) share a common location, and integrative problems are intimately linked to the fact of territoriality. A territorial grouping tends to become a collectivity and hence requires representative agencies.

There is a close link between representation on the one hand and stratification (on the significance of this see, further, Apter, below, pp. 117 ff), and authority on the other. Representative agencies must evoke sentiments which are related to the common valies of a corporate group and must symbolise these values in postive fashion. Individuals participating in the agencies must share in this high positive valuation. They must be drawn from those possessing a generalised high status in some form, or else the roles they fill must themselves have sufficient prestige to confer upon their incumbents high status. They must have the capacity to commit the collectivity to action if they are to be able to perform co-ordinated acts for the collectivity's general welfare. (It would appear from this that the integrative function of the 'representative agency' must be performed successfully as a *means* to action, i.e. the achievement of goal-gratification.) For all this, representative agencies must have a peculiarly high and not easily attainable kind of legitimacy.

These territorial representative agencies Sutton calls *Political Institutions*. If they are the core of political systems, 'the study of political systems becomes the study in the first instance of representative agencies over territories,' their structure and functioning. Sutton claims that Weber's distinctive feature of the State, its 'exclusive control over the legitimate use of force' is implied in this statement. Representative agencies become the ultimate agencies of social control. But most of the discussion of political institutions is more concerned with their character as representative agencies than with ultimate sanctions.

This emphasis on representation suggests that there is a special connection between political institutions and problems of social integration (one means of achieving which is social control). Sutton would not, presumably, disagree with the opinion that the integrative sub-system is the most diffuse of the four which we have discussed, nor that the legal profession, religious bodies, and, indeed, probably almost every group, help to perform the integrative function. But, while admitting that the existence and character of political institutions are intimately (perhaps ultimately) dependent on the general state of social integration, he would argue that they in turn serve very important (perhaps decisive) functions in maintaining that integration.

No society is perfectly integrated, and although any social system is built on conformity of its members to expectations, this conformity is not automatic. The process of socialisation is never completely successful—whether as regards a particular individual or group or as regards certain individuals or groups as such. Diverse functional problems and cultural residues (cf. below, Chap. 2.) prevent the structures from having perfect clarity, consistency, and effectiveness; delicate problems arise from the balancing and inter-meshing of solidary groups in the total society and strains are inevitably set-up.

Forms of symbolic participation, regular elections, and other political devices, reinforce the ideologies of the government as representatives of the people. Political institutions, whether associations built on elective offices or on bureaucratic hierarchies, come to depend on national sentiment rather than on the class status of the incumbents of political roles. The resistance of local particularisms is reduced or removed (and, possibly the appeal which neighbouring states may have for them). Political institutions, thus strengthened, become involved in integration in two ways. They serve as an agency for the control of individual deviance; they provide a means of control and co-ordination among the imperfectly integrated groups in the total social system. The magnitude of the integrative problems facing the government will depend on the degree of integration of the underlying social structure. This may also affect the *kind* of political system which will emerge (cf. below, Shils's analysis of different political systems, pp. 70 ff). It is almost otiose to refer to the new states of Africa in this context.

Social controls over 'deviant roles' may be maintained to a greater or lesser extent through various social structures, without the use of representative agencies. But important control functions are always performed by the political system. As the 'ultimate' agency for control it possesses especially effective control of mechanisms such as the police and the courts. Political institutions are of special importance in the 'total integration of all the tangle of social systems and processes encompassed within a society'. As representative agencies over a territory, political institutions serve as a 'common reference' point for all the social systems within the territory. As examples of problems that lie within the field of integration through the political system we may cite the existence of *immobilisme* in France, the uncertain reputation of parliamentary government in Germany, and the magnitude of the Communist vote in many countries outside the 'Iron Curtain' area, as well as the various problems of the developing countries.

Integration, as we observed earlier, is not an end in itself. Deviant behaviour may be related to effective goal-attainment, whether in the definition of goals or in the methods whereby their realisation is sought. The harmonisation of conflicting

13

interests and rival contenders for power may be studied under the broad heading of integration or the narrower one of goal-attainment. The examination of political systems throughout this study will not reveal any fundamental inconsistency between Sutton's analysis and that of others, but merely a difference of emphasis.

Meanwhile, we return to our analysis of function and structure and, having considered functional sub-systems, examine structural sub-systems.

IV: STRUCTURAL SUB-SYSTEMS OF SOCIETY

Whereas functional sub-systems are abstract or analytical concepts, structural sub-systems are made up of concrete groups. These, however, as we have noted, may overlap and operate in more than one functional sub-system. Modern developed societies have achieved a very considerable degree of structural differentiation of the various functional sub-systems, though even in them such differentiation is far from complete. In our detailed examination of 'the political system' we shall see that Almond, in particular, emphasises the multi-functionality of political structures in all systems. But, analytically, every society has the four functional sub-systems and if the functions are there the structures must be, although in traditional societies they may be almost entirely undifferentiated and operate only intermittently. One important enquiry to which this statement leads, in respect of any concrete society, concerns the kinds and degrees of structural differentiation and fusion which any given society has in relation to the four functional problems. Nor is this enquiry of interest only in respect of developing countries. There is, for example, a very considerable degree of fusion between the polity and the economy in totalitarian systems.

In some societies certain structures in other sub-sectors may perform some of the functions which in other societies are allocated to specialised institutions in the goal-attainment sector, the polity. For example, feudal institutions perform mainly integrative functions although they are also concerned with goal-attainment. In primitive societies the structures are even less differentiated, or more multi-functional. Within the polity itself there may be a greater or lesser degree of structural specialisation; for example, general governmental institutions may perform administrative or even judicial functions or political parties may perform some governmental functions. These observations support an approach to the analysis of the political system which is, it is suggested, more fruitful than one through the traditional 'separation of powers', although the conceptual frameworks put forward as a substitute for the latter do not normally reach a high level of sophistication as yet.

Any concrete social system or structure, then, copes with a multiplicity of functional problems. There is no simple correspondence of differentiated social sub-systems or structures to functional problems. Political institutions, for example, will not have a unique functional significance, whether it be for integration, as with Sutton, or for goal-attainment as with others. Nor will any given 'political problem' be nicely localised in any system, although, by definition, it must at some point arise in the political system. Nevertheless, it must be repeated, to a greater or lesser degree, that there is a specialisation of social sub-systems and structures about particular functional problems.

We must add, at this point, that it often appears to be an implicit, if not explicit, assumption of functional analysis, at least as applied in recent years particularly by American political sociologists, that the greater the degree of specialisation of the political system and of the specific structures within the political system, the 'more efficiently' will the political problems of a society be met. Whether this has empirical justification or is a value-judgment based on the (again implicit or explicit) assumption that the 'Western model' *should* be followed, we enquire later. At the moment, it need be said only that the answer will in part depend on what the goals of the society are, and what order of priority is assigned to them. For example, if economic modernisation is an over-riding goal it may be that the Western political system is not the best means to its achievment.

So far as the actual development of societies and political systems is concerned it can be shown that action systems may become very specialised as institutions, though in some writings it is not always clear whether the term 'institutions' is being used to describe 'strong normative patterns' or 'more differentiated concrete structures'. Again, this is a matter for later investi-gation. Meanwhile, we turn to the last question in this general chapter. This is concerned with the broad ways in which social structures or patterns of interaction, and especially those involved in the political system, may be compared. We shall consider, especially, 'pattern-variable analysis', which Sutton, among others, claims provides 'a standard means of describing the role-expectations and value-standards in *any* social system'.

V: COMPARISON OF SYSTEMS—PATTERN-VARIABLE ANALYSIS

Pattern-variable analysis is a suggestive basis both for des-cribing the patterns of interaction or the structures in any given system and for comparing the structures of different systems. Its starting point is the existence in social systems of alternative norms or role-expectation patterns, or structural predispos-itions. It attempts to arrive at standard ways of describing social structure or the relationships between actors performing roles in any social system. These standards are related to the existence of recurrent and contrasting patterns in the norms of social systems. So far as the political system is concerned, it is argued that the varying processes or structures through which are performed the political functions will affect both the form and the stability of the political system.

Many pattern-variables, in opposed pairs, have been used as a basis of analysis and comparison. We deal first with the four most fully developed by Talcott Parsons, and then consider others which have been used, notably by Seymour Lipset.

These first four have been divided into two sets of pairs which deal respectively with 'locational problems', and with 'attitudinal problems'. The first set of pairs poses (1) the alternatives of *universalism* and *particularism*, (2) *achievement* and *ascription*. In general terms the first pair of alternatives is con-cerned with whether an actor in his relationships with another focuses on a universally accepted precept or on one particular to the situation. Are the laws applied without regard to persons, do the judges operate according to the 'rules of the game'; or do particularistic factors such as family, kinship, or social position enter into such relationships? Are all people treated according to the same standard, e.g. equality before the law, or according to their personal qualities, or their particular membership in a class or group? Are value standards highly generalised or are they significant for a particular actor in particular relations with particular objects? Recruitment and promotion in the civil service, the selection of party candidates ('merit' or a 'balanced ticket'), informal relations within the legislatures, the selection of ministers (N.B. the ironic remarks about Mr Harold MacMillan's 'extended family' when he included so many of his relatives in his Cabinet, or Mr Baldwin's determination to form a government 'of which Harrow might be proud!'): all these are examples related to the political system where such analysis might usefully be applied.

The second of the first two (locational) pairs, achievement and ascription, or as some prefer, performance and quality, is concerned with whether the actors in a system focus on the achieved aspects of others, or on ascribed qualities such as birth or class. There may be some overlap between this pair and the previous pair. But the emphasis here is either on what a person can do, or on what he is. (There may, of course, be an admixture of the two since, for example, a king or chief may have an ascribed role but be expected to maintain a certain level of achievement or performance or otherwise be compelled to abdicate or to be de-stooled.) The contrast asserted by the two sides of the pair stresses the difference between ability or performance or achievement on the one hand, and race, birth or social status, on the other; between the achievement of certain goals, like a Western education and a degree or at the other extreme a sentence of imprisonment under an imperialist regime, and the mere possession of attributes like being the father of many children or an hereditary peer not of the first generation. It is again clear that the nature of political relationships and, possibly, the degree of their effectiveness, will be influenced by the emphasis which is placed upon one or other of these standards. (Sir Alec Douglas-Home gave up his 'ascribed' quality as a 'belted earl' and relied upon his 'achieved' status as a successful politician. The fact that he had *been* an earl, however, may have brought him as much support from some electors as his—probably less well known, at least to those same electors—achievements as Foreign Secretary.)

To turn to the 'attitudinal' aspects, the two pairs of alternatives are (1) *affectivity* and *affective-neutrality*, sometimes des-cribed as intimacy and avoidance, and (2) *specificity* and *diffuseness*. The first of these pairs postulates a contrast between situations in which an actor seeks immediate gratification, and those in which he renounces this in order to serve instru-mental or moral interests, or in which some discipline to this end is imposed. More generally, does a role permit certain kinds of expression of feelings (affect), or does it require such feeling to be held in check (self-control). Sutton's down-to-earth illustration of this is the contrast between the 'loving' attitude to a wife and the 'business-like' relationship with a secretary. (Norms are not always respected!) An example from political relations would be the theory propounded by some British civil servants that they must take an objective, 'statistical' attitude towards e.g. the problem of unemployment, because otherwise their feelings might affect their judgment. Hard cases make bad law.

The second of the (attitudinal) pairs, specificity and dif-fuseness, postulates a contrast between a relationship in which the actor's scope of interest is based on some specific factor, or is broadly based on another's wider, diffuse significance. Is the relationship bounded by the obligations of contract, strictly limited to specific obligations, or by a limited scope of interest in the object, with no obligation beyond the scope indicated in the contract; or is there an undefined range of obligations, an indefinitely large number of obligations, diffuse obligations, such as those, for example, between close kinship roles (which the Nazis, for instance, sought to destroy in order to ensure strict loyalty to the Party, even to the extent of betraying parents)? When a chief enters the electoral arena, do voters judge him on his specific qualities as a prospective assembly man or on his diffuse chiefly qualities? How are the relations between ministers and civil servants, or between members of the bureaucracy conceived? Or between local administrators and the various sections of the public which they serve, which may include family, caste, or tribe demanding 'generalised' or diffuse attention as opposed to specific services.

Talcott Parsons has also suggested another pair of contrasted patterns, that of *self-interest* and *collective interest* or self-orienta-tion and collectivity-orientation. It is usual to cite business and government to illustrate this contrast—though such an example may be 'culture-bound'; indeed, even in Western countries many large corporations strive to create an image of 'service to the public' (witness the reaction of some firms to Mr Brown's pleas to keep down prices in 1965); while not every government decision is taken purely in the 'public interest' (in so far as this can be defined!) nor is every public official necessarily and solely concerned with the 'good of the community'. There may, of course, be a value-judgment that this *ought* to be so. Social norms (and political norms) may define as legitimate the pursuit by an actor of his own private interest (e.g. on the argument that each man by pursuing his own self-interest will thereby ensure the interest of all). Or they may obligate him to act in the interest of a group—though in this case the actor may claim that 'what is good for General Motors is good for the country'. This kind of problem is of particular importance in relation to integration and exists peculiarly, though not solely, in 'new nations'.

Lipset[10] has added two more contrasting pairs to the above. The first of these is *instrumental* and *consummatory*, a broad distinction between the pursuit of means or of ends. In any given situation, however, it is clearly necessary to define the extent to which the actor is (or is presumed to be) looking ahead. What are means in one context, may be ends in another, and vice-versa. There also appears to be some overlap between this and one interpretation of the contrast between affectivity and affective-neutrality. Indeed, some writers have used 'instrumental' in this pair instead of affective-neutrality.

The second is the contrast between *egalitarian* and *elitist* patterns of relationships. Again, there is some overlap between this pair and the achievement-ascription dichotomy, although the egalitarian pattern stresses respect for another as a *person*, irrespective of either his achieved or ascribed position, while the elitist attitude is related to the acceptance of 'superior' positions, on either basis. Certainly this contrast is of great significance in political systems.

Almond has criticised the use of pattern-variable analysis, although, as we shall see, he uses the descriptive terms in dealing with styles of politics and of the performance of political functions by various structures. He believes that the contrasts tend to exaggerate the differences between political systems, and especially between those of 'Western and non-Western Nations'. All political systems, he claims, are transitional and mixed. It is certainly true that in all political systems there are varying admixtures of the two contrasting pairs of attitudes, though affectively-neutral, universalistic, specific, and achievement patterns tend to go together and to be found more frequently or more influentially in Western systems. Lipset contends, however, that Almond's warning is primarily important as a safeguard against reifying such concepts. When applied to empirical systems they are still useful analytically, as Lipset himself proves in the 'First New Nation'.

They may be used, he suggests, either to characterise whole epochs e.g. feudalism *v* capitalism; or whole nations e.g. the United Kingdom and the United States; or sub-systems within nations e.g. the state and industry. We add that they may also be applied to sub-systems e.g. within the political system. Bureaucracies and political parties, for example, may show different combinations of the various patterns of relationships within themselves, and this will affect their inter-relationships.

Finally, actual social (or political) structures are the resultants of the interaction and integration of the various value-pattern systems with other components of the system. To pursue this further, we turn to the notion of 'political culture'.

NOTES

[1] The two general works on sociology, which the author has found most useful are H. M. Johnson, *Sociology, A Systematic Introduction*, Routledge & Kegan Paul, 1961, and H. C. Bredemeier and R. M. Stephenson, *The Analysis of Social Systems*, Holt, Rinehart, Winston, 1962. Much more advanced is Marion J. Levy, Jr., *The Structure of Society*, Princeton University Press, 1952.

[2] Lloyd Fuller, 'Equality, Modernity, and Democracy in the New States', *in Old Societies and New States*, ed. Clifford Geertz, Free Press of Glencoe, 1963.

[3] R. Robertson on Talcott Parsons, *New Society*, 14 January, 1965.

[4] In La Palombara, ed. *Bureaucracy and Political Development*, Princeton U.P., 1963, pp. 168 *et seq.*

[5] 'Social Theory and Comparative Politics', pp. 67–81 *in* Eckstein and Apter, eds. *Comparative Politics*, Free Press of Glencoe, 1963.

[6] For the political aspects of this cf. H. Hyman, *Political Socialisation*, Free Press of Glencoe, 1959.

[7] *The American Polity*, Free Press of Glencoe, 1962.

[8] 'Voting and the Equilibrium of the American Political System' *in* Burdick and Brodbeck, eds. *American Voting Behaviour*, Free Press of Glencoe, 1959, pp. 86–120.

[9] *Government by Constitution*, Random House, 1959.

[10] *The First New Nation*. Heinemann, 1964.

2

Political Culture

THE concept of culture is fundamental to anthropology and sociology. Tylor defined it as 'that complex whole which includes knowledge, beliefs, art, morals, law, custom and other capabilities acquired by man as a member of society'. 'It is abstract,' says Johnson, 'in the sense that it is manifested in behaviour and in the results of behaviour but is neither the behaviour itself nor the tangible results.' We shall not enter into a discussion of the distinction sometimes made between 'material' and 'non-material' culture except to say that we adhere to the view that 'artifacts' or 'culture objects', like behaviour, are cultural, but as concrete objects they are not part of culture as we use the term. Culture, simply, is part of the common orientation of two or more people.

Orientation includes three elements. First, the cognitive i.e. the knowledge of the physical and social world of those who share the same culture—the 'cognitive map'. Ideas about how society works, about its social organisation, may be only partly true (as confirmed by logical and empirical methods) but they are none the less real to the actors concerned. Different actors may have different cognitive maps. Secondly, there are beliefs which in empirical terms are neither true nor false. Knowledge and belief, of course, may be mixed up in the same concrete acts. Thirdly, there are values—difficult to separate from attitudes, and overlapping with one another. We are concerned with values that are directly or indirectly involved in social relationships especially those which have been to a greater or lesser extent institutionalised.

When we attempt to define the values of a society and to study their inter-connections, it is useful to use again the four functional sub-systems which we examined above. 'The social activities implied in the very concept of function,' says Johnson, 'must be shaped to some extent by values, more or less stabilised culturally.' But no society is likely to stress all four sub-systems equally at the same time. 'The values most character-istic of one sub-system (or perhaps two) must therefore pre-dominate in any particular society'. It has been suggested, for example, that Japan, between 1600 and 1868, emphasised 'political values' i.e. the attainment of system goals and loyalty to the government. The Soviet Union is perhaps another example of a society in which such 'political' values, though in different forms, are predominant, and the same may be said of many of the new nations. Even where goal-attainment is of primary concern, the content of the goals may, of course, differ widely. For the predominance of different values, we might consider whether the implication of 'affluent society' is an emphases on adaptation i.e. on 'economic' goals.

Parsons has argued that every society ranks the four func-tional systems, stressing one or the other and ranking them all in some order. The relative emphasis on the four sub-systems in any particular society would determine subtle differences in the ranking of occupation. Our query about the affluent society appears to receive an affirmitive answer in the United States where the business-man has always ranked higher than the politician. For the political system it is clearly important in any assessment of authority and legitimacy, to know in what general esteem leaders, politicians, and officials are held, relative to other positions in society e.g. as above the business-man, or the intellectual, or the witch-doctor. High prestige for political roles may make the political system more 'functional' for the total system.

In addition to cognition, beliefs, and values, an important place may be occupied by the common sharing of certain signs, symbols, and rituals, in terms of which the participants react to one another. This is, again, important for the political system, with its use of flags, anthems, historical monuments, and public buildings, its anniversaries and festivals. The virtual cessation of public controversial political activity during the last stages of Sir Winston Churchill's illness, culminating in the great unifying ceremony of the lying-in-state and the funeral in 1965, may have served to strengthen feeling for 'the political system' which, after all, could produce such a man. In many new nations the charismatic leader may maintain his position as much by being a symbol of the nation, its saviour, its *Osagyefo*, as by being efficient in the achievement of concrete goals; though continuous failure in the latter respect may weaken and destroy the symbol.

For further discussion of the general concept of culture and culture systems in general, readers are referred to sociological writings on the subject. For our purpose it is more important to consider the attempts which have been made to develop the notion of 'political culture'. According to Almond, who has perhaps done most to formulate and define this notion, political culture is not the same thing as general culture, although related to it. It is a differentiated part of general culture and has a certain autonomy. We examine first its broad meaning and then its detailed content.

II: ALMOND ON POLITICAL CULTURE

Since Almond's ideas about political culture are intimately bound up with his concept of 'the political system'[1] we must first briefly examine his description of the latter, although this involves some repetition of the material presented in Chapter I.

'A political system,' he says, 'is a system of action' i.e. it includes empirically observable behaviour and norms or institutions as they affect behaviour. Political institutions or persons performing political roles are viewed in terms of what they do, why they do it, and how it is related to what others do and affects what they do. It includes the totality of the relevant units, and involves an inter-dependence between the interaction of those units and a certain stability in this interaction. The unit of the political system, as we have seen, is the role, which Almond, following Parsons and Shils, defines as 'that organised sector of an actor's orientation which constitutes and defines his participation in an interactive process'. It involves a set of complementary expectations concerning the actor's own actions and those of the others with whom he interacts. So, the political

3   23

system is a set of interacting roles, or a structure of roles ('structure' being understood as a convenient form of shorthand for 'a patterning of interactions'). Role, says Almond, is more inclusive than institutions, organisations, or groups; it can include formal offices, informal offices, families, electorates, mobs, as well as persistent groupings.

Following Weber, Almond regards as the distinguishing property of the political system the fact that it exercises 'the legitimate monoply of physical coercion over a given territory'. (We discuss this further, below, Chaps. 4–5.) For this it possesses a specialised apparatus, and the interacting roles of the participants in the system affect the employment of such physical force. This is not all that governments do, of course, but the employment of ultimate, comprehensive, and legitimate physical coercion is the monoply of the State, and the political system is uniquely concerned with the scope, direction, and conditions of its use. So, the political system is the patterned interaction of roles affecting decisions backed up by the threat of physical compulsion. To describe the political system it is necessary to characterise all the patterned interactions which take place within it i.e. all the roles, defined in action or in behavioural terms, and their inter-dependence; which means that a significant change in any one role affects changes in others, and therefore changes in the system as a whole.

At this point the notion of political culture must be introduced. The political system is embedded in a set of meanings and purposes. There are influences such as attitudes to politics, political values, ideologies, national character, ethical standards. To cover all these Almond suggests the concept of 'orientation to action' and the pattern-variable approach. Similar notions are contained in Beer's 'political culture',[2] though this appears to be somewhat wider than Almond's, in Easton's 'environment', which is discussed below (pp. 120 ff) and in Spiro's 'political styles' (*op. cit.*)

Every political system, then, is embedded in a particular pattern of orientations to political action, that is, in a political culture. A political culture does not necessarily coincide with one particular system or society. We shall see, for example, that Britain and the 'older' Commonwealth countries have a common political culture but separate and different political systems. On the other hand, in Western Europe, there are countries such as France which include within one political system more than one different political culture, each of which also extends beyond the particular political system.

It is important to distinguish this concept of political culture from other terms, and, in particular, from 'ideology' and from 'political party'. The former involves a systematic and explicit formulation of a general orientation to politics which is typical of a militant minority rather than of all the members of a society, though attempts may be made to indoctrinate everyone in the ideology, while its influence will be felt to a greater or lesser extent throughout the society. But general political culture would include members' orientation to the minority ideology and the elite which was attempting to spread it. Party systems are unsatisfactory, by themselves, as a basis for comparing political systems as a whole. Not only may the party-system be a reflection of other factors in the political culture; 'party' in totalitarian systems, and perhaps in some of the new one-party authoritarian states, does not perform the same functions as parties in other systems. In the Anglo-American systems, for example, the two parties are organised manifestations of a homogenous political culture, while the multi-party systems of Western Europe may or may not be organised manifestations of different political cultures. The notion of political culture may be needed to explain different party systems as *one* of the features which distinguish different political systems.

III: THE APPLICATION OF 'POLITICAL CULTURE' TO
EMPIRICAL SYSTEMS

Almond has attempted to apply the concept of political culture as explained in the previous section to empirical systems, both in the article referred to above and in his Introduction to *The Politics of the Developing Areas.*[3] Taking these two accounts together, he distinguishes four broad types of political culture. There are (1) Anglo-American Political Systems (2) Continental European Political Systems e.g. France, Germany and Italy (the Scandinavian systems and those of the Low Countries are separately categorised) (3) some non-Western or Pre-Industrial Political Systems and (4) Totalitarian Political

Systems. We referred earlier to the difficulty of separating 'culture' from 'structure', and Almond's account of these four systems appears to involve a consideration of both factors. Since, in his analysis, these are not readily separable, we summarise the whole of his argument, although this involves some repetition in our later study of Political Systems rather than Political Culture (below).

In Britain, the relation between the diffuse, affective, particularistic and ascriptive elements on the one hand, and the specific, instrumental, universalistic and achievement elements on the other, is one of *fusion*. Modern and pre-modern attitudes combine to produce a *homogeneous political culture*, both secular and traditional. British political structures such as interest groups, political parties, parliament, cabinet and monarchy show the same *fusional dualism*, This homogeneous, secular political culture is multi-valued, rational-calculating, bargaining, and experimental, but there is a wide sharing of both political means and ends. The great majority of the actors accept as the ultimate goals of the system some combination of freedom, mass welfare, and security; though at times some groups stress one value at the expense of another, while at times one value is stressed by all groups. Such balancing is often below the surface and not explicit. A quotation from a letter from Mr Attlee to Harold Laski[4] is in point here. 'I count our progress much more by the extent to which what we cried in the wilderness five and thirty years ago has now become part of the assumptions of the ordinary man and woman. The acceptance of these assumptions has its effect both in legislation and administration, but its graualdness tends to hide our appreciation of the facts.'

This secularised political culture involves the individuation of, and a measure of autonomy among, the various roles; arm's-length bargaining; and the atmosphere of the market. There are groups of electors with votes to 'sell' for policies. The holders of office in the formal-legal role-structure tend to be viewed as agents, or instrumentalities, or brokers. Policies are viewed as hypotheses, while the consequences of legislation and policies are rapidly communicated within the system (by what Easton calls the 'feedback' process from output to input, from polity to society) as crude tests of these hypotheses. There is the atmosphere of a game—witness the metaphors in current

26

use—the outcome is in doubt, and the stakes are not too high. As the late Lord Simon[5] commented, 'our parliamentary system will work as long as the responsible people in different parties accept the view that it is better that the other side should win than that the constitution should be broken'.

Role-structure in such a system is complex and highly-differentiated. Formal government agencies, political parties, pressure groups, the media of communication, and the 'publics' of various kinds pursue specialised purposes and perform specialised functions. They are autonomous though inter-dependent. Role-structure is also manifest, organised, and bureaucratised. Most of the potential interests are thus characterised, though there are also what David Truman has called 'the public interest' and 'latent interests'. There is a high degree of stability in the functions of the various roles. Those of bureaucracies, armies, and parliaments are not ordinarily substitutable, and the political division of labour is at once complex, explicit, and stable.

Most of this comment also applies to the United States. There are, of course, differences between Britain and the United States, but great similarities between the two in contrast to other systems. In the United States the division is at once more complex and less stable. There are more pressure groups and types of pressure groups because of size, complexity, ethnic and religious heterogeneity. There is more substitutability of function: more policy-making by pressure groups and the media of communication, more intervention in policy-making through 'public moods'. Britain has a more centralised and predictable role-structure. But in both countries there is a diffusion of power and influence within the system as a whole, not only in the legal realms of democratic suffrage and representative government, but through mass communications, the mass media, and representation by interest groups.

The political systems of France, Germany and Italy (those of the Scandinavian and the Low Countries being between them and the first type considered) tend to show *isolative* features. There is a polarisation of political culture; some elements and regions are traditional, others 'rational'. Traditionality and modernity are concentrated in different parts of France, for example, and their relationship is isolative. This

27

fragmentation of political culture is due to an uneven pattern of development, to significant survivals or 'out-croppings' of older cultures with their own political manifestations, though they also have common roots and a common heritage, unlike many of the pre-industrial systems. The political sub-cultures are of key significance. There are the surviving pre-industrial sub-cultures, for example the Catholic 'Ancien Regime' areas in France, Southern Italy and the Islands, and parts of Bavaria. The middle classes in the nineteenth century failed to carry through a thorough-going secularisation of political culture. In the Fourth Republic, the Socialist Party and the Mouvement Républicain Populaire, with many items of policy in common, could nevertheless differ sufficiently on such traditional issues as State aid to Catholic schools to break up left-of-centre governments and let in right-wing elements to which they were generally opposed. This is but one aspect of the continued existence of the older anti-clerical middle classes who are still primarily concerned with the secularisation of the political system itself. Then there are the modernised and industrialised parts which emerged in an only partially secularised political culture and therefore found their potentialities for 'political market' behaviour thwarted. This is one reason for the strength of the Communist Party in France, Italy, and pre-Hitler Germany. Rapid industrialisation and improved welfare policies might well reduce this 'alienation' from the political system. We are, perhaps, at present witnessing a new stage in such progress with the emergence of a Centre-Left Government in Italy and the first Socialist President (though with many strains and no certainty of continuity); with the faint signs of a possible rallying around M. Deferre as a rival to President de Gaulle in the 1965 presidential election: and with the possibility of a Social Democratic victory over the no-longer-religiously-oriented Christian Democrats in Western Germany.

Up till now, however, political issues have involved the very survival of the various sub-cultures and the basic form of the political system itself. Political actors have not come to politics with specific bargainable differences but with conflicting and mutually exclusive designs for the political culture and system. There is thus a further fragmentation at the level of ideology and of political organisations. The pre-industrial, partly Catholic element has an adaptive semi-secular and an anti-secular wing. The middle classes are divided into a conservative wing in uneasy alliance with clerical pre-republican elements, and a left-wing in uneasy friendship with socialists. The industrial workers are divided according to the degree of their alienation from the political system as a whole. The result is the development of movements or sects rather than political parties. Political affiliation is 'more an act of faith than of agency'.

The most pronounced characteristic of the political role-structure is its general alienation from the political market; the political culture pattern is not adapted to the political system. Actors are not oriented to parliament and popular elections and they come to the market not to exchange, compromise, and adapt, but to preach, exhort, convert, and to transform the political system into something other than a bargaining agency, except through 'under-counter' transactions. The only normatively and morally confident actor is the militant. Nor is there an individuation of political roles; they are embedded in the sub-cultures and tend to constitute separate sub-systems of roles. Catholic and Communist parties alike have their 'churches', schools, propaganda organisations, trade unions, parties and press. Socialists and 'liberals' also have the same linked organisations, though they tend to be less well developed and exclusive. The centre of gravity in these political systems is not in the formal-legal role-structure but in the political sub-cultures. This tends to produce the phenomenon of *immobilisme*. As one French Premier put it, 'my business is not to solve problems but to prevent people from raising them'. There is also a higher degree of substitutability of roles than in the U.S.–U.K. system, though it is lower than in the non-Western systems. Parties may manipulate pressure groups and make decisions for them; interest groups may manipulate parties and may operate directly in the legislative process. (This, of course, happens in the U.S. and, to a lesser extent, in the U.K.) There is a predominance of the bureaucracy in policy-making. Yet, politically, there is the ever-present threat of the 'Caesaristic' break-through—the emergence of a charismatic nationalism with a totalitarian potentiality. This analysis of Almond's, with its final 'warning', was, of

29

course, made before the collapse of the Fourth Republic and its replacement by the Gaulist Fifth. So far as Western Germany and Italy are concerned, little has happened in the last few years to suggest that this analysis needs to be modified.

There has been some argument as to whether there is, in fact, a distinctive 'Non-Western Political Process'.[6] We shall not pursue it here, but merely examine what Almond considers are features of *some* non-Western or pre-industrial systems. In them we find a modern culture in the cities and large-scale modernising efforts in the villages, though with vast areas untouched. The pattern is *incorporative.* The two cultures are not fused, but neither are they sharply antagonistic. The process of acculturation continues and the result eventually may be either fusional or isolative. These, then, are mixed political cultures and systems. In them, parliaments tend to be something other than what they are in Western systems; parties and pressure groups behave in unusual ways; bureaucracies and armies often dominate. There are 'unpredictability and gunpowder'. Everywhere there is a minimum of two political cultures, Western and pre-Western. The particular amalgam will depend on the type of traditional cultures involved; the auspices under which westernisation was introduced (e.g. by western colonial powers or by native elites); the particular functions of society which have been westernised; the tempo and tactics of the westernisation process; and the type of western cultural products introduced.

A third type of political culture—though some would prefer to call this 'system of authority'—the charismatic, may emerge. Powerful forces are released by the erosion of the traditional political culture; anxieties, rootlessness, and a potential for violence develop. Charismatic nationalism is a movement towards accepting a new system of political norms, or towards a reaffirmation of traditional ones, or often towards peculiar combinations of both. The new forms of legitimacy must provide a powerful affirmation capable of breaking up deeply ingrained habits and replacing earlier loyalties. It must cope with old or traditional political cultures, new or Western-rational political culture, and the transitional or resultant phenomena. There are most serious problems of communication and co-ordination. Large groups have different 'cognitive maps' of politics and apply different norms to political action. Instability and unpredictability are not, in Almond's view, pathologies, but inescapable consequences.

Role-structure shows a relatively low degree of structural differentiation. Political interest often tends to be latent, and when it emerges into politics may lead to spontaneous, violent action. Political parties are unstable; they fragment and consolidate, appear and disappear. There is only a rudimentary specialised system of communication. The bureaucracy is only partially developed, unless it has been left behind by the colonial power and even then it tends to run down as fewer 'expatriates' are left to manage it and a hurried process of 'nativisation' with promotion of inexperienced men occurs. There is an absence of a stable and explicit role-structure and a high degree of substitutability of roles. Political parties may pre-empt policy-making functions; bureaucracies may either take over or be merged into parties. There is no stable political division of labour. Political role-structures are mixed; parliament is based on legal norms and regulations, but operating within it there may be a powerful family, a religious sect, or a group of tribal chieftains, operating by its own traditional norms. Western norms and expectations should not be expected in such a political system; for example, corruption and nepotism may be normatively oriented conduct—indeed, it has been argued that, to some extent, such conduct may be functional for the political system.

We need not examine at such length totalitarian political systems, but merely indicate some of their most significant features. The homogeneity of the political culture in such systems is highly synthetic, although it is difficult to determine at what point in time it may have become 'internalised' and positively accepted, say, by a new generation. There are no voluntary associations; communications are controlled from the centre; the system tends to be non-consensual, though not completely, or else it could not persist. The characteristic orientation to authority tends to be conformity and apathy, though, again, with time, more positive orientations may develop. Totalitarianism, Almond holds, is tyranny with a rational bureaucracy, a monopoly of the modern technology of communication and of the modern technology of violence. Role-

31

structure is based on the process of atomisation from the bottom to the top, which aims to destroy solidarity at any point in the system and to avoid all stable delegations of power which might reduce the freedom of manoeuvre of those at the centre. There is a predominance of coercive roles and a functional instability of power roles—bureaucracy, party, army, secret police; though there is greater stability in economic allocative roles. The electoral process and 'self-criticism' are largely devices intended to create a façade of consent.

But there are 'politics' in such systems. Leaders have to accept some limits to their capacity for retaining obedience to their policies. Roger Pethybridge's 'Key to Soviet Politics'—a study of 'the crisis of the anti-party group'—reveals interest groups at work: the party-apparatus, the government bureaucracy, the economic and technological elite, the army, the secret police, the intelligentsia—even the students; Old Bolsheviks against the new men; localities as supports for rivals or obstacles to leaders. Even rigid institutions take on some flexibility with Kruschev's appeal from the Presidium to the Plenum of the Central Committee. There is no more 'palace politics', no more secrecy, no more inevitable progress to a foregone conclusion than in the 'evolution' (delightfully apposite Darwinian terminology) of the Conservative Party Leader and Prime Minister, Sir Alec Douglas-Home—a sort of survival of the least unfit.[7] If a detailed analysis of the events of 1964, leading to the downfall of Kruschev, were made, it would doubtless reveal many of the same forces at work in the same manner.

Almond's analysis of the totalitarian political system, is, in our view, the most inadequate and incomplete of his attempts to apply the notion of political culture to empirical systems. But we do not intend to take up the difficult problem of whether, and in what form, a transition from totalitarianism to a 'freer' political system may occur. Such an attempt would take up too much space and involve more specialist knowledge than the author possesses. (But see also the further analysis of totalitarian regimes, below, pp. 91 ff.)

IV: THE CIVIC CULTURE

Almond and Verba[8] have elaborated and generalised the concept of political culture in much greater detail in their study of the political culture of Britain, the United States, Germany, Italy, and Mexico. We attempt here to develop the main points of Part I, 'The Theory and Method of the Study', as a further introduction for those not familiar with the use of the concept. The reader must consult the rest of the study for its detailed application to the countries concerned.

The authors first further define political culture as the specifically political orientations, the attitudes towards the political system and its various parts, and to the role of the self in the system. The political culture of a nation is the particular distribution of the patterns of orientation towards political objects. It involves a cognitive element—knowledge of and beliefs about the political system, its roles, their incumbents, its inputs and outputs; (see below, pp. 120 ff, for further development of this); an affective element—feelings about the above; and an evaluational element—judgments and opinions about the **above.**

The following classification of the objects of political orientation is offered:

1. The general political system—about which members may, for example, feel either patriotism or alienation; that it is large, small, strong, weak, democratic, constitutional, socialistic etc.

2. The component parts of the political system, which may be broadly designated as:

   (*a*) Specific roles or structures of e.g. legislature, executive, bureaucracy, party.
   (*b*) the incumbents of roles i.e. particular monarchs, presidents, party leaders, etc.
   (*c*) particular public policies, decisions or enforcements.

These can be classified again as (1) the political or 'input' process and (2) the administrative or 'output' process.

3. The orientation towards the self as a political actor— sense of obligation, competence, etc.

33

Thus we are concerned with the cognitive, affective (or cathectic) and evaluative orientations towards the political system in general, towards the input structures and functions; towards the output structures and functions, and towards the self as a political actor. The usual warning is repeated that this static analysis must not obscure the continuity of the political process or the multi-functionality of political structures.

To sum up, Almond and Verba have aimed to enquire what political objects individuals are oriented to, how they are oriented to them, and whether these objects are predominantly in the 'upward' flow of policy-making or in the 'downward' flow of policy-enforcement. They are concerned with the knowledge, feelings, and judgments of individuals about the political system in general; about the structures, roles, political elites and policy proposals; about the downward flow of policy enforcement; and about the individual's own rights, powers, and obligations. They suggest three broad *types of political culture*, which are expressed diagrammatically thus:

	System	*Inputs*	*Outputs*	*Self*
Parochial	o	o	o	o
Subject	I	o	I	o
Participant	I	I	I	I

The *parochial political culture* exists, for example, in African tribal societies and in autonomous local communities. There are no specialised political roles but only diffuse politico-economic-religious roles. There is a comparative absence of expectation of change as initiated by the political system. In the centralised African chiefdoms and kingdoms some more specialised roles developed. But even larger-scale and more differentiated polities, like the Ottoman Empire, may have predominantly parochial cultures. Individuals are aware in a dim way of the central political regime; they are affectively and normatively rather than cognitively oriented towards it.

In the *subject political culture* there is a high frequency of orientations to the differentiated political system and to its outputs, but very little to its inputs or to the self as a political actor. The relationship is passive. When there are democratic (input) structures, the affective and normative reaction may be against them, as, for example, with the French royalists.

34

In the *participant political culture*, individuals are oriented to the system as a whole, to its input and output structures, and to an 'activist' role for themselves in the polity—though this may take the form either of acceptance or of rejection.

Almond and Verba make it clear that this analysis does not postulate an historical or evolutionary development from one culture to another; it certainly does not mean that each one replaces the former. It adds to it; moreover, the earlier orientations are affected by the additions. The new and the old orientations become combined, fused, or meshed together and different political cultures and systems emerge from different degrees and methods of admixture. Nor is there any implication of homogeneity or uniformity of political culture: parochials, subjects and participants continue to be mixed in any political system; the individual himself may have a mixture of all three orientations; the political culture itself is a mixture of the three types.

When political culture is clearly described and fully ascertained, the very important question as to the degree of *congruence* which exists between it and the structures of the political system can be raised i.e. the question of the degree to which cognition is accurate and affect-evaluation favourable. Generally speaking, the parochial culture fits best with a traditional political structure; the subject culture with a centralised authoritarian structure; and the participant culture with a democratic political structure. Since political systems change, structure and culture often become incongruent with each other. This may also be expressed diagrammatically:

CONGRUENCE—INCONGRUENCE

	Allegiance	*Apathy*	*Alienation*	
Cognitive	+	+	+	
Affective	+	o	$-\big\}$	(negative)
Evaluative	+	o	$-$	
	(Strong)		(Weak)	

The three attitudes, of allegiance, apathy, or alienation can, of course, apply in any of the three political cultures. Almond and Verba suggest that the above scale is also one of stability–instability.

35

There are different kinds of incongruence, each with its own effects. It may involve a simple rejection of a particular set of role-incumbents—a particular dynasty or oligarchy. The consequences for the system will depend partly on how easily changes can be made. Or there may be a 'systematic' change from a simple pattern of political culture to a more complex one. Here we may note that 'systematically mixed' political cultures may stabilise at a point which falls short of congruence i.e. political cultures may remain systematically mixed for a very long time, as in France, Germany, and Italy; though there will be strains and structural instability. Following upon this, Almond and Verba proceed to examine three types of systematically mixed political cultures.

The first is the *parochial-subject culture*. In this type a substantial portion of the population has rejected the exclusive claims of diffuse tribal, village, or feudal authority, and has developed allegiance to the more complex political system with its specialised structures. This kind of admixture occurs most frequently during the process of kingdom-building out of relatively undifferentiated units. But the culture may for long remain mixed, as in the loosely-articulated African Kingdoms or the Ottoman Empire. There are various admixtures between the extremes on a continuum. For example, Prussian absolutism went far in suppressing all parochial orientations; the Ottoman Empire never went very far; Britain preserved a much more balanced admixture.

The *subject-participant culture* poses a different set of problems. In it there is a need to create a sense of national loyalty and identification, and a propensity to obey the regulations of the central authority. If the parochial and local autonomies survive, they may contribute to the eventual development of a democratic infra-structure. This happened in Britain, in contrast to Germany. A substantial part of the population in this mixed culture has acquired specialised input orientations and an activist set of self-orientations. But the rest are oriented to the authoritarian governmental structures. France, Germany, and Italy provide examples of this. There is structural instability which affects the cultural patterns, because the legitimacy of participant orientations is challenged by the subjects. Thus the participant-oriented section cannot become competent, self-confident, and experienced; they tend to remain, rather, democratic *aspirants*, with alienative tendencies. On the other hand, the authoritarian-oriented group must give the appearance of 'playing the democratic game' and this accounts for the populistic overtones of their attitudes. The use of the referendum by President de Gaulle and, indeed, the general use of plebiscitary techniques by those seeking to achieve or maintain power in a mixed political culture of this kind, provide evidence of this point. It is linked with Almond's earlier references to the Caesaristic break-through.

The *parochial-participant culture* is especially to be seen in the emerging nations. In such a mixed culture there is need to develop specialised output and input orientations simultaneously. Parochial systems must be penetrated without their being destroyed, on the output side. On the input side they must be transformed into interest groups which are oriented to the political system and its decision-making structures.

As with general cultural systems so with political cultural systems: there are always sub-cultures. Even the most fully developed participant cultures contain surviving strata of subjects and parochials, and even within that part of the culture which is oriented to participation there are significant and persistent differences in political orientation. Almond and Verba refer to two types of sub-cultural change. First, there are population strata which are persistently oriented in *one* way to political inputs and outputs (the phenomenon of life-long allegiance to one political party and opposition to the other(s)); though they are allegiantly oriented to the political structure. The Left-wing of the Democratic Party and the Right-wing of the Republican Party in the United States provide one example; the miners and the Labour Party in Britain, perhaps, another. These represent *policy sub-cultures* and are relatively unimportant in this kind of broad sociological analysis of political systems, although policy sub-cultures may turn into structural ones, as in the differences which led to the American Civil War. This is also frequently the case with alienated revolutionary socialist, syndicalist, and anarchist sections of society.

A more serious problem is found in *systematically* mixed systems where for example, the parochials are oriented to diffuse traditional authorities, and subjects to the specialised central

37

system. Here we may have an emerging subject sub-culture as well as the persisting separate sub-cultures of the formally mixed traditional units. Similarly, there is the subject-participant mixture. In England, the older Commonwealth countries, the United States, and the Scandinavian countries, the issues of political structures were resolved in the nineteenth and twentieth centuries. Subjects and participants combined—indeed, each individual was in large part himself a mixture of the two, and perhaps of the parochial as well—and homogeneous political cultures developed. Policy sub-cultures, however, remained. There was one school of thought in Britain, particularly in the 1930's, which believed that policy sub-cultures would become structural sub-cultures; that the 'capitalist' section would not accept the achievement of socialism as a policy through parliamentary means, because it would involve the dominance of a structural sub-culture unacceptable to them. The result would be the ending of the parliamentary system either by a 'dictatorship of the Left' or one of the 'Right'. The latter alternative was at that time held to be the explanation of Fascism and Nazism, which were regarded as the last determined effort of the 'capitalist' order to prevent the triumph of socialism (which, for tactical reasons, was represented as 'communism' i.e. not merely a question of policy but of a 'way of life'). Lipset's studies of working-class authoritarianism have pertinently questioned such interpretation.[9]

France is the classic case of the subject-participant type of political cultural heterogeneity. After the French Revolution, which has been described as a 'revolution stopped half-way', there remained differences between the participants (at least aspirants) and the subjects and parochials. The former further fragmented into socialists and communists, the communists, save for exceptional periods of the Popular Front, tending to be alienated. The Right Wing divided into a 'rallied' and an 'unrallied' part i.e. in relation to the Republic. French political history has been a continuing comment on this theme, and the de Gaullist Fifth Republic has by no means completely resolved the dilemma.

Within the political culture, there is the question of the *role-culture*. In the more complex political systems there are specialised structures of roles—bureaucratic, military, political executive, party, interest group, media of communication. These centres of initiative and influence tend to produce political cultural heterogeneity. For example, the elites who perform these various roles may be recruited from particular political sub-cultures. Further, the process of socialisation and induction into the various roles produces different values, skills, loyalties, and cognitive maps. This is particularly true of what Coleman calls 'terminal colonial democracies' but it is also a problem in some 'advanced' political systems. In Germany and France the bureaucratic and military elites have been recruited from aristocratic and authoritarian sub-cultures, and the process of role-socialisation which they underwent reinforced their authoritarian tendencies. In Britain, while top level civil servants were for long recruited exclusively from upper social and educational groups, they were socialised into a political culture which stressed the subordination of the bureaucrat to the political head (and the significance of his warnings of 'what the public would not stand'), and this persisted even with the extension of the suffrage and the emergence of new political elites. Hence the problem which some outside observers (and some inside, also!) professed to see—that the civil service would not serve their Labour masters with the same loyalty—never emerged. In the new nations these same elite elements may, on the other hand, be the 'progressives' i.e. ardent supporters of modernisation, though they may weary of trying to produce a participant culture, and prefer a large element of the subject. What they will certainly not want is a predominance of the parochial.

Role-structures may involve differentiation among the incumbents of the specialised roles either as regards their structural orientation, or their policy orientation. In France, the higher civil service and the military have tended to be ranged against the political parties, the interest groups, and the communication elites in structural orientation, though also on policy. On the latter, however, they could for long operate a 'go slow' technique, especially since the opposing political structures were so unstable and intermittent. We may note the regular fall of governments and the sometimes prolonged period between governments—as well as the weakness of governments even when in office; the civil servants could refrain from implementing political policies, or pursue their own, while the military could pursue their colonial wars with little or no control by their political masters at home. But when the structural weaknesses became too obvious to tolerate, the civil service and military elites found a new set of structures in the person of de Gaulle and the machinery—devised by a civil servant—of the Fifth Republic. The Fourth Republic, with its political parties and unstable governments significantly became known, derogatorily, as 'the system'.

Other differences of orientation have been noticed. In Britain and elsewhere for example, the elites may be strongly opposed to each other, the masses of their supporters not. Or, conversely, the elites may have more in common than the rank-and-file, and be engaged in what the more ardent describe as a 'sham fight'. We may note the alleged community of interest between the 'Front Benches' in the British House of Commons, and the unwillingness of either Government or 'Alternative Government' to accept procedural changes which might increase the power and influence of back-benchers. There is also the difference between the parliamentarians and the 'outside party', typified in the French remark that there is more in common between two deputies, one of whom is a Communist, than between two Communists, one of whom is a deputy. Or, again, there is the perennial argument as to whether the Parliamentary Labour Party (a) is and (b) ought to be subject to Annual Conference, with its different orientation. More generally, all students of political parties have noted the differences between the 'militants' and the rank-and-file, and between those who are formally attached to a party (even if not militants) and those who merely vote for it.

Throughout this section, so far, we have examined the general basis for a study of political culture. It is now time to look specifically at the type of political culture which Almond and Verba call the *civic culture*. This is a mixed culture. Political theorists from Locke to Laski have frequently appeared to be arguing in favour of what has been called the *rationality-activist* model of political culture. According to this model, a successful democracy requires that citizens be involved and active in politics, informed about them, and influential. Their decisions, including that of voting, should be based on a careful

40

evaluation of evidence and careful weighing of alternatives. The passive, non-voting, poorly-informed, or apathetic citizen may weaken democracy. Such a model clearly emphasises the participant orientation to politics, and especially to political input, and minimises or ignores the subject and parochial. Such rational-activist citizens are undoubtedly to be found in greater numbers in successful than in unsuccessful democracies. But the model describes only part of what Almond and Verba mean by the civic culture.

To the rational-activist citizen (or to that element in any *one* citizen), the civic culture adds the allegiant-participant who is not only oriented to political input but also positively to the input structures and the input process of the particular system in which he lives. Secondly, participant orientations do not replace subject and parochial orientations. The former ensures acceptance of authoritative decisions and co-operation with authoritative decision-makers. The latter limits the individual's commitments to politics and makes those commitments milder. To quote Mr Balfour on Britain, 'it is evident that our whole political machinery presupposes a people so fundamentally at one that they can safely afford to bicker, and so sure of their own moderation that they are not disturbed by the never-ending din of political conflict'. In the civic culture, traditional attitudes are maintained and fused with participant attitudes, while subject attitudes produce ready acceptance of political outputs and the role-structures involved in them.

We conclude this section with a brief summary of the contribution to political studies which Almond and Verba consider their 'political culture' approach has to make. Political culture, they contend, provides the connecting link between micro-politics and macro-politics. It is possible to locate the special aptitudes and propensities for political behaviour among the different parts of the population, or in particular roles, structures, and sub-systems i.e. in the political system as a whole, *and* in the special orientation groupings, the sub-cultures, *and* in the role-cultures, the key points of initiative and decision.

Polities may then be compared (1) according to their structural-functional characteristics and (2) according to their cultural, sub-cultural, and role-cultural characteristics. It is possible to study the degree of congruence which exists between culture and structures, and on the basis of this, perhaps, to lay down certain guide-lines with regard to dissonant political role-management—a matter of special importance in rapidly changing and fragmented societies. It is possible to study the frequencies of specified kinds of orientation to the various subclasses of political objects: to the nation and to the political system as a whole; to the input objects such as media of communication, interest groups, political parties, legislatures and executives in their political aspect; to output objects including again, legislatures and executives in their governmental and administrative aspect, the military, the police, and many other functional varieties of civil roles. Finally, the impact of a political culture on the political system of which it is part may be examined. Why does the 'Westminster model' fail or become radically altered when adopted in Commonwealth countries outside Britain? What justification is there for the contention that 'constitutions are not exportable'? Differences of political culture alone will not provide a complete answer to these questions. But they are likely to have greater explanatory value than explanations in terms of race or colour, or vague notions like 'national character' or 'capacity for self-government'.

V: ANOTHER APPROACH TO POLITICAL CULTURE

Little work has been done on this side of the Atlantic on the concept of political culture. Professor S. E. Finer, however, has utilised the concept in order to study the problem of the role of the military in politics.[10] His distinction between countries of mature, developed, low, and minimal political cultures (which he reached entirely independently and without knowledge of Almond's contemporary work) is valuable as a general idea, as well as in its relation to what Finer calls the four levels of military intervention: influence; pressures or 'blackmail'; displacement (of one civil ruler by another); and supplantment.

The level of political culture is high, he argues, when the *political formula* i.e. the belief or emotion by virtue of which the rulers claim the moral right to govern and be obeyed, is generally accepted; or, when the complex of civil procedures and oragns which jointly constitute the political system are recognised as authorative i.e. duty-worthy, by a wide consensus; or, when public involvement in and attachment to these civil institutions is strong and wide-spread. These are virtually three ways of stating the same basic idea.

There are various criteria whereby the level of political culture, as thus defined, may be assessed. There is the degree of public approval of the procedures for transferring power, and of the corresponding belief that no exercise of power in breach of these procedures is legitimate. There is the degree of public recognition as to who or what constitutes the sovereign authority, and of the corresponding belief that no other person or centre of power is legitimate or duty-worthy. There is the question of the size of the public which is involved in the above sentiments and beliefs, and the extent to which it is well mobilised into private associations such as cohesive churches, industrial associations and firms, labour unions, and political parties. When all these three conditions are met to a satisfactory extent the level of political culture is said to be high; to the extent that they are not, it is correspondingly low.

As Finer says, these conditions are obviously better satisfied in Britain than in, say, Iraq. But is is not so easy to determine whether they are better in Britain than in, say, Sweden. Moreover, his notion of political culture is not unitary. It is a complex of the three conditions, and these can be ranked in different ways. One country might have a weak and ill-organised, but reasonably united public; in another the public might be disunited but strongly organised. No attempt can be made, therefore, to arrange political systems in a continuous rank-order.

Political systems may, however, be grouped in a number of broad categories of descending orders of political culture, though border-line cases may still exist. In the first group, where the order of political culture is highest, all three conditions are fulfilled. In these systems the intervention of the military would be regarded as a wholly unwarrantable intrusion. Public sanction for such action would not be forthcoming. This group, with a *mature political culture*, includes Britain, the United States, the Scandinavian countries, Switzerland, Canada, Australia, New Zealand, Eire and Holland. It will be noted that the group broadly coincides with Almond's 'Anglo-American' fusional political cultures, together with some European countries which he places between this category and that of the Western European Continental systems with their isolative political culture.

In Finer's second group, with a *developed political culture*, civil institutions are highly developed. The public is a proportionately wide one, well organised into powerful associations. Civil procedures and public authorities are well rooted. But, unlike the first group, the legitimacy of the procedures for transferring political power, and the question of who or what should constitute the sovereign authority, are both in dispute. This group includes Germany from the Empire to Hitler's accession, Japan between the two wars, France from the Third Republic onwards. Finer also includes the U.S.S.R. in this category. In such countries the military would have to reckon on strong public resistance to their interventions.

Finer's group with *low political culture*, comprises those countries in which the public is relatively narrow and is weakly organised, and where the institutions and procedures of the regime are also in dispute. Opinion would not be strongly resistive to military intervention; this opinion, being weak and divided, is in a fluid state. At the top of this category come countries like Turkey, Argentina, and Spain; at the bottom, countries like Egypt, Syria, Pakistan, Iran, the Sudan (though here the civil revolt against General Abboud, and the re-establishment of a, perhaps, shaky civil regime in 1964 should be noted), and South Korea.

Finally, there are countries of *minimal political culture*, in which for all practical purposes any government can ignore public opinion, because the politically articulate are so few and weakly organised. Mexico and Argentina in the first half-century of their existence (though the former is clearly excluded now, if we accept the analysis in 'The Civic Culture'), Haiti, Paraguay, and the Congo (and perhaps other West African countries where military coups have occurred) are of this kind.

Finer adds, in a footnote, the '*ante-diluvian*' (*i.e. pre-French Revolution*) political culture, which exists in traditional monarchies or 'proto-dynastic societies' where allegiance is owed to the dynasty. The public, as an active and organised force, does not exist. Traditionally structured opinion exhibits a passive consensus on the mode of transferring political power, and on the sovereign authority. Even in Finer's examples, however, (the Yemen, Saudi Arabia and Ethiopia) these features are perhaps beginning to change. It does not entirely remain the case that military intervention would only be exercised in the name of the dynasty, as it was in Ethiopia in 1960. (Although we are concerned with Finer's analysis of political culture, and not specifically with the role of the military in each type, it is useful to note that Peter Worsley, *The Third World*, Weidenfeld & Nicholson, 1964, pp. 185–187, has noted that most of Finer's striking cases of military intervention are taken from Latin America, where its intention has been to preserve conservative regimes. In some Middle Eastern countries, however, it has taken the form of modernising military oligarchies whose role is quite different and whose leadership has been at the 'colonel' level. The key here is not so much 'low political culture', as 'social backwardness'; the simple social structures make it more easy for military administration to cope with the problems raised.)

Although these various analyses of 'political culture' differ in detail, they suggest that the functioning of political structures can be understood fully only in a setting of values and attitudes —orientations to politics. Although we have separated out the notion of 'culture' for analytical purposes, as, indeed, we also separate out the notions of structure and function, the total political system can be examined only by the effective combination of all these notions. This will become clearer as our analysis proceeds.

NOTES

[1] 'Comparative Political Systems' *in Journal of Politics*, Vol. 18, 1965; reprinted in Eulau etc. eds. *Political Behaviour*, pp. 34–42 and Macridis and Brown, eds. *Comparative Politics*, pp. 439–454.

[2] S. H. Beer *et al.*, *Patterns of Government*, Random House, 1958, espec. Ch. 3.

[3] Almond & Coleman eds. Princeton U.P., 1960, pp. 3–64.

[4] 1 May, 1944. Quoted in Kingsley Martin, *Harold Laski*, Gollancz, 1953, p. 161.

[5] Quoted by L. S. Amery, 'The Nature of British Parliamentary Government', *in Parliament: A Survey*, ed. Campion, Allen and Unwin, 1952, p. 40.

[6] cf Lucien Pye, 'The Non-Western Political Process', *Journal of Politics*, xx, 1961. Reprinted *in* Eckstein and Apter, eds. *op. cit.* pp. 657–665.

[7] The above passage is taken from the author's Inaugural Lecture 'Government, Politics, and Political Science', University of Exeter, 1963.

[8] Gabriel A. Almond and Sidney Verba, *The Civic Culture*, Princeton U.P., 1963, espec. pp. 3–78.

[9] cf. *Political Man*, espec. Chapters IV and V.

[10] S. E. Finer, *The Man on Horseback*, Pall Mall Press, 1962, espec. Chaps. 7–9, and espec. pp. 86–89.

3

Typologies of Political Systems

MANY attempts have been made to develop a typology of societies, sometimes including their political aspects among the criteria of differentiation. One of the contributions which the philosophy of history made to the development of sociology was the conception of society as something more than 'political society' or the State. This necessitated an attempt to make a valid and clear distinction between the State on the one hand, and what the philosophers of history designated as 'civil society'. An examination of the relationships between the two then became possible; further, a classification of political systems related to the different forms of civil society could be attempted. Early sociologists, however, were chiefly interested in the origins and development of the State, regarded as one association within society. 'However little we now may accept these schemes of unilinear evolution, the classification of political systems remains a primary task of political sociology, as a basis for generalisation, and much can be learned from the nineteenth-century writers.'[1]

The evolutionary sociologists made a distinction between those societies which had, and those which had not, a political system, though they made it in different ways. Spencer distinguished within the category of 'simple societies', those with no headship, and those with only occasional or unstable headship. At the stage of 'doubly compound societies', an elaborate political organisation had developed. Hobhouse distinguished between three types of society on the basis of their 'fundamental bonds'; those based on kinship, those based on

47

authority, and those based on citizenship. He also found some correlation between the level of economic development, increasing social differentiation, and the emergence and consolidation of a regular political authority. Marx and Engels elaborated a classification of societies in which the State came into existence only at a stage of economic development where antagonistic classes appeared.

Both Spencer and Comte found the explanation of the emergence of the State in the increasing size and complexity of societies, in which warfare was a major factor. F. Oppenheimer considered that the origin both of social classes and of the State was to be found in the conquest of one tribe by another. Recent sociological and anthropological study has confirmed some of these theories and modified others. It is generally agreed that some primitive societies lacked a 'political authority', though Schapera has argued that political organisation is more prevalent than many sociologists believe; it is the 'State' which is lacking.[2] (For further consideration of this point see below, Chap. 4.) Certainly the role of kinship as a means of maintaining social unity appears to have been exaggerated and that of the 'territorial tie' underestimated. Where a separate political authority exists, however, it is closely bound up with kinship, religion, and other institutions.

Two points made by the evolutionary sociologists still remain important. Firstly, there is some significance in the relationship they saw between the State and military conquest, and also between economic or religious developments and the emergence of the State. Secondly, they discerned, in Western civilisation, a development from authoritarian states to less coercive types of political system. In examining this development, they analysed the relations between political authority and other social phenomena e.g. economic power and social stratification, in ways which are still valuable. We do not examine here the various classifications which they attempted on the basis of these enquiries, but reproduce a somewhat more comprehensive classification taken from Bottomore (*op. cit.* p. 150) as an illustration of the kind of contribution sociologists make to the analysis of political systems.

48

Typologies of Political Systems

1. Primitive Societies.

    (a) without a distinct and permanent political structure.

    (b) with a distinct and permanent political structure, but strongly influenced by kinship and religion.

2. City States.
3. Empires based on City States.
4. Asiatic States with a centralised bureaucracy.
5. Nation States.

    (a) modern democratic states.

    (b) modern totalitarian states.

6. Empires based on Nation States.

Mr Bottomore himself admits that this classification is largely descriptive. Also, as we shall see later, the simple dichotomy between democratic and totalitarian states is not really very useful. But it does take into account the scale of societies, the economic system, social stratification, religion, and other factors important in determining political structure.

A more general scheme was suggested by Ginsberg in his 'Evolution and Progress'.[3] His classification was based on (a) the type of social structure and (b) whether domination or consent is embodied in legal and institutional arrangements. But the political scientist needs a more elaborate taxonomy than this, and one less 'concretised' than Bottomore's. To some such suggested schemes we now turn.

II: WEBER'S 'IDEAL TYPES'

One frequently used criterion is the nature of authority in the political system, or of the government's claim to legitimacy. This was the basis of Weber's three *ideal types* of authority: rational-legal, traditionalistic, and charismatic. Since most later typologies, to a greater or lesser extent, have contained within them something, whether directly or indirectly, of these categories, some account of them is necessary here.[4]

Briefly, in *rational-legal* systems, the government claims obedience on the grounds that commands fall within the impersonal, legally-defined scope of their office; authority inheres in the legal order itself, and only by derivation in the office-holders. *Traditionalistic* authority on the other hand, rests on the sanctity of tradition alone, on the immemorial past, on precedent. Whereas in the rational-legal system laws are considered as effective means of achieving certain goals, in the traditionalistic type they are sacred in themselves. In the former, laws are changed and new legislation is constantly bringing the system up to date; in the latter, prerogatives and obligations change little. Further, in the rational-legal system the laws constitute a perfect system of abstract rules, logically consistent and comprehensive; in the traditionalistic system they are discrete precedents not necessarily related to one another in systematic fashion. There is a large element of discretionary power allowed to the ruler, and, consequently, greater scope for arbitrariness.

The *charismatic* type of authority mainly emphasises the supposedly unique or very unusual qualities of the ruler. A charismatic leader with the 'gift of grace', inevitably opposes traditionalism or a rational-legal order; he is essentially revolutionary.

Two general comments may be made. First, these are 'ideal types', and all empirical systems are mixed in terms of this typology. Secondly—a specific application of the previous point —charismatic elements, in particular, can be mixed with either traditionalistic or rational-legal elements. So, in Britain, for example, traditionalistic elements persist side by side with rational-legal (and a Churchill may bring charisma into this mixed system). Pareto noted the English adherence to certain forms even when the substance is radically changed. Bagehot described the English as a 'deferential' people. Almond and Verba noted the inclusion of subject and parochial orientations in the 'civic culture'.

The three types need further elaboration.[5] The American phrase 'Not under men but under laws' expresses the rational-legal ideal, though it is not an exact description of American practice. In England, the different admixtures are perhaps even clearer. The monarchy is a traditionalistic element. The Prime Minister is the effective head of government. He and his political colleagues occupy legally-defined roles but are likely to possess elements of charisma. Below them, the bureaucracy rests almost entirely upon a rational-legal basis. 'The rule of law' a rational-legal concept, is bolstered up by the pomp and panoply of the judges; the importance of precedent in common law countries tends to enhance the traditional element; but the jury system is essentially charismatic. Elections are based on a rational-legal system, but there is an element of charisma in the appeal and personality of the candidate as well as in the 'aura of democratic sanctity' they confer on a political system. The referendum is even more likely to reinforce charisma, as with President de Gaulle. Nevertheless, democratic systems probably rest more clearly upon a rational-legal than upon any other basis. There is a definite limit set by law to the arbitary exercise of power by rulers, and an enforcement of their responsibility to the citizens. Relations between government and governed, whether individuals or groups, are defined by law, though there are from time to time complaints of 'unfairly used' discretion through administrative jurisdiction, and a demand for something like an administrative court of appeal or an *ombudsman*. At the extreme, of course, rational-legal safeguards may be destroyed by the 'populist' form of democracy, leading to either a left-wing or a right wing dictatorship.[6] In traditionalistic systems the ruler usually assumes office through some form of hereditary succession, though there are variations in the precise methods by which the 'rightful' heir is discovered; there may be some traditional limits on his power and even some provision for 'de-stoolment'. In any case, the traditionalistic chief expects obedience within an imprecisely defined range of action and always possesses a traditional sphere of 'arbitrary grace'. His administrative staff will consist largely of persons bound to him by personal ties of loyalty, and as kinsmen, freedmen, slaves, or simply favourites or paid 'household' servants. Their rewards may be a mixture of status, rights to fees or other incomes, allowances, maintenance, and other not clearly defined privileges; neither in recruitment nor advancement are rational-legal arrangements normally found. There are, of course, variations in the degree of centralised authority possessed by the ruler. Feudalism is a decentralised traditionalistic system far removed from the 'patrimonial' system like that of the Ottoman Empire. Even in such patrimonial systems, however, the administrative staff may acquire considerable power outside the chief's control. Various elements in society may also have means of resisting or ignoring chiefly control, the more so the further removed they are from the centre of his power, particularly when communications are bad. Some features of regimes of this kind are examined more fully in our analysis of Eisenstadt's study of 'Historical bureaucratic empires' (below, pp. 129 ff).

The pure type of charismatic authority is, as we have said, revolutionary. Whether we examine profound revolutions like the French, Russian, or Nazi German, or minor revolutions which are little more than coups d'état of the Latin-American type, they all involve at least two features of political significance. The institutionalised pattern for acquiring or exercising governmental power has in some degree been ignored, and new leaders have been able, for a longer or shorter period, to wield supreme power which rests on a *new* basis. Apart from these two basic features new ideologies may or may not be elaborated as an *ex post facto* justification for the new regime, and the social structure may or may not undergo considerable changes. The success of new leaders, whatever the actual extent of the changes made by them, inevitably endows them with some element of charisma. Hitler and Mussolini substituted charisma for the institutions which they had overthrown. Charismatic leaders such as these choose their staffs on the basis of personal loyalty, enthusiasm for the cause, and the possession also of some kind of charismatic quality. The leader's authority is absolute, however much in practice he may delegate.

But a system such as this is essentially transitional. Charisma must be 'routinised', and this means that it must move towards a traditionalistic, a rational-legal, or a mixed system. Tasks of administration require more than enthusiasm and adulation. Some kind of developed organisation is necessary to perform the essential tasks of government and to produce those concrete results by which charisma must seek to justify itself. Differences of opinion will inevitably emerge and the decision-making process must to some extent be rationalised. The problem of the succession will at some time have to be solved. If the leader tries to legitimise his position by plebiscites, these will come to possess some 'authority' as a basis for choosing leaders, and this may tend in a democratic direction. Bureaucracies will inevitably emerge, though the extent of their influence will depend not only on the power of the leader but also on the nature of the society and on past traditions. Or the use of traditional forms to strengthen the leader's authority may enhance their independent influence, and to some extent resuscitate them, albeit in changed form. It is not possible to pursue this argument further without going into illustrative case studies for which we have no space here.

This is, however, a convenient point at which to consider a criticism of the whole concept of charisma as a type of authority, made by Mr K. J. Rattram of the University of Singapore.[7] In Weber's account, the important factor in charisma is 'how the individual is actually regarded by those subject to charismatic authority, by his "followers" or "disciples"'. But Weber also stresses the importance of the need for a leader exercising charismatic domination to give some *evidence* of his qualifications in order to sustain his authority. Moreover, when the question of a successor arises, 'the right person who is truly endowed with charisma' has to be found. Shils has interpreted the general notion of 'grace' to include such qualities as having a 'strikingly vivid personality' and being 'extremely sensitive'. There may also be other qualities involved in charisma. Mr Rattram certainly argues that *more* than 'an exceptional personality' is required, if this be understood only to include appearance, manner, and style. Further, 'the type of leader generally called charismatic gets his support very largely from the *issues* he is associated with, the *grievances* he seeks to put right, and the *manner* in which he proposes to do so, and the *time* he chooses for making those issues and grievances the passionate concern of those whom he thinks will be his followers.' (Our italics.)

There must be inspiration, there must be a bond between leaders and followers, there must be popularity. Followers must provide intense support for leaders who, apparently, 'just occur'. But, Mr Rattram goes on, in how many cases have leaders described as charismatic 'just occurred'? There are *explanations* of the rise to power of men like Hitler, Nasser, Nkrumah, and the rest. Such explanations may include the vulnerability of some groups to particular pressures and appeals; propaganda; the elimination of opponents; powers of oratory; and, more generally, the conditions of the society itself in which these leaders 'occur'. 'We must not', argues Mr Rattram, 'fall into

53

the error of believing that leaders whom we regard as charismatic are individuals whose exceptional qualities come to be spontaneously recognised by their populations. They are often persons who succeed more than others in exploiting the situation around them.' In this situation propaganda and skilful management are of vital importance.

He then proceeds to test these generalisations by reference to some of the new states. Apter, for example, in his study of 'The Gold Coast in Transition', holds the view that Nkrumah's role as a charismatic leader was essential in ensuring that Gold Coast nationalism used the electoral and parliamentary procedures developed by the colonial power, thus endowing such procedures with legitimacy—through his 'gift of grace'. Shils has argued that political equilibrium in the new states *after* independence 'has depended on a great charismatic personality who, at the peak of the governmental mountain, offsets the distaste for bureaucratic legal rule'.[8] But, Mr Rattram pertinently asks, how can we know what type of equilibrium could normally have been expected, and how the presence of popular leaders like Nehru, Sukarno, and Nkrumah has produced something better—if, indeed, it is clear what kind and degree of 'equilibrium' they have, in fact, produced. We might, further, ask what charismatic leader ensured respect for the constitution in Nigeria after the controversial elections of 1964. Since the answer is 'none', then what ensured at least temporary 'equilibrium', and would it have been better if President Azikiwe had tried to resuscitate his erstwhile charisma? Finally, the three authors of another study[9] believe that the decline in respect for indigenous ruling houses and aristocracies—'a withering of the deep emotional roots of respect for traditional authorities'—provides the basis for the emergence of charismatic leadership. But, as Mr Rattram rightly says, these things did not 'just happen'; the 'charismatic' leaders were often the agents who *caused* the lessening of respect for freedom.

The argument that charismatic leaders are necessary to create unity and consensus may also be over-done. Any government (without charisma) by successful large-scale economic reconstruction, without *too* many sacrifices, might achieve the same end. 'While national unity may often appear to be a function of effective leadership, we should nevertheless be

54

aware that it is not dependent on any particular quality of leadership, and that in many cases the role which individual leaders play is conditioned by their social and political environment.' The further claim that certain individuals come to be regarded as 'symbolising the nation' is, Mr Rattram argues, mainly a rationalisation. As for Shils's argument that socialism in the new states grows 'fundamentally' from a feeling for charismatic authority, why should it have grown from different roots than those of the socialist intellectuals of the West?

We end with Mr Rattram's own concluding paragraph '. . . We are not very certain of what exactly we mean when we say that a leader is "charismatic", in other words, what it is that distinguishes him from other leaders. A vivid personality seems to be a necessary component, but certainly not the only one. Otherwise there is no reason why we should not just say that such and such a leader is very popular "because he has a vivid personality", without having to use the word "charisma". Then again, if popularity were the only index of "charisma", we do not know how popular an individual has to be, or how attached his adherents have to be to him, before we call him "charismatic". It seems certain, however, that the type of popularity generally associated with "charisma" relies at least as much on the issues taken up by a leader as on his personality. Propaganda, too, is of some real consequence. And finally, attempts to analyse the "role" of charismatic leaders seems to be based very largely on speculation, without much regard to the environment which produces these leaders and in which they function'.[10]

Other, more recent, typologies, although in some cases they are based on 'the nature of authority', and make some use of Weber's ideal types, including the charismatic, are basically concerned with 'environment', the social system of which the political system is a sub-system. To these we now turn.

III: AGRARIA AND INDUSTRIA

Most recent typologies of political systems have been based upon a combination of pattern-variable analysis applied to the patterns of interaction or the structures within the system, and the political culture approach. One sophisticated form of this, of course, is the attempt to investigate the degree of congruence between structure and culture.

Such typologies may derive from a study of societies, and are then adapted to the study of the political sub-system; all, however, are concerned with the relationship between the two, society and polity, and particularly with the influence of the former upon the latter. One early such typology, and one which influenced Almond, among others, is the broad distinction between *Agraria* and *Industria*, developed by F. X. Sutton.[11]

AGRARIA is the name given to a society based upon an intensive agricultural economy. It has four distinctive features which, following Sutton, we list and then discuss.

1. A predominance of ascriptive, particularistic, diffuse patterns of interaction.
2. Stable local groups and limited spatial mobility.
3. A relatively simple and stable 'occupational' differentiation.
4. A 'deferential' stratification system of diffuse impact.

Such a society is distinguished by the importance of status and of custom, and a relative absence of specialisation. Its norms are ascriptive; there are stable patterns of assignment of individuals to roles on the basis of birth, sex, age etc. There is continuity of status and in access to facilities and rewards with strong ties to locality and a predominance of particularistic groupings. Role differentiations may be numerous, as in India, but they are at a lower level of differentiation than in economically more advanced countries, and show ascriptive patterns of recruitment, which are not subject to 'generalising' influences. Class stratification has a diffuse significance and an occupationally concrete character (cf. the 'estates' in feudal Europe). The society is deferential rather than egalitarian. Sutton holds that Weber's 'traditionalistic' type is implied in this description especially through the predominance of ascription.

INDUSTRIA is broadly described as a complete opposite to Agraria. Its basic features are set out below.

1. A predominance of universalistic, specific, and achievement norms.
2. A high degree of social mobility.

3. A well-developed occupational system, insulated from other social structures.

4. An egalitarian class-system based on generalised patterns of occupational achievmeent.

5. A prevalence of associations i.e. functionally specific non-ascriptive structures.

We must emphasise, in such a society, the great importance of universalistic and achievement norms andthe correspondingly marked restriction of the significance of kinship systems. These norms are a solvent to the barriers among local, ethnic and other particularistic groups. There is access to many different possible statuses, and occupations can be compared by their norms, their monetary rewards, etc. The prevalence of associations is of particular significance because of their non-ascriptive and specific patterns of interaction. There are fewer discontinuities in the class-structure, though many *specfiic* hierarchical rankings. Sutton holds that the elements of Weber's rational-legal type are contained in this description.

There are, of course, mixed systems. Almond, indeed, argues that all systems are mixed and transitional. Although in modern Western systems the secondary structures and relationships are far more differentiated and significant, while the primary structures tend to be affected and modernised by the secondary ones (note, for instance the new role of castes as pressure droups in the political system of India); yet there is an *interaction* between the differentiated specialised structures such as parliaments, bureaucracies, courts, political parties, interest groups, and the media of communication, on the one hand, and the 'pre-modern' structures, on the other hand, which persist as political structures of great importance. If we take legislatures as an example, in the West the loyalty of the M.P. to formal parliamentary norms is greater than to kin, regional or religious groups; the secondary structures are more effective. Yet primary groups based on these latter factors and on interests of various kinds, or simply friendships, influence M.P.'s also. In the non-West, different kinds of informal structures based on aristocratic and family ties, caste, religious sects and other primary groups, operate and frequently affect the decision-making structure more than legislative committees or parties.

Comparison between systems, therefore, does not rest upon a rigid dichotomy between Agraria and Industria, any more than between Weber's three ideal types. Empirical systems must be compared according to the various admixtures of the different characteristics which they contain.

IV: FUSED, PRISMATIC, AND REFRACTED SYSTEMS

Fred W. Riggs has developed Sutton's approach further, though in somewhat different terms, as indicated by the title of this section.[12] The use of the term 'Public Administration' does not indicate the scope of Riggs's study, which, in fact, attempts to formulate an overall theory of economic, social, and political change in the partially and peripherally modernised societies. His conceptual framework is based on structural-functional analysis. A basic pattern of activity which is repeated is a structure, the result of any such pattern of activity is a function. Riggs holds that certain functions *must* be performed in any society if it is to persist; as examples of such functions he cites the satisfaction of wants, the allocation of power, and the distribution of influence.

Societies may be classified according to their degree of functional differentiation. Traditional societies—Riggs cites as an example the Thai Kingdoms before the 19th century—are functionally diffuse. Kings, priests, officials, and family heads play many-faceted roles, involving political, economic, administrative, and other functions. There are few organisations whose role is specialised to a single function. At the extreme, where all functions are performed by a single structure, societies may be described as *fused*.

In highly industrialised societies, functional differentiation is great; churches, trade unions, political parties, scientific organisations, administrative agencies, communication media, parliaments, have each a fairly narrow range of specific functions. At the extreme, where every function has a correspondingly specialised structure, societies may be described as *refracted* (by analogy with the spectrum which separates out all colours).

In Asia, Africa, and Latin America today, societies are like neither of the two above models. They are *prismatic* (as the

58

prism refracts fused light). In one sense, such prismatic societies are at a midway point between the two extremes of a continuum. But Riggs's interest in 'mixed' or 'transitional' systems has led him to analyse a number of unique features of such systems, which derive from the fact that functional differentiation has developed much further in certain areas of society than in others. Both the fused and refracted models are relatively homogeneous and realistic. i.e. their norms correspond to concrete structures. The prismatic systems show more heterogeneity.

In such systems, three types of phenomenon are characteristic: 'formalism', heterogeneity, and overlapping. 'Formalism' implies a marked discrepancy between the prescriptive and the descriptive structures. Rules, laws and declared policies bear no correspondence to the 'behaviour' which they purport to regulate. As a simple example, education may be compulsory for all children between certain ages, but, in fact, only fifty per cent of such children are in school. Or, public service recruitment is purportedly based on merit, but actually depends on connections.

Heterogeneity refers to the familiar situation in which modern urban behaviour is intermingled with traditional village behaviour to form complex new patterns. These same patterns are often examples of overlapping i.e. of the reciprocal dependence of such functionally distinct structures as exist. For example, prices are determined only partly by market supply and demand; various social, political, and other aspects of the relationship which exists between buyers and sellers also affect them. Salaries of public officials are determined neither by status nor by work done, but by rank, which includes factors both of achievement and ascription. One prominent feature of the mixed system is the 'clect', a term used by Riggs to describe a group which uses modern associational methods, but for diffuse and particularistic goals. Weiner's work on modern India suggests that there caste tends to develop these mixed characteristics.

An important historical comparison emerges from this analytical approach. In Asian, African, and Latin-American societies, changes in formal institutions precede changes in behaviour, whereas in European countries during the modernisation phase, changes in behaviour generally came first. Since the formal institutions do not possess the necessary strength and persistence and may not elicit the necessary public interest and influence, one result, in the former group of countries, is the disproportionately rapid development of bureaucracies, which are not effectively checked by non-bureaucratic social forces.[13]

It should be noted that Riggs's scheme does not cover all the variables in the social system. For example, fused systems may be either bureaucratic empires or feudal societies; in the former, there is a consolidation, in the latter, a fragmentation of power. Refracted systems may be either autocracies or democracies.

Readers who wish to examine in detail the application of these concepts to empirical systems should consider Riggs's treatment, especially, of Taiwan, Thailand, and the Philippines as well as, by way of contrast, the United States. Such examination will reveal 'the wealth of unconventional formulations [suggested by Riggs] . . . It stands as a challenge to the terminological conservatives who insist that human society be analysed in the language of common sense and admit new concepts only when the lexicographers do.'[14]

At the risk of repeating some of what we have already considered in our exaimnation of Almond's notion of political culture, we include, at this point, some of his applications of the Agraria-Industria, or refracted-fused-prismatic typology. In the British political system, Almond maintains, the relation between the diffuse, affective, particularistic and ascriptive elements, and the more specific, instrumental, universalistic and achievement elements tends to be one of *fusion*, (not to be confused with Riggs's fused systems). Modern and pre-modern attitudes combine to produce a homogeneous political culture, secular and traditional in content. British political structures—interest groups, political parties, parliament, cabinet and monarch—manifest the same fusional dualism.

In France, however, there is a polarisation of political culture; some elements and regions are traditional, others 'rational'. Traditionality and modernity are concentrated in different parts of France and their situation is *isolative*.

In some non-Western countries, modern culture prevails in cities, while despite large-scale modernising efforts the villages tend to maintain traditional forms, although they are constantly being eroded. Here is an *incorporative* 'pattern, not fused but not sharply antagonistic. The acculturation process is continuing and the result may eventually be either a fusional or an isolative culture and system. Almond considers that this kind of analysis, which, of course, resembles that of Riggs, especially in his 'mixed' or 'transitional' system, is more realistic than the sharp contrast between two syndromes: that of universalism-specificity-achievement-affective-neutrality, on the one hand, and that of particularism-diffuseness-ascription-affectivity, on the other. We pursue this later, in our study of Almond's 'political system' (below, pp. 134 ff).

A similar approach has been used by La Palombara in his account of some characteristics of political change and of political systems, partly as an attempt to distinguish 'change' as such from 'modernisation'.[15] His criteria are four in number. Firstly, there is the degree of structural differentiation of those institutions involved in the performance of political functions which may be defined generally in Easton's terms as 'the authoritative allocation of values' for a society. This criterion is also that of Almond and is comparable to Riggs's degree of 'refraction'. It is concerned with the creation of new structures and roles for the performance of political functions, the development of specialisation, and a division of labour between those responsible i.e. the political role-incumbents. For example, there will emerge a separate group of new administrators, functional specialists, for rule-application. Usually, though not always, there will be similar differentiation and specialisation in other sectors of society. On the other hand, despite the formal differentiation of political structures, the political function itself may be largely handled by structural arrangements that carry over from the past, as for example, in Southern Italy.

Secondly, there is 'magnitude', by which La Palombara means 'the ratio of political activity, however institutionalised, to all other activity in society'. Generally, differentiation and magnitude vary with each other, although the latter is greater, for example, in totalitarian societies. The question to be asked here is, 'how extensive a role does a particular social system ascribe to specific political institutions?' The answer to this, however, does *not* measure degrees of 'modernity'—otherwise the U.S.S.R., India, and Pakistan for example, would be more 'modern' than the U.S.

Thirdly, and in line with Parsons and Almond, as well as Sutton, La Palombara considers the degree of achievement-orientation applied to political recruitment and role-differentiation. All systems combine ascription and achievement (as also the other contrasted pairs in pattern-variable analysis). We must enquire what patterns of interaction for political functions are related to other structural elements of the system, and how they are related. For example, a 'modern' single-party might nevertheless be recruited on an ascriptive basis; or there might be class recruitment (or caste, or ethnic) to the civil service.

Finally, there is the degree of secularisation and rationality in performing political functions, a criterion which we have already sufficiently considered.

Like Riggs, La Palombara emphasises the need to introduce other variables, if we are seeking to include *political* development in such a way as to enquire into the possible emergence of a *democratic* system. There is no 'magical connection' between *any* of the four above criteria and Anglo-United States democracy. We examine these other variables at greater length later (below, pp. 191 ff).

V: FURTHER CRITERIA FOR COMPARATIVE ANALYSIS

Eisentadt, in his study of historical bureaucratic empires[16] has suggested a somewhat different approach, though there are some similarities to the foregoing typologies and also to Almond's scheme, which we consider below (pp. 134 ff).

First, he says, we must examine the extent to which the major political activities are organised in special roles, and differentiated both from other roles and/or groups in the society, and from each other. Secondly, and closely related to the first, we must examine the extent to which different political activities are organised in specific collectivities or groups, or are embedded in others, for example ascriptive kinship, territorial, or status collectivities. Thirdly, we are concerned to examine the goals of the polity: their content, their origin (in various groups); the criteria by which they are defined—whether, for example, political or non-political values are sought; and the nature and extent of participation in their definition. Finally, we must examine the types of legitimation and sanction in the society. This last clearly involves similar considerations to those relevant to Weber's three ideal types as well as to other approaches such as that of Binder (see respectively, above, pp. 49–55 and below, pp. 65–9). But it also involves, more specifically, the patterns of accountability i.e. the question of which are the reference groups for decision-makers in the political system.

All these variables are intimately concerned with the extent to which the polity is articulated as a sub-system of society; with the main direction of the system's political activity; and with the main points of inter-dependence between the political and the other institutional spheres.

On the basis of these criteria, Eisenstadt develops a far more comprehensive typology of political systems than we intend to examine in detail in this study. We therefore list his categories, but comment in detail only on the last two. The full list is as follows:

1. Primitive systems (not divided, as with Bottomore, above, p. 49).
2. Patrimonial Empires e.g. the Carolingian, the Ahmenid, the Parthian.
3. Nomad or Conquest Empires e.g. the Mongols, the Arab kingdoms under the first Caliphs.
4. City States.
5. Feudal Systems.
6. Centralised historical bureaucratic Empires.
7. Modern Systems, which may be divided into:

    (*a*) democratic.
    (*b*) autocratic.
    (*c*) totalitarian.
    (*d*) under-developed.

As regards (6), which is the main focus of Eisenstadt's extended study, we note merely that there is a limited autonomy only of the political sphere, and a limited level only of differentiation of political roles and activities. This brief description, however, provides a useful starting point for a further examination of (7), the group of modern political systems.

63

Typologies of Political Systems

In all four of these there is far greater differentiation of political activities, of the roles of rulers and ruled, and considerable development of the division of powers. There is a wider distribution of political rights and a much broader scope of political authority. (La Palombara's 'magnitude'.) There is a potentially active participation by various groups in the determination of political goals, and an extensive development of specifically political and administrative groups, but especially of party political groups. There is a weakening of the traditional hereditary patterns of legitimation, and a growing institutionalisation of competition for the right to exercise the various powers within the system, and for the attainment of ruling positions. The rules of the political system articulate the political aspirations and the goals of the system, while non-political factors (economic, cultural, social, organisational etc.) supply both 'free floating resources' (which must be mobilised by the political system for goal-attainment), and generalised power (which must be channelled through the political system to produce 'authoritative' decision-making). Clearly, these characteristics exist in different degrees and in differently balanced combinations in the four types of 'modern' political system.

Generally, however, Eisenstadt notes, at the present time, a weakening of the distinction in many political systems or, more accurately, societies, between the goals of the rulers and the political aspirations of the ruled, with a concomitant development of types of political institutions and processes which are directed towards incorporating the social and political aspirations of different groups into the goals of the polity. The formal claim to legitimation is that the polity represents the values and aspirations of the various groups in society. The developing inter-relation of political and other institutions and the absorption of groups into the polity may, he suggests, lead to totalitarianism. This pattern concerns not only the developing nations but also the many advanced societies in which collectivism and socialism become preferred values. We take up this point again later. Eisenstadt's detailed analysis of political systems is also discussed further, since it leads into our consideration of such approaches as those of Easton, Mitchell, and Almond to the notion of 'the political system' as such (below, Chap. 4).

64

VI: SYSTEM-LEGITIMACY CLASSIFICATIONS

In the introduction to his study of Iran, Binder[17] has developed another alternative conceptual framework and approach both to a typology of political systems, and to the actual working of the political system. We deal with the former here. It includes elements both of Weber's ideal types, and of the more sophisticated pattern-variable analysis. Binder distinguishes three broad types of system, the *traditional*, the *conventional*, and the *rational*.

The first of these follows very closely Weber's 'traditionalistic' ideal type. In such systems there is patriarchal leadership, a haphazard delegation of authority, a religious justification for the arts of government, a belief in the inscrutability of God's will and a pre-scientific notion of causation. The existing order of society is seen as pre-ordained, and its origin is referred to the distant past. The ruler is responsible to God alone; if he acts in an 'ungodly' way, this may lead either to rebellion, or to an acceptance of such conduct and its consequences as a 'punishment'. There may, indeed, be centres of power which are in conflict within the system, but these are not seeking a new form of legitimacy.

Possible conflicts are 'contained' by suitable delegations of authority, consultation, contractual agreements (compare the frequent 'confirmations of the charter' in mediaeval England), grants of audiences, honours, rewards, marriages etc. Individuals and groups attempt to use 'pull', lobbying, the seeking of appointments, and similar means of obtaining gratification. They may be given access to the decision-making process through consultations, or even through membership of administrative bodies. System-maintenance depends almost entirely on religious ceremonials. At a later stage, however, *controlled* democratic or constitutional (purely consultative, not deliberative) ceremonials may be added. Where such procedures fail to satisfy, there will be protests, boycotts, and work or service stoppages. But it must be noted that rulers can also inspire such anomic activities in order to frighten political opponents into believing that 'the people' are with them, the rulers.

Patterns of interaction are diffuse, with emphasis on kinship

65

ties. Parties and elections, where they exist, are linked with religion. Authority may rest, in part, on charisma (which, as we have seen, may be associated with ascriptive positions); opposition to it may take the form of 'palace revolutions', assassinations or coups d'état. 'Personal power' rather than conventional processes will determine decisions. Parties are short-lived and may be closely associated with, or virtually consist of interest groups, and there is a predominance of fragmented and compartmentalised structures within the power relationships. Primary groups, ethnic groups, and demographic classes are the dominant reference groups. Patriarchal leadership penetrates these structures, and bargaining (of the bazzar rather than of the market type) will take place between leaders. There are few specialised associational groups, and in bureaucracy, military, or clergy, there is particularistic-ascriptive role-orientation. This kind of system, Binder holds, is in a state of 'neutral equilibrium', with only mild changes occurring.

Binder's typology, it will be recalled, distinguishes between the *conventional* and the rational system (although many features of both these categories are contained in the more orthodoxly defined 'rational-legal' system). We now describe the former, which is 'a working constitutional democracy'. We may note that in Binder's view—following Aristotle's notion of the polity, and the views of many other political scientists—constitutionalism is 'a practical modification of democracy'. The modification is in an 'undemocratic' direction, in the interest of making the system work, although an attempt may be made to justify the institutional limits laid down by 'democratic' arguments. Binder asserts that intolerance is a heritage of the age of reason, and that 'ideal' democracy is as ideological as Marxism, and possibly as 'immature' or authoritarian. 'Democrats', he claims, in the Middle East and in similar areas, have frequently adhered to this view of democracy with its populist overtones[18] —hence, perhaps, the eventual emergence of authoritarian one-party, or even communist regimes. In Western democracies, on the other hand, *constitutionalism* accepts a certain ambiguity and falling-short of 'ideal' standards (or perhaps, rather, an unwillingness to push 'basic principles' to their 'logical' conclusion) as being 'mature'. There is some comparison between such systems and the 'civic culture', as described by Almond and Verba.

The pattern of power-relationships in conventional systems is fluid; change, indeed, is generally viewed with favour. There are conventionalised procedures for achieving legitimisation of new or changed power-relationships. There is broad consensus on ultimate values, often very broadly and vaguely defined, but no certainty about their more detailed content, or about how they are to be realised in any given case. There is tolerance for the pursuit of self-interest and for deviations from the norms. Freedom is essentially defined in political terms, and the laws are temporary compromises. Society is pluralistic, and this reinforces the purely political checks and balances; there is a polyarchal distribution of power and influence. Such systems define their goals, and means to those goals, through the normal procedures of legislation, adjudication, and administration; but there is greater emphasis on consultation, especially of interest groups, although elections, fought on 'general' issues, moderate group influence. Pragmatism is the keynote of the operation of such systems.

The *rational* system (which, we repeat, is clearly neither Weber's 'rational-legal' system nor the civic culture of Almond and Verba) seeks absolute justice and shuns compromise. It is organised hierarchically, and administrative regulations strictly control all the associations within the system. Both traditional and rational systems may have admixtures of the conventional. The former have 'frequently acquired some of the paraphernalia of conventional systems', such as elections, cabinets, regulatory agencies, and a centralised judiciary. Contrariwise, conventional systems may retain certain traditional myths. Rational systems often pay lip service to democratic ideals. They may indeed claim, like the 'people's democracies,' to be more fully realising those ideals. Critics of such systems would argue that this is the tribute which vice pays to virtue. Finally, there may be an admixture of the traditional and the rational, which Binder considers is the case in Iran, for example. Tradition is rationalised by the subordination of the aristocracy to a personalised source of legitimacy, which is itself identified with a logically ordered set of values.

In hybrid systems there is confusion and conflict about the

legitimacy of the system. When legitimisations do not accord with power relationships, then administrative implementation needs to be extremely efficient, through the use of 'adjustment', or of force, or of a combination of both. This efficiency, however achieved, is of vital importance if far-reaching changes are introduced into the system.

Binder also discusses the distinction between 'developed' and 'under-developed' systems, which he considers cuts across his three-fold classification with its mixed systems. Normally, he holds, there is a relationship between traditionality and under-development, on the one hand, and between conventionality or rationality and development, on the other. Referring to the use of various indices of modernity or development e.g. literacy, industrialisation etc. as used by Lipset and by Coleman (cf. below, sections on Coleman and Lipset, Chap. 6), Binder points out, like La Palombara, that *political* development must be related to the *impact* of incremental change in such factors as these *upon* the components of the political system. Among such impacts, he suggests as important the fact that power-relationships will be more often translated into legitimisations (i.e. 'processed' through the political system) and less frequently left outside the political sphere; and that there will develop better defined and fewer forms of obtaining such legitimisation. Institutional groups, such as the bureaucracy, will develop greater skill and new groups and channels of information will be formed. An examination of the *conditions* in which transition to democracy occurs is of fundamental importance to any assessment of what political system is, in fact, likely to emerge from a process of economic and social modernisation.

In this context, we must note, firstly, the importance of environment, including especially the social environment, as a cause of change. This will include such factors as changes in the international situation, and in the 'colonial' situation. Next, there is what may be described as 'normal system eccentricity'. In general this refers to the necessary deviations of the legitimis-ations from the actual power-relationships they are supposed to legitimise (i.e. express in authoritative formulae); these deviations arise from the fact of changing power-relationships. Thirdly, systematic change may arise from dysfunctional system-maintenance activity, which also leads to legitimacy confusion.

68

Where the government is responsible to a small elite which has effective control over the military, the bureaucracy, and the associational groups and change towards a more democratic system, for whatever reason, occurs, then whether or not there is a charismatic interlude—three things are necessary, if breakdown is to be avoided. Firstly, there must be socialisation into new roles, adequate and suitable to the new functions or to the new procedures for performing such functions. Secondly, there must be actual practice in working the democratic institutions associated with representative government and pressure politics. Thirdly, there is need for institutional efficiencies; the new institutions must not merely be worked in accordance with their required norms, they must produce satisfactory results. Transition to democracy depends on the willingness and the ability of the military and bureaucratic elites to decide, rationally and consciously, to establish and work certain democratic institutions.[19] A more fully-worked out conceptual framework and theory for this transition is given below in our account of Binder's definition and description of 'the political system' (below, pp. 171–81).

Meanwhile, we add merely that all the above reasoning holds for either revolutionary or traditional-rational mixed systems like that of Iran. Lipset has suggested, however, that democratic institutions are more easily sustained where elements of traditional legitimacy are maintained. This also appears to be the argument of Almond and Verba in relation to the civic culture. Lerner[20] has argued that modernisation leads to the 'contemporary participant society', i.e. the 'developed political system'. But such system, as La Palombara and others would agree, need not be *democratic*. On the other hand, it is doubtful whether in present day transitional systems the means of 'totalitarian' control exist, any more than they did in the days of divine-right monarchy or of enlightened despotism. Another factor, on Lerner's argument, is that economic development must *precede* political development, unless the administration can more or less simultaneously achieve both economic and political development. If the latter outruns both economic development and administrative achievement, then democratic systems are liable to founder because they do not produce satisfactory results as regards goal-achievement.

69

VII: A SIMPLE TYPOLOGY

In his Introduction to the 'Politics of the Developing Areas' Almond adopts a classification originated by Shils[21] of the political systems of the 'new states' of the non-Western world. This classification is of interest in itself as a typology of political systems, and also because each type implies a particular condition of governmental structure and can be applied to systems other than those of the new states. In this section we concentrate upon the typology; the detailed structural features are dealt with in our account of Almond's analysis of 'the political system' and its functions.

We have said that, although Shils is primarily concerned to examine possible alternative courses of political development for new states, his types can also be used for the purpose of comparing *all* political systems. This is due, among other reasons, to the fact that the elites of the new states have before them as models, contemporary existent modern states. They are impelled by their own ideologies, and by the structure of the contemporary world, to attempt a transformation of their own societies into modern polities such as there are elsewhere in the world. The systems they are striving to build, therefore, bear some considerable resemblance to other existing systems. These *new* systems, in their various stages of development are, therefore, not merely compared in theory to existing models by the new elites; they can, in fact, be compared in this way empirically by political sociologists and political scientists.

We consider first some general points. The predominant visible model which commands by its achievement, and by the prestige of its 'earthly embodiment', is that of a regime of *civilian rule,* through *representative institutions* in the matrix of *public liberties*—modern democracy. The new states began their career, at least in very large degree, with such a model, though with differences of detail according to whether they achieved sovereignty under the aegis of, for example, France or Britain. They diverge from it only from a feeling of urgent necessity, although having done so, 'ideological' justifications for such divergence may be offered, as well as more empirical explanations such as those based on social structure. Alternatives include oligarchy—civilian, military or mixed; a traditional-istic order—monarchical, absolutistic or feudal; or a modern theocracy. There is also the dictatorial communistic regime which now also provides variants—the U.S.S.R., China, Yugoslavia, Poland. But purposive deviation from the model is most likely to take the form of an oligarchy—including the communist oligarchy. The other alternatives are rather con-tinuing pre-democratic systems, which may be *maintained* or *resuscitated*, even if only in part, through doubts concerning the relevance of democracy, but which can seldom be *reverted* to *in toto*, after democracy has been found wanting. Such regimes, as also the oligarchy which is adopted under certain conditions, protest their 'fundamentally modern and democratic aspira-tions'.

We mentioned that the new states have normally begun their career under a 'Western type' democratic model. Their elites, of course, have not made careful studies of different types of regime; that which they know best is that of the colonial power which ruled them. Their demands for self-government have taken the form of a demand for such regime. The Ceylon-ese Ministers, for example, refused to contemplate the con-tinuance of the 'London County Council' type of system of the period 1928 to 1946, and demanded full responsible cabinet government on the Westminster model. (It is true, of course, that some of them, including the late Mr Bandaranaike, later expressed doubts concerning its suitability for Ceylon). Generally speaking, the colonial elites have insisted upon the full Westminster system; it has not been foisted upon them. Some of their leaders, however, notably President Nyerere, have expressed doubts concerning some of the features of the model, such as a formal opposition and a non-political civil service. More generally, if it appears that the over-riding goal of 'modernisation' is difficult to achieve under the democratic system, the elites are ready to introduce substantial admixtures of oligarchy, a readiness which is enhanced by socialist aims and the (little understood) example of the communist model. Given these circumstances and emerging problems, it is possible to 'delineate certain types of regimes which might be the outcome of the interplay of a zealously pursued ideal and intractable necessity'. But these types are all related, positively or negatively

6   71   P.S.

to the 'civil regime' described above. Adaptations of the model 'will run towards concessions to the traditional order, toward the heightening of oligarchical tendencies as a means of overcoming the refusal of the traditional order to enter the modern age, and toward the invention of new institutional arrangements through which liberal and democratic inclinations can find hitherto unknown forms of expression'. We now examine each of Shils's models in more detail.

Political Democracy is the regime of civilian rule through representative institutions and public liberties. Its components are first, a legislative body periodically elected by universal (adult or male) suffrage, empowereg to initiate legislation through private members, committees, or the executive leaders, and to enact or repeal legislation initiated by the executive. The latter is subject to review and control through debate, enquiry, and budgetary provision. (This itself is an idealised model. For 'deviations', especially as regards Executive-Legislative relations in Britain, cf. the author's *Parliament and the Legislative*, Routledge & Kegan Paul, 1965.) The executive carries out its policies throudh a hierarchically organised non-political bureaucracy, which is answerable to its political heads and, through them, to the legislature.

Candidates for the legislature are normally members of contending political parties, the party which wins an overall majority of seats (or achieves one in coalition) dominating the legislature of which its leaders may be members. (There are, of course, variations such as the Presidential model.) Executive and legislative action is subject to periodic review through free elections, as well as being continually scrutinised by free organs of public opinion. Within the legislature, opposition and minority rights are guaranteed, and governments can be changed by regularised procedures of election. There is, further, an independent judiciary to protect the ridhts of citizens against the government as well as against each other. There may or may not be a written constitution; in either case, traditions and conventions regadring the conduct of the executive, the legislature, the civil service, the army, and the police, as well as the judiciary, are well known and generally respected.

More important than this somewhat stereotyped and institutional description of a well-known political system, are the preconditions for such a system which Shils attempts to set out. Firstly, there must be stability, coherence, and effectiveness of the ruling elite. Governments must receive sufficient support to give them confidence that their policies are likely to be approved and effectively carried out. Authority will in large part depend upon reasonable effectiveness in the promulgation and execution of policy. Coherence and organisation are essential in both the alternative parties or groups, between which mutual and fundamental trust is also essential. The political leaders must be attached to representative institutions, and regard themselves as generally answerable to the electorate. The legitimacy of the elite must be accepted by a very substantial proportion of the population, particularly those sections who are politically conscious. Both competence and integrity are essential as a basis for this. Nor should the 'outside party' or its bureaucracy be able to turn the parliamentary party into its mere mouthpiece. Responsibility is maintained through Parliament, the 'centre of gravity' of the system.

Secondly, there must be a fairly coherent and responsible opposition, which is accepted as a necessary part of the political system. Its criticism should be constructive, not merely obstructive, and it must certainly eschew all methods involving conspiracy and subversion. Where one party is overwhelmingly in control, Shils argues that adequate opportunity for dissent within the majority party *on the floor of the house* should be permitted. Together, majority and opposition must form a preponderant block against either 'traditionalistic' or 'progressivistic' extremists. The difficulty of maintaining a 'Centre' coalition in the French Fourth Republic, or in present-day Italy, emphasises the significance of this requirement.

Thirdly, there must be adequate machinery of authority, which requires a well-trained and organised civil service, detached in its political orientations, loyal to any constitutional government, yet independent enough to offer strong and objective advice which politicians feel compelled to take into account. Conversely, civil servants must never despise politicians. It has been said that a civil servant who does not get on well with politicians is unlikely to be promoted, and does not deserve to be! It goes without saying that freedom from corruption is essential. As part of this machinery, it is necessary only to refer to the need to maintain 'the rule of law', particularly as regards an independent judiciary. It is also necessary that though there should be an effective police force, a reliable military force, and other organs of law and order, these must all accept a binding obligation to the prevailing political authority.

Fourthly, there must be a self-confident and self-sustaining set of institutions of public opinion—press, university, civic and interest associations, professional bodies, trade unions, and local government bodies—widely spaced throughout the classes and regions of the country. Information available must not be solely from government sources; there must be freedom of expression and of association. Shils argues also that there must be a 'modern civilian intelligentsia', and a fairly numerous, moderately educated, and reasonably politically concerned section of the population, 'primarily middle class but also with some peasants (sic) and working-men among them'. There must be a fairly comprehensive and elaborate system of private and voluntary associations, though none must become so powerful as to hold the rest of society to ransom. There is thus created 'an infrastructure of decision and authority . . . which reduces the amount of authority exercised and of decisions made by the State', and also 'keeps in check tendencies towards the "politicisation" of life that are inimical to the regime of civilian rule, representative institutions, and public liberties'.

Finally, 'continuity is essential to civil order'. Insoluble problems which arouse passionate conflicts harm political democracy; they produce crises which encourage 'martial law' and a suspension of the guarantees which are an essential part of the system. There is need for a sense of community, a sufficient degree of interest in public affairs, a general acceptance of the legitimacy of the existing political order, a sense of dignity and rights as well as of obligation on the part of citizens, and a sufficient degree of consensus regarding values, institutions, and practices. All this creates what Shils terms a 'political society', one in which 'polity' and 'society' approximately coincide in their boundaries in the sense that no part of society is excluded from access to the polity. (Not in the sense that there is no 'boundary-maintenance' between the political sub-system and society, cf. below, Chap. 4.)

No existing society, of course, actually fulfils all the pre-conditions for the continuously effective working of the system of political democracy. But in the new states the distance from the pre-requisites of the system is rather greater. Shils considers that in India, for example, only the outstanding qualities of political leadership and of a few journalists, together with the remarkably efficient civil service and the ingrained civil sense of the officer corps have kept the regime as close to political democracy as its inheritance of cultural, economic, and political obstacles permit. In other new states, tribe, religion, language, and traditions of parochial hierarchy and acquiescence have prevented the emergence of a 'civil order'. Nigeria and Malaya, perhaps, in Shils's opinion, have adequate compensation for their deficiencies as political societies, though doubt was thrown on both during 1964–65. In Iraq, Indonesia and the Sudan, the elites have lacked internal solidarity, not only among parties but within parties and cliques. Opposition has been recalcitrant and factious, and governments correspondingly impatient. Almond, on the other hand, includes Japan, Chile and Israel in his list of political democracies. In most cases, the tasks of modernisation, the doubts and ambivalence of the elites, the narrowness of public opinion, have all helped to bring about a greater concentration of authority than political democracy would countenance.

Tutelary Democracy exists where elites, while recognising the difficulties of a system of political democracy, wish to retain as much of its institutions as possible, though they introduce modifications in order to maintain an effective and stable government and to modernise the economy and the society. Some have gone so far as to establish a much stronger executive and to reduce considerably the power of the legislature and of the political parties, while still retaining the rule of law and basic civil liberties. But even with restrictions on representative institutions and the free expression of public opinion, the elites do attempt to keep the system going more or less democratically through very strong executive initiative and continuous pressure from the top. The 'guided democracy' of Indonesia is a deliberate and drastic attempt to concentrate political life into a restricted elite, while keeping some parliamentary forms—

75

though they are continually being eroded. In Burma after 1958 the Army maintained something like a system of tutelary democracy, though after one attempt to restore the old system there was a reversion once more. Ceylon has maintained parliamentary forms, and was holding yet another election in 1965, nearly twenty years after independence, though it has been deemed necessary to impose considerable restrictions on the press and on public liberties. Almond placed Ghana in this category, though it would appear now rather to belong in some ways to the next category, of modernising oligarchies. Tutelary democracy is more authoritative than political democracy. It appeals to men brought up to believe in democracy and who have considerable attachment to democratic institutions, but who have little confidence in their people's present capacity to operate them. The system may retain all, or most, of the institutions of political democracy but adapt them all in the direction of a greater preponderance of the executive. Executive and party move closer together, and discipline is maintained in both state and party by strong personalities. Parliament has fewer powers and less influence, since it is either dominated by the executive or by the party. Opposition is discouraged, if not entirely suppressed. The Press may be restricted, and public information largely under the influence of government-controlled media of communication. But the rule of law, at least so far as a degree of independence of the judiciary is concerned, is likely to be maintained. (It is the absence of this feature, to a great extent, which makes it appear that Ghana is no longer in this category.) But freedom of expression, assembly, and association, is not likely to be complete.

There are a number of pre-conditions of this system which may not be very easy to fulfil. As in political democracies, the elite must be effective, and therefore stable, competent, and internally coherent. In the absence of these qualities, even the 'proto-democratic' features of tutelary democracy are likely to disappear. Success, especially in modernisation, is one important foundation for legitimacy; so, too, is probity—hence the sometimes puritanical attitudes in ruling circles which are not always found in political democracies. Ghana and Nigeria provide a contrast here. The elite must also have a firm grip on the machinery and the affections of its supporting organisations.

Tutelary democracy aims to provide a more disciplined and stable regime than is possible, given the social and economic conditions of the new states, under political democracy. If it appears to be failing in this essential task, it will quickly become more oligarchical unless the system begins to break down altogether. But throughout this period the elite must continue to be attached to the *idea* of democracy and it must be willing to renounce some of its powers as the democratic capacities of society increase.

The elite must also minimise its use of coercive means of achieving consensus. The opposition must not be treated as 'pariahs, cranks, or enemies' and at least the principle of opposition must be accepted. The opposition, for its part, must not take refuge in obstruction and subversion, even though it sees little opportunity of achieving power. A further condition of success is the existence of a competent civil service, loyal, as in a political democracy, to the executive, but not unwilling to accept the possibility of a new elite emerging, if the tutelary democracy does eventually become a political democracy. Dispassionate and informed criticism is essentially a task of the public service, in the absence of effective parliamentary and public criticism. Nevertheless, the civil service must remain subject to the controls of the political executive, and not itself immune to judicial control. Indeed, 'in a tutelary democracy [the] educative role [of the judicary] is of the first order'. Again, as in a political democracy, police and military must be firmly under the control of the civilian political elite.

One of the greatest differences between political and tutelary democracy is the absence in the latter of strong public opinion and of private and voluntary associations. But the regime must encourage education, thought and aspirations and must be receptive to the first signs of an alert and forceful public opinion. 'This is, indeed, the evidence of the good faith of the tutelary elite.'

Such a regime clearly presupposes a reasonable 'civil' population and a general inclination to acknowledge the legitimacy of existing authority. Apathy, on the other hand, as much as fractiousness, will cause the regime to become oligarchical. Shils, in fact, considers that 'we might even go so far as to question whether tutelary democracy is a possible alternative'

77

political system in the new states. In India, the elite has been sufficiently devoted to the principles of a democratic polity to carry out its tutelary functions well. But Burma, Lebanon Turkey, and the Sudan are the only outstanding examples where political democracy has been *reinstated*, and the return to such a system is not always permanent. It is almost impossible to judge to what extent, for example, Senegal and the Ivory Coast are examples of tutelary democracies or of modernising oligarchies with but a façade of democratic institutions. Mali and Guinea almost certainly are not the former. 'Our experience thus far may be interpreted as supporting the view that deliberate restrictions on the working of the institutions of political democracy traverse a road which allows no easy retracing of steps once taken.'

Modernising Oligarchies emerge from conditions where the gap between polity and society and the dangers from the 'reactionary mass' of the traditional society make a concentration of authority appear to depend on some form of oligarchy, even to those who would prefer parliamentary democracy but realise how far removed from its possibilities their societies are. Representative institutions appear likely to be too unstable and too likely to provide a means whereby traditional elements can hinder modernisation, to commend themselves to politicians, military men, and intellectuals who desire to speed up the pace of change. In the Sudan, Iraq, Egypt, Pakistan, and among certain elements in Indonesia, Ceylon, and even India, as well as in many of the new African states, 'oligarchy is believed to be the only way to create a modern society with rational honest administration, and decisive action for social progress'. 'Modernity' entails a preponderance of public authority, especially where there is the great 'gap' between polity and society, and the heavy counter-weight of traditional beliefs and practices. 'Oligarchy is the "natural" theory of the radical "progressivists" of the new states.' Yet there is little or no theoretical exposition of all this, it is a reaction to circumstances as they are perceived by the relevant elites.

For its success, such a system obviously depends on the existence of a well-organised elite, 'clique-like' in structure, relatively closed, watchful over its new members and aspirants

78

to membership. If it is a civilian clique, it must possess a firm ascendancy over the military. If it is a military clique, it must of necessity obtain the co-operation of the civilians whose expertise it needs.[22] Any oligarchy eliminates parliament as a deliberative organ with autonomous powers and reduces it to 'acclamatory and ratifying roles', with perhaps advisory functions, but certainly no opposition is permitted. Political parties, except that needed to support the oligarchy, will either be legally dissolved or bullied into submission.

Modernising oligarchies need an elaborate machinery of bureaucratic administration. They will normally compromise with the pre-existing civil service, and promote new men to key positions. Even military oligarchies will have to utilise existing bureaucrats. A regime such as this is usually unwilling to tolerate an independent judiciary, which is part of the 'slow-moving' regime they wish to replace. In addition, the oligarchy normally wishes to dispose of 'spies' and 'traitors', for which the rule of law and an independent judiciary are inconvenient. There is always a danger of conspiracy in a society where open criticism is impossible. A stable oligarchy must therefore rest heavily on the police and the army, both of which will have a 'political role' far more prominent than in either political or tutelary democracy.

As in both the previous systems described, the elite must be stable, coherent and effective. Its purpose is to 'clean up the mess', and it must strive for outstanding achievements, whether economic or in foreign policy. Moreover, any lack of unity in the oligarchy would encourage divisions in 'public opinion', and perhaps encourage the otherwise discredited politicians. 'The elite must be cast in an heroic mould [and] appear to live on a level on which the self is transcended on behalf of a higher good.' The modernising oligarchy is not a 'conventional tyrant'. It is more akin to the 18th-century enlightened despot, but without the aura of hereditary right to rule. Practical achievements such as land reforms, more equitable taxation, improved irrigation, as well as a high level of administrative efficiency and integrity, are essential.

Opposition, we have said, cannot be tolerated. It must be dealt with by suppression, by being associated with 'foreign enemies' or by 'tension-alleviating' economic and social policies which leave no grievance on which oppositions might capitalise. On the other hand, all suspicion of corruption must be eliminated, at least at the higher levels. Firm control must be maintained over the police and the army, and an efficient intelligence service must be able to detect any centres of dissatisfaction and deal with them vigorously. In systems where oligarchy is established, there is likely to be little independent and informed public opinion, and what little there is will either be rigidly controlled, suppressed, or organised so as to ensure that it will reinforce rather than hinder the oligarchy.

The elite does not require active political participation, or what Shils calls 'civility'. Rather does it demand assent and enthusiasm. If there is any element of democracy in the system it is 'populistic', and the oligarchy will make use of plebiscites, processions, demonstrations, and even 'organised' pro-regime anomie! 'Homogeneity of opinion is a desideratum of the modernising oligarchy.' A practical consequence of this is that sectionalism and communalism must be reduced to a minimum and traditional ties and practices removed as much as possible. A 'mobilised, unitary, national will' is demanded, and in achieving this the intellectuals are expected to place their services at the disposal of the regime. To justify this unity, a sense of national emergency will be constantly encouraged, and 'heroic' measures demanded.

Among the new states which clearly have an inclination towards oligarchy, Pakistan, the Sudan (subject to the changes in 1964), the United Arab Republic, and Iraq all went in this direction from imperfect and unstable forms of political and tutelary democracy. As we have suggested, there are signs that Ghana is travelling the same road, not to mention many of the ex-French West African states. Nor need it be doubted that oligarchical regimes are capable of persistence, even though the particular group in control may change from time to time. More doubtful, however, is the nature of the results likely to be achieved by such regimes and, in particular, whether they can succeed in their efforts to modernise society, rule with stability and effectiveness, and continue to mobilise enthusiastic support. Certainly in many cases there is already evidence of some success e.g. in improving transport and communications, reforming land tenure and introducing irrigation schemes and other civil engineering projects. More doubtful are the prospects of modernising the rest of the economy, especially industrial production. Apart from foreign interests, in the absence of a strong indigenous entrepreneurial class, the elites are often to a great extent tied up with traditional and conservative interests and unlikely to take sufficiently radical steps to encourage new private enterprise.

There is a greater likelihood of effective reform of the machinery of government and the maintenance of public order. Yet even in this sphere the residues of the previous regime are not easily removed, or even contained, and new tensions are likely to be set up. Further, there is ample evidence to suggest that even military oligarchies are subject to constant threat and occasional overthrow, often by a combination of other military cliques and communist groups. On the other hand, Pakistan and the United Arab Republic, for example, have shown a remarkable degree of permanence and an absence of serious threats of replacement. Against this, however, 'although the external power of traditional authorities can be broken by oligarchies, there is no necessary correlation between this and the eliciting of a zealous affirmation of the modernising oligarchical elite which supplants the traditional elite'. Centres of dispersed authority, related to particularism and tradition-ality, cannot be tolerated, yet they are not easily suppressed permanently.

Totalitarian oligarchy 'is oligarchy with democratic airs'. It is legitimated by a coherent doctrine which, as the creation of intellectuals, has some appeal for intellectuals. In such a system a small clique exercises rule and refuses to admit the legitimacy of public opposition. No compromise is possible with religious communities, kinship groups, or even local traditional authori-ties; every sphere of life must be dominated, and every centre of previously independent authority annulled. So far, no new state has become communist (it is clear throughout that Shils is concerned only with *communist* totalitarianism), 'though accusations have been made against such regimes as that of Guinea, Mali, Zanzibar, and even Ghana.' But many have adopted methods of organisation which bear considerable re-semblance to those used in avowedly communist countries and it is sometimes difficult to distinguish between the new 'authoritarian' regime and the totalitarian model.

There must, in such a regime, be a strong, well-disciplined, highly coherent elite, constituting a party which is internally united and convinced of its historical mission. A powerful bureaucracy normally controls both party and state. The party controls a monopoly of power and can tolerate no other independent party. Parliamentary institutions are used for purely acclamatory and ceremonial purposes and both legislation and execution are in the hands of the party. Popular elections or plebiscites do not determine the membership of the elite, nor do they have any 'mandatory significance'. The rule of law is dispensed with, at any rate in 'political' matters—which may be very broadly defined indeed—and there can be no independent judiciary. Public opinion cannot exist as an independent factor and there are no autonomous civic or interest groups.

A totalitarian elite is likely to strain the resources of the economy and the society far more than a modernising oligarchy of the type previously described and for this reason it must keep a firm grasp on the machinery of order and enforce very strict discipline both within itself and throughout the system. Since opposition is not to be tolerated, there is always the danger that 'intra-elite' opposition may become subversive (or regarded as such by the majority): any such element among the existing leaders is likely to be suppressed. The ruthless action needed for rapid modernisation requires a vast administration apparatus, which may suffer from over-centralisation due to over-pressure. Party supervision over the bureaucracy then comes to be regarded as even more essential.

Although free public opinion must be suppressed, since the totalitarian regime is populistic it demands an expression of widespread popular support for its policies. The elite, too, will be more distrustful of traditional elites and of the practices of traditional authorities, than any other type of governing elite. There will be a widely ramified machinery of organisation, propaganda, and control, penetrating into every sphere of life. A situation of crisis or emergency must be constantly maintained in order to justify such measures. All this implies that 'the polity would become not just congruous with society . . . but identical with it and superior to it'. The result is not a 'political society', but an 'ideological society'.

This kind of model has its attractions for new states. It appears to offer the prospect of rapid progress. But its chances of success may be less favourable than the appearance. Could such an oligarchy, for example, face a much greater rate of saving and investment than a vigorous elite in any of the three previous types of regime which we have examined? Might it not create *more* alienation and active hostility? Would it possess the necessary administrative skills, which are so lacking in most of the new states, whatever their political system? If coercion fails, the modernisation programme is endangered and this must eventually produce disharmony in the elite and unrest in the population. Particularistic loyalties, never completely destroyed, would re-emerge and unity be destroyed. So far, we have insufficient experience of such regimes in the new states to be able to fill out these generalisations in more detail.

Traditional Oligarchy has persisted in many of the new states, though not in the form of large-scale bureaucratic empires such as those described by Eisenstadt, sometimes with the encouragement of the colonial power; it has 'led a crippled and dwarfed existence under the toleration of foreign rulers', without enlisting the support of the modern sectors of society. However much sympathy for the traditional culture there may be, there is always a strong desire for modernisation, which requires centralisation and active intervention in all spheres of life. Traditional oligarchy, therefore, seems unlikely to have a strong permanent appeal; yet 'below the surface of deliberate choice, traditional oligarchy is powerfully magnetic,' and some traces of it will be found in most of the political systems of the new states.

Shils has little to add to our previous accounts of this kind of system. Authority rests on a firm dynastic constitution buttressed by traditional religious beliefs. The ruler may be chosen entirely on a kinship basis, or with some element of choice at least by the 'elders'. His counsellors are selected on the basis of kinship or personal choice. There is no need for a legislative body, since what few new laws are required will be

83

enacted by the ruler and his advisers, though 'proto-parlia-ments' or advisory assemblies, carefully controlled, may be established. The civil service will be restricted in size and largely maintained as a household retinue. Large tasks will not be undertaken and major emergencies will be difficult to cope with. Local kinship or territorial groups will exercise a considerable degree of independent power. Critical, informed public opinion is lacking and popular participation, at least above village level, is not expected.

The elite is not concerned with any aspect of modernisation; indeed its apparatus is inadequate for such policies, and if such apparatus were created the position of the oligarchy would be undermined. Divergencies of opinion within the elite are not likely to threaten the regime, and 'traditional conciliar mech-anisms' will be adequate—at least until a strong 'modernising' opposition emerges. The machinery of order, again, is adequate until the latter tendencies appear. These are not likely to do so, however, unless an 'intelligentsia' can develop (this may, in fact, appear first at student level) or urbanisation proceeds. Unless and until the latter phenomenon appears there is un-likely to be even a small politically-conscious section in the community. Meanwhile, the traditional feudal and kinship structure will serve to maintain the oligarchy, albeit on the basis of highly decentralised power.

It is unnecessary to stress the obvious fact that such a traditional oligarchy is unsuited for modernisation. 'To become modern means to renounce its own nature.' If a traditional ruler decides to modernise, he might for a time carry his proposals on the basis of his existing traditional legitimacy. But 'in the end, the result would be one in which the traditional regime would survive only interstitially and vestigially'. It will be interesting to test this generalisation in, for example, Afghanistan as progress under the new constitution established in 1964–65 is watched.

Finally, it is important once again to emphasise the signifi-cance of 'traditionality' in all new states. 'The vestigial survival of traditional oligarchy would be characteristic not only of regimes modernised by traditional rulers but by modern elites as well. The traditional order in the new states is too deeply-rooted to be extirpated, even by the most impressive measures.

It will constantly reassert itself in the most modernised bureaucratic structures, in modernised party systems, and in the
political conception of modern intellectual and political elites.'
If Ghana may prove to be the exception to this rule, Northern
Nigeria and the Ivory Coast, among others, continue to illustrate it. But we must constantly remind ourselves of Almond's
insistence that *all* political cultures and political systems are
'mixed', and in a certain sense 'traditional', and that if pattern-
variable analysis were applied in detail to the empirical
political systems outlined by Shils, it would not reveal a simple
dichotomy of syndromes.

The continued existence of 'mixed' systems, and the difficulty
of clearly distinguishing, even analytically, between the various
models, is well brought out by Shils's addition of the category
Traditionalistic or *Traditionalistic Revivalist* systems. Such a regime
'while purporting to embody and enforce traditional beliefs and
practices, actually destroys the traditional structure of government, and replaces it by an oligarchical constitution'. A
traditionalistic oligarchy appears to be resolutely opposed to
modernity, and seeks legitimacy on the grounds that it is
protecting the traditional culture. But it ends up by leaving
little of the looseness of the traditional system. There are
nationalistic overtones in such regimes, since the 'superiority'
of inherited practices and beliefs is insisted upon, and their
revival is regarded as a means of strengthening the nation. But
it is also recognised that certain of the practices of modernity are
essential in order to strengthen the nation further. This applies
especially to modern technology, and above all to modern
military technology.

But modern technology and administration are, in the long
run, inimical to traditionalism, especially since they involve the
emergence of a modern intelligentsia. 'A traditionalistic regime
in the present age would therefore be inevitably unstable.' This
is even more likely to be true, if, as in present-day Afghanistan
and Nepal, some elements of 'constitutionalism' are added, with
whatever safeguards, to the administrative and technological
innovations.

Although in analysing the five or six different political
systems suggested by Shils, and adopted by Almond, we have
inevitably illustrated the system largely by reference to new

85

states, the above analysis has, of course, not been intended as a complete study of their political systems and certainly not of the conditions for their emergence or continuance. Readers are advised to consult Shils's own work, as well as that of Almond and Coleman and the many other studies of the problem of the 'developing areas'—including one of the most recent, Worsley's 'The Third World'—in order to test for themselves the usefulness of the suggested typology for an understanding of empirical systems.

VIII: POLITICAL CHANGE

We have, however, included as a further guide, a summary of two other suggestive approaches to a taxonomy of political systems, although each is concerned with transitional problems rather than with static typologies. The first is based upon the work of J. H. Kautsky[23]. Although the primary purpose of the book which he has edited is to examine the possible relationships between nationalism and communism, it does contain a description of five political systems which is very similar to that of Shils. They are set out below:

1. The traditional aristocratic authoritarianism.
2. The transitional stage of domination by nationalist intellectuals (Communism).
3. The totalitarianism of the aristocracy (France).
4. The totalitarianism of the intellectuals (Stalinism).
5. Democracy.

The validity of some of these categories is examined further in our next section. But Kautsky's detailed analysis of what he means by a democratic political system has several points of interest. He begins by examining the interest-group theory of politics, which sees politics as a conflict of interests with competition among people with different interests, generally united in groups defined by an interest, for the limited resources, such as wealth and prestige, available in the governmental arena. Government is made up of the contestants, or the representatives of conflicting interest groups, though like David Truman, Kautsky would presumably agree that the Government can also represent something called 'the public interest' even if this is merely the peaceful compromising of conflicting interest through agreed procedures.

In the new states the 'contestants', according to Kautsky, are chiefly social classes, the aristocracy, the peasantry, the old middle class, the capitalists, the workers, the new middle class—though these divisions are not, in his opinion, based on the Marxist class conflict (cf. again, Peter Worsley *op. cit.*). This approach to an analysis of the political system, he claims, is empirical, not 'rational', and it is based upon the statement that actors performing political roles *do* behave in certain ways, not that they *ought* so to behave. The one general variable which affects the course of political development, Kautsky holds, is the economic conditions of the society.

Although this latter assertion seems to overlook the point raised by La Palombara, for example, that particular ways of achieving economic modernisation do not *necessarily* lead either to democracy or to any other form of political organisation (see, further, below, Chapter 6, Section II), Kautsky has made one important contribution to the argument about democracy which is a valid reply to those who refuse the name democracy to any system which does not embody all of the features of the 'Anglo-American' system.

Democracy, he says, is a political system in which all, or the most significant, groups in the population participate in the political process and have access to effective representation in the process of making governmental decisions i.e. of allocating scarce resources. *Parties, elections* etc. are more or less reliable *symptoms* of the existence of democracy, rather than factors *producing* it. This seems to be a useful addition both to Shils's analysis of 'political democracy', and to the argument about what exactly is meant by 'political' (as opposed to economic) modernisation.

Our second approach in this section is specifically concerned with the process of transition. It is taken from Apter's study of Uganda,[24] in which he also refers to his study of Ghana. Apter starts from the fact that changes in Africa represent a process which has a much longer history than European intervention and that a 'set of abstractions' is needed to guide us through this process. Stated briefly, Apter sees three types of political leaders operating in three different political systems. In Ghana and Guinea, for example, leaders have sought to *mobilise* the total resources, physical and human, of their countries. In Nigeria and, for a time the Mali Federation a kind of *consociation* has been sought so that political unity might provide a means of bringing together a number of groups for purposes of common action. In Buganda, 'change is filtered through the medium of traditional institutions, and is in the hands of a *modernising autocracy*'. Each of these three types of political tendencies may be considered as a 'consequence of political arrangements which sort themselves out in the politics of contemporary Africa'. Each has developed as a result of the great challenge posed by the extension of political democracy to Asia and Africa. 'What remains to be accomplished in Africa is the creation of new civilisations.' This involves 'religion or cosmology as well as a defined system of political and social organisation'. The three systems indicated, however, represent the latter rather than the former.

The nationalism of all three is 'political in its materialism and its concern for rapid development'. The mobilisation system is related to 'Marxism as a secular religion'. The modernising autocracy retains 'traditional religious ties, absorbing and filtering modifications in social structure through the screen of Islam and Christianity'. Pan-Africanism, in Apter's view is not, as yet, a religion or a fully developed ideology. It rests upon the idea of political independence, economic and social development and reaction to colonialism. 'It is . . . at the mercy of traditional factors in African society and is vulnerable to the immediate politics of parochial nationalism.' It relies heavily on the political form and on the state as *more* than just a political form.

The mobilisation systems, Apter argues, have the greatest affinity with the new pan-African state. Consociational systems cut across pan-Africanism by substituting for its ideology a loose political framework of co-operation. Traditional systems sustain powerful sentiments for local and parochial institutions, but may be no less nationalistic than the pan-African state. There may be 'strange combinations. . . . In Nigeria, in the North, a theocratic state collaborates with a mobilisation system in the Eastern Region and all are within a consociational framework'. Nor are all modernising autocracies alike in every

88

respect. Buganda shows a form of 'secular traditionalism'; it includes the pan-Africanistic emphasis on modernisation but seeks to maintain the stability of traditional institutions.

Apter compares the system with the early European monarchies. But he reminds us that the modernising autocracies of the Western world gave way to representative government; this latter may be a threat to the African modernising autocracy. 'Its most distinguished characteristic is a hierarchical principle of authority which admits a two-way claim of communications but bases its legitimacy upon the right of a monarch to rule.' In Buganda, moreover, the political forms and social institutions are virtually identical. Apter seeks, in his detailed study, to discover the possibilities for survival of such a system. We do not re-examine his assessment in the light of subsequent developments, which appear to have made at least possible the acceptance by the Kabaka of Buganda of the status of a constitutional President; the break up of the Kabaka Yekka Party, based on personal allegiance; and the acceptance by Buganda of a co-operative role in the representative (tutelary?) democracy of Uganda. Instead, we turn to an examination of the key-features of each of his three systems.

The 'types of authority patterns' are based on five variables: (1) patterns of legitimacy; (2) loyalty; (3) decisional autonomy; (4) distribution of authority, and (5) ideological expression.

In the *mobilisation system* a party or regime is concerned with the drastic and thorough reorganisation of the society. The elite is unrestrained by the constitutional order. It assumes that the social structure of society must be altered so as to create a new system of loyalties and ideas. Its perspective approaches that of a revolution and it attempts to lead 'a wholesale assault on the problems that lie ahead'. Power resides at the top of the organisation, generally in a single leader who monopolises legitimacy. Conferences and assemblies give his decisions formal validity; all agencies in society are concerned with the mobilisation of consensus. Total allegiance is demanded of all adherents to the party. The party itself is 'tactical—rather than policy-oriented' and combines the maximum freedom of action with the minimum of accountability. No other solidarity groups are tolerated except those subordinate to the regime. In so far as an ideology develops it is primarily concerned 'to give

89

perspective and justification for what already appears necessary'. But opportunism prevails and 'the political "culture" of
the members is based upon their common oreanisational
affiliation'.

The *consociational* model places a high value on compromise
among divergent groups. It 'sacrifices precision in organisation
and militancy in outlook in order to allow diverse interests to
congregate'. The nature of the 'consociation' may vary from
loose confederations to federal states. Consensus is based upon
acceptance of a common denominator or shared set of interests.
Compromise and accommodation are essential in such a system.
There is a danger of *immobilisme* because of lack of common
agreement, and crisis and fission are always a threat. Events in
Nigeria in 1964, expecially, aptly illustrated all these characteristics. Authority is pyramidal; power is dispersed and shared
between the units and the centre. Legitimacy rests upon the
representative principle and leadership is collective. Multiple
loyalties function on various levels and political groups and
parties cannot demand unqualified allegiance to either a leader
or a set of aims. The necessity for compromise already noted
leads usually to a minimal programme of change. Ideology is
extremely important as a means of maintaining broad consensus and favourable orientation to political roles and structures. 'Negritude' in French West Africa is an example of such
ideology.

The *modernising autocracy* rests upon the acceptance of existing
authority, but for modernising purposes. It requires 'a profound
solidary core with an ethnic or religious basis', as a basis of
support for leaders or ruler. The system can tolerate wide
changes in social and economic life, though it cannot cope so
easily with 'new social and political groups which demand a
change in the system and principles of legitimacy'. If economic
advance seems likely to involve political democracy, the former
may be resisted. Authority is hierarchical but it 'is the institutionalised property of the leadership role', rather than of a
particular individual. Institutionalism generally implies some
limits on discretion. Membership of the unit is virtually tantamount to citizenship but members may belong to a range of
voluntary associations and political groups. Leaders can 'plan
long-term strategies' but are not as able as in mobilisation

systems to be opportunist; they must be aware of the consequences of change and seek to control them. Power cannot normally be shared except by delegation subject to recall. The ideology will be 'neo-traditionalist' or revivalist, but will allow for innovations. Roles in the system must be instrumental, though the hierarchical pattern of authority must be secure. Apter suggests that Japan was 'the most clear-cut example' of such a system. Ethiopia and Morocco, he cites as further examples, and also Tsarist Russia.

We repeat that readers who wish to follow in more detail the application of the theoretical framework must consult Apter's studies of particular countries.[25]

IX: FURTHER CONSIDERATION OF TOTALITARIAN POLITICAL SYSTEMS

We have already commented at various points on certain analyses of totalitaria sysntems (e.g. Almond p. 31; Shils p. 81), and also on the broad distinction made between such systems and those of democracy. Advocates of a sophisticated analysis of political systems have consistently argued against what they regard as an over-simplified dichotomy between 'democratic' and 'totalitarian' political systems. This protest has not simply been based upon the difficulty of defining the 'democratic' system, although the emergence of what are claimed to be new forms of 'democracy' in some of the new states has enhanced this difficulty for all except the 'purists', as we saw above in our brief reference to Kautsky. It is also based upon a belief that 'totalitarian' systems are not all sufficiently alike to be contained within one category—a belief which, again, has been strengthened by the obvious practical desirability of discovering what differences, if any, exist between the various kinds of one-party states, as well as other 'authoritarian' systems, on the one hand, and 'totalitarian' systems on the other. An even older justification for a more sophisticated analysis, though this has been couched in political and economic rather than sociological terms until recently, has been the desire to distinguish between Fascism or Nazism and Communism. To complete this even more complicated picture, there is now the necessity to distinguish, within an increasingly 'polycentrist' category, between different 'communist' systems, and not merely between those of Russia and China.

We shall not attempt a comprehensive typology which would cover all these possible variations in political systems. But it does appear useful at this point to refer to a powerful analysis of the 'totalitarian' category advanced by Robert C. Tucker[26]. He argues that the concept of totalitarianism has two weaknesses. First, it fails to direct attention to significant differences between the closely resembling political phenomena of communism and fascism. Secondly, it fails to direct attention to significant resemblances between both these phenomena and a further class of phenomena belonging to the same genius i.e. single-party systems of the nationalist species. As examples of the latter, he cites Turkey under Kemal Ataturk; Nationalist China under Sun Yat-Sen and Chiang-Kai-Shek; Tunisia under Bourguiba; Egypt under Nasser, and Ghana under Nkrumah. He proposes a definition to include all the regimes covered in the preceding analysis—'*the revolutionary mass-movement regime under single-party auspices*'. Totalitarianism is *one* of its forms.

Tucker first considers the 'revolutionary' phase of such regimes, since all those in which he is interested were born in a revolutionary struggle; once in being, they strive to maintain their revolutionary momentum. A movement to displace a pre-existing system of order becomes a revolutionary movement for national renovation, or to carry the revolution beyond the national borders, or both.

There follows the 'post-revolutionary revolution'. In its internal aspect, this is a constructive process of far-reaching change and reform. In its first phase, it is directed either against a foreign colonial regime, or a regime of foreign dependency, or against an indigenous order which is treated as though it were foreign. An ideology will be constructed (or an existing one adapted) to provide both a philosophy of the revolution and a programme for the revolutionary struggle. (We may, not too invidiously, compare the Communist Manifesto— or, perhaps more appositely, some of Lenin's writings—with Nkrumah's 'Consciencism,' or Nasser's 'Confession of Faith'.) This ideology provides a political orientation and a powerful organising instrument in the hands of the leadership. Tucker holds that this phenomenon may be traced back to Mazzini, to 18th-century France, to Cromwellian England. It may develop out of the mass-movement during the struggle, or even after the conquest of power. It may even be a 'political artifact or pretence'. (cf. Apter on ideologies in 'mobilisation' regimes, above, p. 89.)

Whatever the origin or the nature of the ideology, the mass-movement-regime will be organised on the basis of a militant, centralised, revolutionary, or 'vanguard' party— Mazzini's 'party of action'. This is headed by a disciplined elite, which is connected with the mass through party-cells; at the top is a 'dominating' leader (normally possessed of 'charismatic' qualities, though with a ruthless efficiency in practice also). The Party becomes the staff headquarters of the new revolutionary movement-regime. Its territorial committees and cells become the units of effective rule. The single-party State is such that it is difficult to distinguish between party and state. Examples of this are provided not merely by the Communist Party under Lenin, but also by the Russian Populists. In other countries, obvious examples are the Liberal Constitutional (Neo-Destour) Party of Tunisia, the Convention People's Party of Ghana, and the Democratic Party of Guinea.

Since the militant centralised revolutionary party becomes the new foundation of political authority, and its cellular structure the 'infrastructure' of the new state, the movement-regime takes on the authoritarian character of the found in organisation. It may become much *more* authoritarian i.e. it may become 'totalitarian'. But the leadership insists that it is 'democratic in a new way'; it demands mass popular participation; and establishes 'transmission belts' (for the *two-way* traffic of ideas and policies, although 'democratic' centralism ensures ultimate party control); it may invent such terms as 'guided democracy'—though in Shils's typology, 'tutelary democracy' would not be applicable.

Tucker emphasises the principle of the transferability of organisational forms among different movement-regimes of various types. He refers to the pyramidal system of 'councils' in Egypt and Pakistan—the machinery of 'anti-Soviet sovietism' to reach the masses. Moreover, the movement-regime 'has no restricted habitat in the world'. There is, however, a rough

93

correlation between antecedent colonialism and the rise of nationalist movement-regimes, or of communist movement-regimes that come to power on a wave of nationalist revolution. There is also such correlation between movement-regimes and conditions of economic and cultural backwardness, feudalism, stagnation etc. On the other hand, the contrast is evident between two groups of countries. Russia, Asia, the Middle East, Africa, Latin America, and Eastern Europe on the one hand; Germany, Italy, Spain, Portugal, and even (since embryonic 'movement-regimes' do occur in limited fashion there) the United Kingdom and the United States.

We may now turn to a *differentiation of the species of movement-regimes*. But it must be emphasised that we are dealing with classes of phenomena which are distinguishable but not fully distinct; there are no conceptually pure 'ideal types'. For example, nationalism is a powerful force in both communist and fascist regimes. The best mode of differentiation, Tucker suggests, is according to *characteristic prevailing tendencies*. Above all, there is the *motivation* of revolutionary policies i.e. 'the revolutionary dynamic'. This, of course, may be lost, as, for example, in Franco Spain. We analyse this 'dynamic' further.

In the revolutionary dynamism of the nationalist movement-regime, the first goal is national independence, and the second modernisation, which involves an internal social revolution. But at the second point it may lose its impetus, and even suffer 'extinction'. The Kemalist movement in Turkey, for example, was carried far enough for orderly further development; not so the Chinese Kuomintang. The future development e.g. of some African states is not yet clear in this respect. We may contrast, at their *present* stage of development, Guinea and the Ivory Coast. Further, a relatively restricted revolutionary 'constitutency' may emerge, based on a *national* ideology. This may include the development of an active neutralist foreign policy, not involving the 'export' of revolution. In so far as Nkrumah originally emphasised pan-Africanism, he has had to moderate his views, partly because they offended some neighbouring African states, partly because of Ghana's own internal problems.

So far as communism and fascism are concerned, these have often been contrasted by the statement that the first has an international 'class' appeal, while the latter has an essentially 'national' appeal. Tucker points out that the attempt to distinguish the two regimes on this ground may be misleading. Both elements commingle in both systems. Fascism in Spain is essentially national. But fascist regimes may attempt to assert a supra-national appeal e.g. the notion of the German Volk, of Mussolini's 'Romanism', of Nasser's 'Arabism'. Any communist regime may also be international in its orientation, while we may see 'national communism' in Yugoslavia (and, indeed, to a greater or lesser extent now in all the communist countries). The obverse side of this is that the emergence of 'communistic' regimes e.g. in Africa by no means necessarily implies the spread of a monolithic 'world communism'.

All the same, fascism does indulge in strident national self-glorification, though the *leader* becomes the driving force of the political mechanism and the ruling party is reduced to the role of an important cog in the state apparatus. Movement-regimes are in general *oligarchical* rather than absolute autocracies. But fascism deviates from this pattern, and shows a pronounced tendency to absolute autocracy, 'statist' in orientation. The State, as personified in the leader, may displace the party as the 'supreme symbol and object of official adoration'—witness the emergence of 'fuhrerism'.

Finally, an *alteration* of the dynamism is possible. Tucker regards Stalinism as a metamorphosis of the original Communist or Bolshevik movement-regime, and the movement since 1953 (de-stalinisation) as one to reconstitute the latter. But readers who wish to pursue this line of thought must turn to Tucker's book. We have offered his introductory analysis as a contribution to solving the problem of arriving at a satisfactory typology of political systems.

NOTES

[1] T. B. Bottomore, *Sociology*, Unwin University Books, 1962, p. 147. The following summary is largely based on Chapter 9 of this work.

[2] *Government and Politics in Tribal Societies*, Watts, 1956.

[3] *Essays in Sociology*, Vol. III, 1961.

[4] cf. Weber, *The Theory of Social and Economic Organisation*, trans., A. M. Henderson and T. Parsons ed. with Introduction by Parsons, O.U.P. 1947, espec. Part III, 'The Types of Authority and Imperative Co-ordination'.

[5] cf. H. Johnson, *Sociology*, Routledge & Kegan Paul, 1961, pp. 323–339, for a fuller treatment.

[6] For a brilliant analysis of Populism cf. Peter Worsley, *The Third World*, Chapter 4.

[7] *Political Studies*, Vol. XII, No. 3, 1964. 'Charisma and Political Leadership', pp. 341–354.

[8] *World Politics*, Vol. 12, 1959–60, 'The Intellectuals in the Political Development of the new States'.

[9] Kahin, Pauker, and Pye, 'Comparative Politics of Non-Western Countries', *American Political Science Review*, vol. 49, 1955.

[10] cf., again, Peter Worsley, *The Third World*, espec. Chapters 4 and 5 on the new states and their leadership.

[11] cf. especially, 'Social Theory and Comparative Politics' in *Comparative Politics*, Free Press of Glencoe, 1963, pp. 67–81, eds. Eckstein & Apter.

[12] cf. 'Agraria and Industria', Towards a Typology of Comparative Administration *in* Siffin ed. *Towards a Comparative Study of Public Administration*, Bloomington, Indiana, 1957. Also *The Ecology of Public Administration*. Asia Publishing House, 1961.

[13] cf. also, La Palombara, ed. *Bureaucracy and Political Development*, Princeton U.P., 1963.

[14] From a review of *The Ecology of Public Administration* by Herbert Feith *in Australian Outlook*, Vol. 16, No. 3, Dec. 1962, pp. 320–321. There is a highly critical review of the same book by W. A. Robson in *Political Quarterly*, Vol. 33, No. 4, Oct–Dec, 1962, pp. 432–5.

[15] *op. cit.*, *Bureaucracy and Political Development*, Notes, Queries and Dilemmas, pp. 39–48.

[16] *The Political Systems of Empires*, Free Press of Glencoe, 1963.

[17] L. Binder, *Iran, Political development in a changing society*, Univ. Calif. Press, 1962, pp. 1–58.

[18] cf. again, Peter Worsley on 'Populism', *op. cit.*

[19] cf. also Fred W. Riggs *in* La Palombara, ed., *op. cit.* pp. 120–167.

[20] D. Lerner, *The Passing of Traditional Society*, Free Press of Glencoe, 1958.

[21] E. Shils, *Political Development in the New States*, Mouton, 1962.

[22] cf. Morris Janowitz, *The Military in the Political Development of New Nations*, Chicago U.P., 1964.

[23] *Political Change in Under-developed Countries*, ed. J. H. Kautsky, Wiley, 1962.

[24] David E. Apter, *The Political Kingdom in Uganda*, Princeton U.P., 1961, pp. 3–9, 20–28.

[25] cf. in addition to the study of Uganda, *The Gold Coast in Transition*, Princeton U.P., 1955.

[26] *The Soviet Political Mind*, Praeger Paperback, 1963.

4

The Political System—1

We now turn from attempts to develop a typology of political systems for comparative purposes, to a more detailed consideration of 'the political system' as a sub-system of society, but also with its own functional problems. Of course, the more clearly the characteristic features of 'the political system' can be defined, the greater the possibility of valid comparison between different political systems on the basis of which of these characteristic features they possess, in what degree and with what variations. Logically, indeed, it might be argued that a comprehensive account of the components of 'the political system' should precede any attempt at comparison. Our own approach, however, has been to examine in general terms the broad ways in which political systems may be compared, which we have now completed, in the expectation that readers will return again to this general analysis when they have considered the more detailed analysis of 'the political system' upon which we now embark.

To define satisfactorily the elements of politics and the basic components of a political system is not easy.[1] Recent writings have provided a number of leads which we take as our starting point. 'Elementary political activity,' says M. de Jouvenel, 'is the moving of man by man.'[2] Things happen because of a relation of 'instigation-response'.

Professor Catlin speaks of 'the control relationship' of will—of 'acts that issue in control and of the structures resulting from the control relationships of will'.[3]

Harold Lasswell, besides providing the general notion that

politics is concerned with 'who gets what, when, how', and with 'influence and the influential', uses an approach based on power, defined as 'sanctioned expectations'. All these leads, however, fail to distinguish the *political* as such. We may, of course, speak of 'politics' in clubs, associations, churches, trade unions, universities etc. But we are concerned with the politics of *the* political (sub-)system of society, and with the involvement of members of society in *this* system. To distinguish between people and groups on the basis of their involvement with politics in this sense, we may use Alfred de Grazia's notion of the 'politists'[4] or, somewhat more narrowly, Earl Latham's 'officiality'.[5] More usefully, we may narrow the field by stating that we are concerned with behaviour 'affecting public policy' decisions. Still more specifically, we may say, with David Easton, that people are 'participating in public life when their activity relates in some way to the making and execution of policy for a society'.[6] A more systematic definition is offered below.

Any political system involves political structures, political roles performed by actors or agents, patterns of interaction between actors, whether individuals or collectivities, and a political process. This is, basically, a continuous series of patterns of interaction between political actors, in which leaders secure the support they need, and get their followers to accept restrictions (power and influence are important considerations here), while followers procure direction and decisions, and give the necessary support. All this operates in a political culture i.e. a set of orientations to politics, which involves the question of legitimacy and of values. There is, as we noted in general terms in our structural-functional analysis of social systems, an interaction between the political (sub-)system and the other subsystems in society. In order further to study the political system, we must separate it (or the polity, or, more narrowly, the state) from society, and distinguish between the 'political' and the 'social'. This is a task which has only recently been attempted with any degree of sophistication, and by political sociologists rather than political scientists.

Aristotle made no distinction between the social and the political—only one between the private and familial on the one hand, and the 'public' on the other. His famous statement ought properly to read 'man is a *social* (not political) animal'. The early theorists of the state were either concerned with the problem of 'sovereignty', or to justify a prescriptive position. Rousseau drew a contrast between 'man' and 'citizen', between the state of nature and civil society, which is not what we require. St. Simon was concerned primarily to distinguish between government and administration and to 'take politics out of government'. Anarchists like Paine failed to recognise that some form of *political* association is necessary to make society possible at all. There were hints of the distinction we seek in Bodin and, even more, in Montesquieu. Marx and Hegel distinguished analytically between state and society, but only in order, in the first case, to destroy the state, and in the latter, to subsume society under the state.[7]

We may begin with the simple proposition that social organisation presupposes that some people must have some power over other people which is recognised by enough of all the people as legitimate. Competition for power must be regulated or institutionalised. To such end the state (we discuss the use of this term in relation to 'political system' later) must have the specific means peculiar to it of the monoply of the legitimate use of force within a given territory. Politics, then, is the striving to share power, or influence the distribution of power, or the power to make 'authoritative decisions'. The criterion of a *political* question is concern with the distribution, maintenance, or transfer of power in this sense. We are now, of course, with Weber. But even Dahl's modification of Weber's definition of the state (though he uses 'government') to read, 'that which successfully upholds a claim to the *exclusive regulation* of the legitimate use of physical force in enforcing rules within a given territory'[8] does not entirely meet our requirements. We need to justify the use of 'political system' rather than state.

Some societies are not anarchic, but have no *centralised* monopoly of the legitimate use of physical force—those, for example, described in Schapera's 'Government and Politics in Tribal Societies', or in Lucy Mair's 'Primitive Government', some of which, though 'none are stable political systems . . . are remarkably more political than others'. (Professor B. Crick, *In Defence of Politics*. I quote Crick because he prefers to confine the use of the term 'polity' to *one kind* of political system—

99

broadly, Shils's 'political democracy', which as we have seen, to Shils, is *one type* of polity only. In our analysis, there are many polities or political systems but only one political democracy.) In such societies, there are definite systems of control neither chaotic nor casual in operation. Runciman would call these 'stateless societies'. (Runciman, *op. cit.* p. 36. We do not discuss his other modification of Weber's definition, to include Durkheim's 'great nomad societies, whose structure was sometimes very elaborate, although they occupied no specific territories'. To talk of 'non-territorial states' and substitute 'centralised' for 'territory' as the criterion of 'statehood' seems an unnecessary complication in this study, which takes no account of such societies.) We prefer the general term 'political system', which may or may not include a *state* as defined by Weber. Almond, as we shall see, expands 'political system' to mean 'that system of interactions to be found in all independent societies which performs the functions of integration and adaptation (both internally and vis-a-vis other societies) by means of the employment or threat of employment, of more or less legitimate physical compulsion'. (In view of Almond's 'structural-functional' approach it is perhaps curious that he excludes 'goal-attainment'.) More briefly, the political system is 'the legitimate, order-maintaining or transforming system within society'.

This use of the limiting phrase 'more or less', enables us to include totalitarian systems, in which legitimacy may be in doubt, revolutionary systems, in which the basis of legitimacy may be in process of change; and non-Western systems, in which there may be more than one legitimate system. 'Physical compulsion' distinguishes political systems from others (if we understand 'legitimate' as 'authorised' by the legal norms of the system), though this does not mean that politics is reduced to force. All the 'inputs' into the political system are in some way related to claims for the employment of legitimate compulsion. All the 'outputs' are related to the exercise of such legitimate compulsion. The term 'system' itself implies three general properties (1) comprehensiveness—it includes *all* the interactions affecting compulsion, and not merely structures based on law (2) interdependence—change in one sub-set of interactions produces change in other sub-sets and (3) the existence of boundaries—points where the political system ends, and other systems begin, though the boundaries between society and polity differ in different political systems.

To sum up, and consciously to indulge in some repetition: we have, then, a complex of people tied together by patterns of behaviour. We speak of a *system*, because this covers all of the patterned interactions relevant to the making of political decisions. The unit of the system is the *role*—that organised sector of an actor's orientation which constitutes and defines his participation in an interactive process. An *actor* may be either an individual or a collectivity. So, a *political system* is a set of interacting roles or structures of roles (structures being understood as a patterning of interactions). *Political* relates to physical compulsion, as described earlier, though this does not reduce all political activity to the use of force. We remind ourselves, finally, that every political system operates within a *political culture* (or more than one, since the two are not co-terminous). Political culture is defined briefly as 'orientation to political action'.

We are now in a position to examine some of the analyses of 'the political system' which are, to a greater or lesser extent, based on the foregoing approach.

II: SOCIOLOGISTS AND THE POLITICAL SYSTEM

The writers of books on general sociology, even those which adopt the structural-functional approach and pattern-variable analysis, rarely devote much space to the 'political system' as such, and few courses in general sociology appear to include much political sociology, at least of the broad 'macro-political' approach which involves consideration of *total* political systems. (They do, of course, include consideration of small groups, interest groups, political parties, bureaucracies etc., which are not our concern here.) There has, however, been a slight tendency of late to apply sociological analysis, particularly of the structural-functional variety, to some aspects of the political sub-system in relation to the total social system. Before considering the works of specialist political sociologists, or of political scientists who have turned to a sociological approach, therefore, we examine two analyses taken from general works on sociology. The first is Johnson's 'Sociology', sub-titled 'A systematic introduction'. (*op. cit.* especially pp. 313–323. We have already noted Johnson's use of Weber's 'ideal types' as the basis of a typology of political systems, above, pp. 49 ff.)

Johnson begins with an examination of the terms '*Government, State and Nation*'. A government, he says (in the terms used by Weber to describe the state), exercises imperative control within a definite territory, and within that territory it successfully claims a monopoly of the use of force. 'Imperative' simply means the issuing of commands, including laws. He proceeds to modify the word 'monopoly', by explaining that there may be a division of the right to use force, e.g. in federal systems, and that the government may within limits permit or tolerate the use of force by other persons. But in the latter case, the government determines those limits i.e. in Dahl's phrase, it claims the right to the 'exclusive regulation' of such force. The existence of a small number of 'deviants' does not, of course, invalidate the use of the term.

'Legitimacy' in a sociological sense is not quite the same thing as legitimacy in law, though the two kinds of legitimacy tend to be associated in fact. The difference which exists is, perhaps, in a way somewhat comparable to the distinction between *de facto* and *de jure* (though admittedly this is itself a recognised *legal* distinction). In the sociological sense, a legitimate government is one that has the support of those who are subject to it (in which case it is likely to receive '*de facto*' recognition). Defeated or exiled rulers may, of course, still claim to be the 'legitimate' authority in the legal sense (and they may continue to be given *de jure* recognition). Legitimacy implies a kind of authority (not simply based on force), which is always a matter of degree. Governments may sometimes use 'illegitimate force' (i.e. 'not authorised by law') but they will not forever continue to enjoy 'sociological legitimacy' if they persistently do so.

Johnson next distinguishes between 'government' and 'state'. The former does not include all persons within its territory, but only the incumbents of 'official roles'. The latter includes both government and governed. Subjects or citizens are all members of the state (we do not consider it necessary to repeat that in such a context we prefer 'political system'), and may enjoy rights not shared by non-members such as aliens. (We do not take up the point that some aliens, e.g. diplomatic representatives, may have *more* rights; nor that citizens are subject to some control by their own state even when not on its territory.) Over its subjects the State exercises sovereignty, which term, when used vis-a-vis other states, is roughly the same as 'political autonomy'. (Again, we do not pursue the problem of limitations on such sovereignty due to international conditions, or to the existence of federations etc.) However extensive and secure such sovereignty may be, it must always be emphasised that the state is an 'abstraction' from the total lives of its members; they belong to a variety of other groups—though some governments may leave relatively little to private discretion.

Johnson next takes up the point that some primitive societies do not have a 'government', in the sense of a group, smaller than the society as a whole, that by recognised right or self-imposition exercises 'imperative' control within a given territory. But, he says, there are probably few societies in which all adults (even all male adults) have an equal part in making decisions which are binding on the group as a whole, or in using force to uphold a traditional order. Such functions are assigned to certain roles or groups, if only 'the informal council of family heads. . . . The very existence of government in a society, therefore, is a matter of degree'. Even quite small functioning groups, however, always have at least some kind of informal leadership.

A nation, Johnson defines as 'a group of people who, normally living in a particular territory, wish to form their own state; if they already have it, then they wish to keep it as the most important social bond that expresses their sentiment of belonging together and sharing a common destiny'. (There are certain difficulties in this virtual equation of nation and state. Do the Scots or the Welsh *not* constitute a 'nation' because none but a few 'nationalists' desire to form their own state? This is quite different from the problem of defining the national characteristics of those people who happen to live in the same state, apart from the fact that they wish to keep it.) We shall not pursue the question of how important such things as a common religion, a common language, or a common 'racial' origin are in relation to 'nationality', except to agree with Johnson that these things individually or together, are not sufficient or necessary to 'nationhood'. Their absence, however, may be an obstacle to successful 'statehood', though a continuous and successful political organisation may well create a 'nation' out of the most disparate elements. However this may be, a nation and a state are not necessarily the same.

We are not certain that 'nation' and 'national character' are very useful concepts in political sociology; 'political culture' or 'orientation to politics' may serve our purposes better. But Johnson does suggest another reason besides those given above why we should distinguish between state and nation. A state includes a government. One of the strongest bonds that may unite a 'nation' is 'common allegiance to the *form* of their government, that is, to the prevailing political institutions'. The people of a 'nation', on the other hand, may desire to have an *independent government*, but disagree as to the *form* that it should take. Both Germany and France provide important examples of this. National tradition in the United States and Britain, on the other hand, is intimately connected with a respect for the basic political institutions in those countries.

Although these generalisations are important, it may be suggested, with respect, that many of them are not peculiarly 'sociological' (unless, perhaps, like M Jourdain and his prose, we have been speaking the language of sociology all our lives without knowing it!). Had sociology no more to offer to the political scientist than this, its distinctive approach would be very limited.

However, Johnson next turns to a topic which has been of deep concern to sociologists, that of *Power and Influence*. Power is defined as the ability to get one's wishes carried out despite opposition. In any process of interaction, some participants usually have more power than others. An actor exercises power very largely by influencing the actions of others; those others need not be the persons against whom the actor is pitting his power. In elections, the successful candidate demonstrates his power by influencing not his opponent, but the electorate. Nevertheless, power consists largely in the ability to influence the actions of other people. There are numerous modes of influence, and also many bases of influence. But despite the importance of information, advice, appeals, inducements, and even 'authority', every government makes some use of coercion and force. These appear to be essential instruments of government in large states. But every government also strives to win legitimacy. The use of force and coercion is ineffective as compared with the exercise of authortiy i.e. 'imperative control recognised as rightful by those subject to it'. Legitimacy and force are to some extent substitutes for each other; the more a government has to depend on the latter, the smaller would appear to be its claim to the former. (For a fuller treatment of this cf. Bernard, below, pp. 224 ff.)

Johnson's general discussion of *political systems* adds little to our earlier discussion in Chapter I. The goals of all the diverse activities of government may be regarded as *societal* goals, though this does not mean that all members of the society agree. Many of them may not even be aware that such goals are being pursued. Further, the leaders' goals may differ from those of the followers, and they sometimes 'mobilise (resources) for purposes that would be rejected if they were made public'. The very concept of politics, as we have seen, implies the existence of conflicting ideas about how the facilities and personnel of government should be used.

> 'A political act is something more than a piece of agreed routine; political situations arise out of disagreement . . . Government is used to resolve conflict in the direction of or prevention of change.'[9]

So the statement that the goals of government activities are goals of society implies merely that the dovernment acts to some extent on behalf of all the people, decides on policies that at least *affect* all the people, and even, to some extent, mobilises all the people and co-ordinates their actions. 'If the "polity" is defined as the goal-attainment sub-system of society, then obviously the government is an important part of the polity.' But Johnson reminds us, as we have already emphasised, that the polity is not 'an explicitly co-ordinated *structural* sub-system of society . . . it is a *functional* sub-system'. The government, however, as a *concrete group*, participates in all four functional sub-systems; at the same time, other groups in addition to the government, participate in the polity. These include parties and pressure groups among others. Governments, in other words, as concrete groups also have integrative, pattern-maintenance, and even economic (or adaptive), as well as goal-attainment functions. Here we have the basis at least of our separate consideration of 'the political system' and its functions and structures.

We discussed earlier Johnson's analysis of the *differences* between political systems, based on Weber's 'ideal types', (above, pp. 49ff). His discussion of the *similarities* between systems is set out here. Firstly, the effective government of every society consists of a small proportion of the population. Rule is always the rule of the few. Secondly, every government consists of a chief and an administrative staff under the chief. Thus no society can be run by one person without assistance, and the members of every government are always unequal in actual power and authority. The 'chief', of course, need not be a single person. Thirdly, every government claims to be 'legitimate' i.e. it regards obedience as being a matter of duty. But the extent to which a government emphasises legitimacy, of course, varies. Though legitimacy is important, however, we must note, fourthly, that it is never the sole basis of the government's power. Both the administrative staff in relation to the chief, and the governed in relation to the government are motivated in a number of ways, as are those who disobey. Differences of motivation are an important factor in any comparison of political systems. Finally, whether a government acknowledges the fact or not, every government is, and must be, concerned to some extent with the welfare of *all* segments of the population. They may be compelled to do this by the institutional structure (e.g. universal suffrage and periodic elections) or simply by enlightened self-interest. In any system, whatever the compulsion, the chief and his staff, however, are never equally concerned with all segments of the population under them. 'Every institutional pattern of government—even more, every particular government holding power under the pattern—depends upon a particular constellation of interests within the population governed.' This statement provides a lead into many detailed points about particular political systems or the differences between them. Before pursuing this in detail, however, we shall look at one further approach by sociologists to the notion of 'the political system', to structures and component parts. Bredemeier and Stephenson,[10] unusually in what they themselves describe as an 'introductory text-book', devote a sizable chapter to 'Politics'; their analysis fits into a general 'structural-functional' approach. To be of use, their framework would have to be applied in much greater detail to concrete political systems, but as an introduction, especially for political scientists making their first acquaintance with sociology, it is extremely helpful. For this reason we include a summary of their approach here.

Starting from the simple point that 'rights' imply 'enforceable obligations', and that the latter, in the last resort, involve 'the use, or the threat of use, of physical compulsion', they proceed to note that if such compulsion could be used by each and every individual, society would face 'Hobbes's war of each against all'. However, in stable societies there are 'political statuses', defined as those with 'a monopoly of the use of physical compulsion'. They then describe the 'basic issues of politics', which stem from these fundamental considerations. These are, broadly, two in number.

1. *Which* of the innumerable claims and counter-claims should be 'rights' and which left to the arena of bargaining, or to the structure of in-group loyalties? And for those rights which are recognised, who should bear the corresponding obligations? This, as we shall see, is another way of enquiring how goals are defined, how the allocation of values and costs is decided, and how controls are exercised. This involves an empirical enquiry into each political system, not a normative judgment of what *ought* to be done. That is, there is no universal criterion of what the functions of the state ought to be or the means whereby its goals ought to be achieved.

2. How are the statuses with the power to decide such questions, and possessing the monoply of physical compulsion to enforce the decisions, defined and filled. For the political sociologist this is again an empirical question, though the political philosopher may express a preference for a particular procedure. His value-judgment, however, is unlikely to be of much use unless he is clear about the empirical consequences and the practicability of his choice.

Among the sources of potential conflict in society, there are those which appear impossible of satisfactory mutual practical compromise between the individuals and groups concerned. e.g. should the resources of South Africa, or those of the Deep South in the U.S., be used 'to protect white supremacy', or to achieve equality? Should the U.S. in its policy of overseas aid seek to spread free enterprise, or to help the countries concerned to industrialise by any means? Many other similar problems, unresolvable by 'computer techniques', might be posed. On such issues there are no 'reasoned solutions' but only *political* ones. Even in less 'basic' issues, the fact that rights are 'inherently scarce', and involve placing obligations on others, means that differences about the choice between the former, and the balance between both, can only be solved *politically*. Again, the cost of social change, e.g. automation, will not fall evenly upon everyone; 'society' must make the decision, at least in these days, when public opinion is intolerant of such tragedies as 'the long drawn-out agony of the handloom weavers' during the industrial revolution. This is particularly true where 'social costs' must be considered, and a balance between present and future generations be preserved. More generally, there is the constant division between those who get more of their demands satisfied, and those who get less—the 'haves' and the 'have-nots'. This involves not only economic, but other values. Again, society must strike a balance which would never be achieved if everyone were left to pursue his own self-interest; few people today believe in Adam Smith's 'invisible hand', and even he would not leave everything to it e.g. education. New nations are especially faced with these dilemmas, and particularly that between serving immediate interests and those of posterity; the latter is part of the problem of modernisation (which, as we have seen, may also involve a choice between rapid economic development and the fostering of democratic procedures). Finally, in any system based upon a division of labour and social stratification, individuals and groups are likely to see problems from the point of view of their own position in the social structure. There may be considerable argument as to who is capable of seeing 'the public interest' (or even if there is such a thing) but somewhere in any society there must be those who are entrusted with the difficult task of trying to see the issue in this way.

This kind of analysis, *mutatis mutandis*, can, of course, be applied to any type of group; we are concerned to pursue it only in the context of the large group which has enough independence and self-sufficiency to be, in most respects, 'master in its own house' i.e. the total social system, or society. In such a system, to resolve these conflicts, some statuses must exist with the responsibility and authority to make binding decisions. These are *political statuses*. As Johnson also pointed out they are always fewer in number than those who are controlled by the decisions. But the decision-making statuses, whatever their number, may vary in certain ways, which are related to (1) what people are to decide who will occupy such statuses and (2) by what criteria? 'The essential difference between a democratic political system and a non-democratic one is that in the former the people to be governed by the decisions are the ones who decide who will make them.' The process, of course, may be indirect as well as direct. In such a democratic system, therefore, leaders must attempt to satisfy their followers, or at least the most influential or the most numerous of them. In the non-democratic system, decision-makers use different standards for making their decisions.

This analysis would appear to do no more than restate the dichotomy between democracy and dictatorship, which, as we have seen, is over-simplified and of little heuristic value. But Bredemeier and Stephenson proceed to suggest sub-divisions of the two categories. There are four major ways in which *non-democratic* systems may differ from one another: (1) in the *degree* to which the decision-makers are independent of the wishes of the governed; they are never totally immune to pressures arising out of the needs and aspirations of their followers and must always temper their orders accordingly, (2) in the *scope* of the subjects' lives that are controlled—too obvious a point to need elaboration, (3) in the extent of the subjects' *sense of* legitimacy of the regime—again a point discussed at length at various points of this study, and (4) in the degree to which decision-makers are independent of *anyone else* (apart from the subjects in general) e.g. a particular group or organisation or section of the community.

There are similar differences within the broad category of democratic systems, and these may be expressed in similar terms: (1) there are differences in the *degree* to which decision-makers, even when elected, are responsive to those who choose them; they 'cannot please all of the people all of the time', and must decide which groups to satisfy; moreover, leaders can manipulate their followers in various ways, (2) there are also differences in the *range* of peoples' lives that are controlled by political decisions; a majority of voters can be as 'totalitarian' as a dictator, (3) there are differences in the subjects' *sense of legitimacy* of the democratic structure, and of the extent to which democratic procedures should be applied e.g. should judges be elected?, and (4) there are differences, even in democratic systems, in the extent to which leaders are independent of influence from *people other* than their constituents who may, indeed, have no opinion on the matter; should the British Parliament, for example, abolish capital punishment when public opinion polls appear to show a majority against such decision?

We noted above that a prior decision to be made is *which* conflicts should be settled 'politically' and which left to bargaining or primary group attachments. Economic questions are likely to be controversial in this respect, so, also, though for different reasons, such things as education or medicare. This point is repeated merely in order to emphasise that a decision as to *which* mode of settlement is to be adopted, is also a *political* decision. A decision *not* to settle a dispute 'authoritatively' is a political decision.

The next point is the obvious one that integration and adaptation (and the degree of success in goal-attainment) of a society, will depend finally on the quality of the decisions made (including the decision *not* to use political means) and on the degree to which they are accepted by the members of society. We examine, first, the factors which may affect the success or otherwise of the decision-makers in relation to adaptation; secondly, to integration (goal-attainment is, in large part, subsumed under one or other of these headings).

A basic requirement for *successful adaptation* is that knowledge about the environment and ideas about its effective use must be developed, and that decision-makers must be motivated to use and apply such knowledge and ideas in the light of a reasonably clear conception of what the 'ideal' relationship is between the system and its environment. There is today considerable debate about the role of science and technology, research and fore-casting, and considerable doubt as to whether governments are as well-equipped to use such aids as they should be. Only some broad generalisations are possible here. The major require-ments for the use of the above tools is that there should be permission and encouragement for all attempts to improve their quality and application; that ideas concerning them should have free and open channels of communication; and that objectivity, based on enquiry, be regarded as essential to right decisions. To use our earlier terminology of 'political culture', while cathexis (emotional reaction) and evaluation cannot and ought not to be excluded from influence on decisions, a pre-requisite is an accurate 'cognitive map'.

But the knowledge thus acquired and the ideas formulated must be communicated to decision-makers who, be it repeated, must be able to use them in the light of their previously agreed criteria of what is the desirable relationship between system and environment. 'On the level of societies as social systems, it is a conception of the *purpose* (goals) of the system that is often missing. The result tends to be for decisions to be based on considerations of what will preserve the adaptive mechanisms, rather than on consideration of what adaptive mechanisms are supposed to be *for*.'

Given that knowledge, ideas, and motivation to act are all present, there remains the problem of getting the resulting decisions accepted and carried out by the members of society concerned. The allocation of resources, statuses, rights, and obligations implied by leaders' decisions, particularly if they are based on long-run rather than short-run considerations, will not necessarily be the allocation which would be preferred by society or by significant groups in it. The solution to this problem, however, is so closely bound up with the general problem of *integration* that we must first consider the latter.

The question of information is also important in this context, because leaders must be aware of the integrative difficulties which may be arising in the society and must be able to form some opinion as to their causes, as well as be motivated to deal with them. The way in which these requirements are met will depend on 'which mechanisms of integration are institu-tionalised'. Bureaucratic mechanisms with specialised statuses are important in this respect, both for the gathering of information, and for communicating it to the decision-makers. (A British version of this is that while ministers tell the civil servants what the public won't stand, the civil servants tell the ministers what won't work!) It must be added that where integration is left either to bargaining or to the functioning of primary groups, then the 'wrong' degrees and types of integration (i.e. those dysfunctional for the society as a whole) may result. A *political* decision is then required as to whether to introduce the alternative method i.e. an authoritative decision through the political system.

We may now turn specifically to the question of acceptance of leaders' decisions by followers. In the general terms employed by Bredemeier and Stephenson, leaders must procure *support for their occupancy of leadership statuses* while their 'disposal' problem is that of *getting their decisions accepted.* Followers have as *their* procurement problem the *obtaining of decisions*; in exchange they offer what the leaders need, *support.* 'The political process is the process by which leaders procure the support they need from followers, and get followers to accept restrictions on their freedom; and it is the process by which followers procure direction and decision, and give necessary support.' There are four possible ways in which this political process may work.

Firstly, there is *Political Exploitation, or Rule by Force.* At the extreme of non-institutionalisation, decision-makers rely on 'might' not 'right', both as regards the occupation of their statuses and the enforcement of their decisions. It has been suggested that examples of such a system are the defeated American Confederacy after the Civil War, the Soviet Union immediately after the October Revolution, Hungary and East Germany today. In most systems, however, the exploitative method and reliance on force is a 'deviance' from the norm, though even a coercing group may exercise some *de facto* if not *de jure* 'authority'.

Secondly, there is *Political Bargaining, or Rule by Compromise.* Such a method, for example, is embodied in the political method of election campaigns; interest groups compete with each other and 'bargain' with candidates. Leaders seek support for their policies by making other decisions which are desired by followers. The success of the ruled in getting their needs met depends on their political bargaining power; this, in turn, depends on the alternatives open to them and the existence of at least a two-party system. (With a multi-party system they may obtain promises of decisions but find that the parties cannot carry them out because they can only achieve power in a compromise coalition.) Groups must, of course, be able to 'deliver the vote'. 'Only those interests are likely to be protected by political decisions that are (a) widespread and (b) expressed by well-organised collectivities.' This requires, in Almond's terms, both 'articulation' and 'aggregation' of interests. In large complex systems, the masses of followers cannot rationally bargain with their leaders. To quote Talcott Parsons, 'there must be mechanisms by which the average voter can come to a "responsible" decision which is meaningful to him. He must not, in too many cases, withdraw to non-voting, nor be susceptible to appeals which would be grossly disruptive of the stability of the system. Since the intellectual problems involved in a rational solution are not practically soluble . . . the mechanisms are typically non-rational. They involve stabilisation of political attitudes in terms of association with other members of the principal solidary groups in which the voter is involved. In terms of party affiliation this may be called "traditionalism". The traditionalistic operation of non-rational mechanisms is a condition of the stability of the system.'[11] Herman Finer has put it thus: 'without parties an electorate would be either impotent or destructive by embarking upon impossible policies that would only wreck the political machine.'

Thirdly, there is *Political Bureaucracy, or Rule by Law*. Whatever trading or bargaining may be involved, a stable system would seem to require the institutionalisation of the actual decision-making process so as to involve a *duty* to accept the decisions as binding. Under a structure of 'rule by law', the right to make certain kinds of decisions is part of the cultural definition of certain 'statuses'. There is an 'authority-structure'. This, be it noted, is different from the procurement of obedience on the grounds of 'authority', meaning 'expertise', although authority in the first sense is unlikely to persist forever, unless 'authority' in the second sense is present in sufficient degree to produce effective results. The converse of the 'right' of leaders to make decisions, is the 'right' of followers to have those decisions made in a certain way, and, perhaps, in certain circumstances, to *require* leaders to act. Courts perform the function of making final determinations (subject to legislative or constitutional over-ruling) 'of who has what duty to whom'. The law must be respected, though it is possible to 'bargain' to obtain an alteration of the law.

Finally, there is *Political Identification or Rule by Loyalty.* Support for leaders in such a system is not given only (or, perhaps, even predominantly) on a rational assessment of what can be obtained from them. A large proportion of voters are 'loyal' to particular parties, though perhaps not many quite so 'loyal' as the English voter who is alleged to have said that if her party put up a pig in her constitutency she would vote for it! In the same category is loyalty which is given to a 'charis-matic' leader, who evokes a diffuse rather than a specific, institutionalised type of loyalty. We have discussed this sufficiently above (pp. 52 ff) and need only emphasise that this type of leadership is most likely to emerge in conditions of *anomie*, when the social structure fails to meet integrative, adaptive, or pattern-maintenance requirements. It is often accompanied by 'scape-goating' tactics, e.g. blaming the de-ficiencies of a system on such factors as 'the wicked plotting of . . .'. McCarthyism in the U.S. owed its success largely to this technique.

The above, then, are four possible ways in which the political process may work; it needs only to be stressed that most political systems will include elements of all four and that no political system can be maintained by only one.

Structural-functional analysis involves consideration of the notion of political equilibrium and disequilibrium. We discuss this problem in more detail later, but it is convenient to con-clude this summary of Bredemeier's and Stephenson's approach by reference to their contribution to such consideration. The mechanisms of the political process reviewed above, they say, operate in equilibrium so that (1) leaders receive all the support they want (2) all the decisions they want to make are voluntarily accepted (3) followers receive all the decisions they want and (4) there are leaders whom they trust and feel able and willing to support. Two major types of breakdown might occur in this political equilibrium.

First, *'inflationary disequilibrium'* where the *disposal* problem of the system are satisfactorily met, but not the *procurement* problems (see above, p. 112). Competitors for leadership-statuses strive to bid support away from each other by stronger appeals and promises and severer attacks on opponents. Followers, in turn, press more and more claims for new and expanded rights. Expectations and demands may, at the extreme, become completely unrealistic; some groups are unwilling to accept the obligations implied in others' demands; leaders are unable to fulfil their promises. This in turn, may derive from their inability to secure the compliance of certain groups, while followers may be unwilling to accept obligations for themselves which arise from their own demands e.g. to pay the cost in taxation.[12] A democratically oriented regime may be supplanted by some form of authoritarian oligarchy.

The second kind of breakdown, *deflation* arises from a situation, in which people cannot find acceptance for the goods and services of which they wish to dispose. Politically, widespread apathy develops. Leaders make no effort to arouse followers to new accomplishments, and competition for political statuses may be perfunctory or even collusive. Followers, partly because of lack of leadership, also become apathetic, and cease to press claims for new rights. The system may 'run-down' and, in the last resort, disintegrate.

We now attempt, very briefly, to examine the causes of either kind of breakdown, and first the *inflationary*. This kind of crisis arises, basically, from a situation in which competition for the available supply of goods and services increases, without an increase in the supply of such goods and services. Competition might increase in *one of two ways*, and first by a *'decrease in the cost of procuring'*. For example, if the prevailing notion of accepting 'that station of life to which it has pleased God to call you', or of 'accepting the decisions of authority' breaks down, because of education or propaganda, there will be less sacrifice of 'respectability', 'pride', or 'loyalty' involved in demanding more rights. Apter cites the break-up of traditional feudal relationships in Africa, as Africans left their villages to work in the mines and factories. Old obligations broke down, new aspirations developed; the processes combined, under the spur of leaders, to produce nationalism. But there may, secondly, also be an *increase in the estimated cost of* not *demanding more*. Films, radio, newspapers, education, the example of others, have all produced the 'revolution of rising expectations' in under-developed countries. A sharper awareness of what is being missed has the effect of 'increasing the cost' of *not* seeking to achieve it. The existing state of affairs is no longer docilely accepted either way.

So far as *deflationary* pressures are concerned, they arise when the competition for goods and services is decreased, without a decrease in their supply. Such pressures may also arise in two ways. Firstly, when people are deterred from asserting political demands through fear of reprisals, ridicule, bureaucratic obstacles etc., or when there are alternative ways of gaining the same or substitute satisfactions, they are deterred from political activities. There is an *increase in the costs of procuring*. Secondly, a decline in political interest also means that *the cost of* not demanding more is *low*, in the sense that deprivation, or failure to improve, is not much felt.

The above analyses of inflationary and deflationary political situations has been presented from the point of view of followers' demands upon the system. Similar considerations apply from the point of view of leaders. *Inflationary* pressures are produced by anything which increases competition among them for support; *deflationary* pressures by anything that decreases such competition (in each case, provided that there are no counter-balancing changes in the supply of support). If competing leaders' estimates of the *cost of trying to win more support decline*, they will increase their demands for support; similarly, if their estimates of *the cost of* not *trying for more support* increase. They will intensify their efforts to influence followers, possibly by 'undemocratic' methods. Conversely, if leaders' estimates of the *costs of procuring rise*, or their estimates of the *costs of* not *procuring support* decline, they will less ardently seek to influence followers; or they might estimate the degree of apathy, ignorance, manipulability etc. in such a way as to feel that they *need* not bother to elicit support.

Bredemeier and Stephenson do not attempt to apply these analyses in detail to concrete political systems and situations, a task which would clearly be outside the scope of an introductory textbook on general sociology such as they set out to write. The first reaction of the political scientist might well be either that the generalisations are too vague to be of much value, or that they simply express the 'common sense' approaches which political scientists have long used in unnecessarily complicated form. It would be an interesting exercise, for which we have no space here, to apply the inflationary–deflationary analysis to a period covering, say, two elections. Meanwhile, it must be said that although none of the conceptual frameworks and theories of the *political system* to which we now turn are based in detail on the approach just outlined, they are in some cases not far removed from it, and may be the more readily understood because of the general outline provided in this section.

III: GOVERNMENT AND THE POLITICAL SYSTEM

In the course of an article in which he seeks to relate systems of of social stratification to the working of political systems,[13] Apter has outlined a scheme for the analysis of 'Government'. Although we have argued for the more inclusive term 'political system', Apter's model, which is based upon structural-functional analysis, spills over, at least indirectly, from 'government' to 'politics' sufficiently to justify an examination of it here. With Apter, 'government' refers to a concrete group. 'In a system (it) is the most generalised unit possessing (*a*) defined responsibilities for the maintenance of the system of which it is a part and (*b*) a practical monopoly of coercive powers'. These two broad categories he calls the '*structural requisites*'. In addition, the manner of participation in government of members of a unit can vary; types of participation patterns he calls *format*; the criterion for differentiation between types is the *degree of representativeness of government*. Although 'government' is a concrete unit, it is distinct from other units in the respect that it is a *concrete structural requisite for any social system*. Government is the most strategic of all sub-structures for the *maintenance* of society. 'We do not say that, if you set up a government, you automatically create a society. Rather, the minimal requirements for the maintenance of government must be related to society in such a way that both can exist.' The crucial concerns of government are those which threaten the existence of the unit of which it is a part. It has an indivisible responsibility, through its monopoly of coercive powers, for protecting the system. If its minimal structures fail to operate, it must undergo drastic modifications and/or the system itself will. Important threats to the system are, first, threats to the ability of the government to work in terms of its structural requisites, and, secondly, threats arising out of inadequate governmental performance.

Some of the broad range of activities which governments undertake are 'vitally' necessary if the unit is to keep going; some of the means whereby these functions are performed are, broadly, the *structural requisites of government.* They are: (1) the structure of authoritative decision-making; (2) the structure of accountability and consent; (3) the structure of coercion and punishment; (4) the structure of resource determination and allocation, and (5) the structure of political recruitment and role-assignment.

Decision-making by government involves the possibility of alternatives and selection between them. It is, presumably, prompted either by demands made outside the government, or by demands arising out of the government's own plans or previous actions. The kinds of questions to be asked are: who makes the decisions?; what is the nature of the issues posed?; what is the range of supervision by decision-makers? We need to know the method of arriving at decisions, the scope of decisions and the degree of centralisation in decision-making. In more detail, decisional legislation may consist either of framework legislation laying down broad principles with the details left to the civil service and other agencies; or supervisory legislation, in which little or no discretion is left to those who apply the legislation.

Patterns of accountability and assent involve 'reference groups' for decision-makers. Such groups may modify decisions at the request of government, or they may require formal approval before a decision is made. In democratic societies, some of these groups are legally defined e.g. standing committees of the legislative and parliament staff, or even statutory advisory committees. Others, like interest groups, or special groups within parties, can sometimes be informally shifted by the decision-makers, who then have more autonomy. Without accountability, formal or informal, decision-makers may lack information, or be unable to predict or control the consequences of their decisions.

Coercion and Punishment may become the more extensive the greater the autonomy of decision-makers. They may take the form of positing new norms or new concepts of 'ideal citizenship' or of social pressures. Their consequences may, again, be difficult to predict, and if their costs, financial or moral, are too high, the system may break down, or at least come to rely too much on party, police, or army. (cf. further on this, Bernard, below, pp. 224 ff.)

The definition, exploitation, and allocation of resources by government are essential to the implementation of their decisions. The consequences of such allocation may be either a general increase in social welfare, or a redistribution of wealth. Receipt of benefits will increase members' commitments to the system. Those who suffer, of course, become less committed, and against them coercion and punishment may be necessary.

Finally, *methods of recruitment to and the definition of, the roles of government* are important for the system. Different types of elections and electoral systems, for example, differ in their effects. But important as this category of structural-requisite is to the functioning of government, it is even more important in relation to 'format', which is itself an indication of the formal responsiveness of a regime.

Format is the degree of representativeness of the system. All regimes, as we have observed many times, are oligarchical in some respects. The important question is whether the oligarchy serves the wider purposes of the system, or is free to serve its own. Even totalitarian regimes, however, have some representative features. As regards format Apter classifies systems as (1) dictatorial (2) oligarchical (3) indirectly representational, and (4) directly representational. Variations which derive from this basis involve differences in the performance of the structural requisites, and indicate the degrees of sensitivity. They also affect the role of political parties (which Apter proceeds to discuss in detail in the rest of his article).

The above analysis emphasises the crucial and strategic role of government in a going social system. Its format in part determines its actions. These actions occur within the framework of the five structural requisites, failure to perform in any one of which entails the breakdown of government itself. 'In so far as government is regarded as a concrete structural requisite of any society, the social system itself will be altered.'

Although, as we said, this scheme takes as its central point 'government', it sees the latter as operating within a political system which is itself a sub-system of society. To the broader analysis of this political system we now turn.

IV: INPUTS, OUTPUTS, AND THE POLITICAL SYSTEM

One of the earliest attempts to provide a working model of the political system is contained in Easton's analysis.[14] He is concerned to enquire how authoritative decisions are made and executed for a society. This takes place through inter-related activities within, but *analytically* separate from, the rest of the social system, and distinct from the environment. The basic scheme may be represented diagrammatically thus:

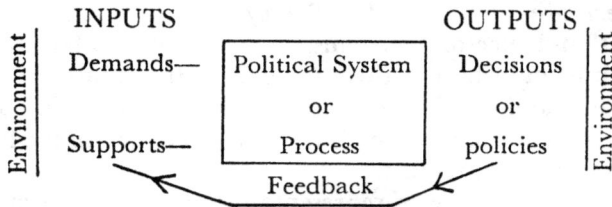

The first requirements are to identify the political system by its fundamental units, and to establish its boundaries. The units are political actions, structured in political roles and political groups. The boundaries are defined by all those actions which are more or less directly related to the making of binding decisions for society. (Binder (see below, pp. 171 ff) considers that a distinction must be made between the *legitimacy* of the *statement* of the decision, and the *effectiveness* of its implementation, but this does not seem to affect the theoretical concept of the boundaries. It might affect 'feedback'.) We next turn to the inputs and outputs of the system. We must identify the inputs and the forces that shape and change them, and trace the process whereby they are turned into the outputs of the system. We must describe the general conditions under which the process can be maintained, and establish the relationship between outputs and the succeeding inputs, established by the feedback process. The system has to make efforts to cope with the changing environment (material and social)—the external variables, but its behaviour will also be affected by the system's own structure and internal needs. Within the system there will be *some* differentiation, some minimal division of labour, which provides the structure within which action takes place. There is also the problem of integration—the need for mechanisms whereby the members of a structural system are integrated, or induced to co-operate in some minimal degree, so that they may make authoritative decisions.

In the ensuing detailed analysis, Easton concentrates almost entirely upon the input functions of the system. He says little further of the process whereby these inputs are turned into outputs (i.e. the structures etc. of the political system 'inside the box'—see diagram) and not much about the output functions. (We shall see later that Almond virtually ignores 'the box' and that he, too, carries his analysis of outputs to a degree of refinement far less than in the case of inputs; the reasons for this will be examined then.)

In the category of inputs, *Demands* provide the raw material or information which the system must process, and the energy (resources, in Mitchell's terminology, below, p. 124) needed by the system. Why should demands lead to *political* activity? Easton gives broadly the same answer as most sociologists: firstly, the demands made cannot all be fully satisfied (even though some are satisfied outside the political system); and, secondly, the satisfaction of some demands requires a special organised effort by 'society'.

How do demands arise, and assume their particular character? They arise either in the environment (external) or within the system itself (internal). The environment includes other systems within the total social system (society)—ecology, economy, culture, personality, social structure, demography. (Apter, for example, would emphasise social stratification.) These constitute the major set of variables shaping demands from outside the political system. But we must also notice the influence of the 'ongoing culture' (cf. Almond and Verba) which shapes the goals, the specific objectives, and the procedures of the system.

This culture embodies the standards of values in society and marks out the areas of potential conflict between and over demands. Internal influences will include, for example, those of the system of representation, the nature of the constitution, etc. The system itself will have its own norms and institutionalised procedures.

Not all problems are recognised as issues, since no one may raise the question of doing anything about them. Like the poor, they are always with us. Not all demands become 'issues', since no conflict may arise and no one will oppose the satisfaction of the demand. How, then, are demands transformed into issues; what determines whether a demand becomes a matter for serious political discussion? General factors of significance here include the relationship between the demand, on the one hand, and, on the other, the location of its supporters in the power structure; the importance of secrecy and timing; the possession of political skills etc. There are also the images held with regard to the ways in which things get done in the political system. We may recall David Truman's point that all interest groups attempt to couch their demands in terms which imply that they are concerned about the 'public interest'. However they arise, and however they become issues, demands are a significant part of the material on which the system operates. They are also one important source of change.

But there is another aspect of inputs, *Support*. This is the energy, in the form of actions or orientations (states of mind) which promotes or resists a political system, or the demands and decisions which are needed to keep the system running. The domain of support may be examined in relation to three objects—an analysis very similar to that of Almond and Verba in their study of political culture. Firstly, the political community; members must support the peaceful settlement of demands and there must be a high degree of national unity or 'consensus'. Secondly, the regime; members must support the rules of the game, the constitutional principles which legitimate action and provide authority. Easton would apparently agree with Spiro that 'procedural consensus' may be more important than 'substantive consensus' (i.e. agreement about *particular* goals and policies). Thirdly, members must support the actual government if it is to be able to perform the concrete task of negotiating settlements; force is not enough. There is clearly an inter-relationship between these three objects of support, but they are probably set out in descending order of importance so far as their significance for the maintenance of the system is concerned. Opposition to the actual government is less significant if there are institutionalised ways of bringing about a change. Opposition to the regime is less important if there are accepted ways of changing the rules e.g. by constitutional amendment through a process which is neither too rigid nor too flexible. Failure to agree on either or both of these matters— and especially the latter, may, of course destroy consensus in the political community itself, and produce a revolutionary situation.

It is not easy to estimate the quantity and scope of support needed to maintain a system. It may be the active support of only a small minority, though one which is quantitatively great in its intensity and degree of commitment. Easton cites India as an example of such a situation. Or it may be the support of virtually all, though in small amounts. Easton cites France as an example here, though he was writing before the downfall of the Fifth Republic. The normal situation in any political system is the existence of both support and hostility (or perhaps apathy); it is the balance which is important. (This kind of problem is discussed in a more sophisticated manner by Bernard, cf. below, pp. 224 ff.)

Easton next discusses the *mechanisms* of support, and it is at this point that he deals with outputs. By mechanisms of support is meant the means for maintaining a steady flow of support for the system. Outputs can be a mechanism of support if the decisions made within the political system satisfy the day-to-day demands made upon it. There may also be inducements, positive or negative (i.e. sanctions), and these will vary, for example, as between democratic and totalitarian systems, and, indeed, within each broad category of systems. Governments or, in another sphere, parties, need not meet *all* the demands even of their most influential supporters; they can call upon a reserve of support—consensus or party loyalty. But *some* demands of the influential members (individuals or collectivities) must be satisfied if the system is to maintain itself. The questions that arise are those of how much?; who are influential?; why?

Easton looks finally at *politicisation* as a mechanism of support. This is the process of steadily manufacturing support, of political socialisation—the equivalent of 'general' socialisation in societies. The patterns of political life are learned by the members of the system; they absorb political attitudes and orientations. Common basic expectations with regard to standards are used by members when making political evaluations. These expectations are reinforced by a common network of rewards and punishments, by means of the communication of myths, doctrines, ideologies, philosophies etc. which affect all members. The system thus comes to be accepted as legitimate.

The kind of analysis developed by Easton has been taken further, sometimes with modifications, and, in particular, by Mitchell in his study of 'The American Polity' to which we turn next. It remains to note that although Easton was an early advocate of input-output system analysis as applied to political systems he is well aware of its dangers and limitations, as will appear from a further contribution of his which is discussed later (cf. below, pp. 221–4).

V: AN ELABORATION OF STRUCTURAL-FUNCTIONAL ANALYSIS AS APPLIED TO THE POLITICAL SYSTEM

In the introduction to his 'American Polity', Mitchell[15] first provides a general outline of structural-functional analysis such as we provided in our opening section, parts of which were, indeed, taken from Mitchell. We now examine the more detailed application of this approach to the political system. The basis of this approach may be expressed diagrammatically in what is, in some ways, an elaboration of Easton's diagram. A simplified account of the above diagram may begin with a consideration of the *Functions of the Polity*. These are listed by Mitchell as follows:

1. The authoritative specification of system goals; we are interested in both their types and their numbers.
2. The authoritative mobilisation of resources to implement the goals; resources include personnel, skills, material, technology.
3. The integration of the system: this involves a consideration of controls, their types, numbers, and enforcement.

4. The allocation of values and costs; this involves a consideration of their types, incidence, recipients and quantities.

As part of the authoritative performance of these functions (three of which are shown in the diagram on the output side and one on the input), the various *demands and expectations*, their types, numbers, sources, and intensity, and the *supports*, their types, levels, objects and intensity, must be taken into

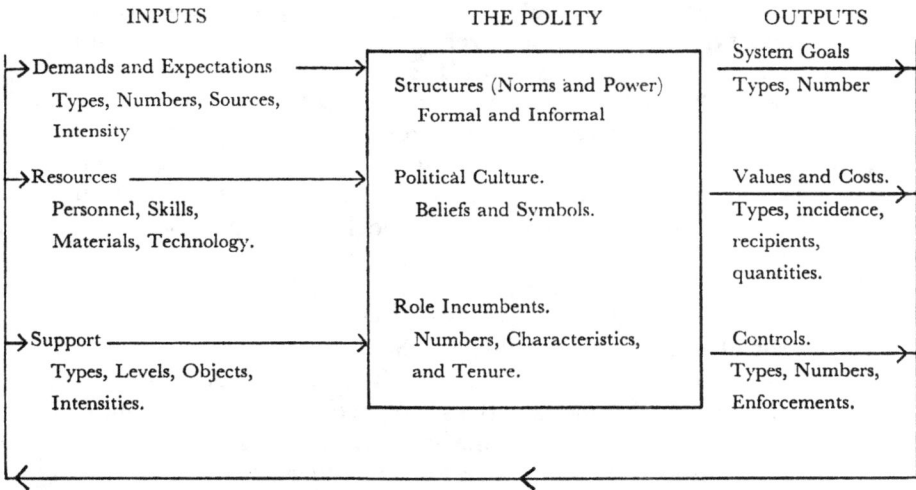

INPUTS	THE POLITY	OUTPUTS
→Demands and Expectations Types, Numbers, Sources, Intensity	Structures (Norms and Power) Formal and Informal	System Goals Types, Number
→Resources Personnel, Skills, Materials, Technology.	Political Culture. Beliefs and Symbols.	Values and Costs. Types, incidence, recipients, quantities.
→Support Types, Levels, Objects, Intensities.	Role Incumbents. Numbers, Characteristics, and Tenure.	Controls. Types, Numbers, Enforcements.

account. These are shown in the diagram on the input side. Each of the four 'authoritative' functions needs further consideration.

Collective goals are sought by groups or by the society, though, of course, they are determined by individuals in the name of society. There is no one comprehensive and generally applicable list of goals for any and every political system, but as illustrations Mitchell cites self-defence, social welfare, economic protection, the management of valued resources, education, protection of consumers, workers, businessmen. Every political system requires authoritative means for the *selection* of goals from the various demands which are made.

The *allocation of values*, (derived from goals) and costs (involved in achieving goals) follows from the fact that each goal imposes obligations on certain members, and provides generalised or particular benefits for members. Allocation of this kind in society is performed as frequently by the polity as by the economy. The polity, at the least, lays down the 'rules of the game', which affect 'who gets what, when, and how'; it frequently decides the *actual* allocation. There is inevitably an imbalance between demands and supplies; the polity is concerned with the distribution of scarce or limited values. The same applies to costs. There are, it must be repeated, other rationing or distributive systems in society, e.g. the stratification system, which, however, is not entirely separate from the polity. Apter (see Section III, above) argues that members of the public join political groups to expand mobility opportunities, by influencing or controlling governments which themselves are 'geared to' the ultimate alteration of social stratification or aspects of it. Conversely, the stratification system affects government. (His 'model' of politics, based on these assumptions is too sophisticated for consideration here.) Nevertheless, there is some functional specificity in advanced societies. The economy is concerned with wealth and income, the social stratification system with prestige; the polity with power—though there are overlaps. The 'ideals' of allocation and the 'realities' are seldom the same; in the polity, for example, the principle of 'one man one vote' may be established but citizens possess unequal power and influence.

The authoritative mobilisation of resources and services involves consideration of such matters as taxation, but also the recruitment of personnel and skills to the polity. The use of controls of various types is important here, since they are concerned not only with integration in general, but with the mobilisation of particular resources and skills. No polity can fulfil the goals of society unless it can obtain from it the *means* whereby the goals are to be achieved.

Finally, although the polity, and the government as part of the polity, may not even be the most important factor in relation to *integration* (though we have seen that Sutton regards this as pre-eminently its function) it is of key significance. Formal and informal processes of socialisation and social control may lie largely outside the polity (though the latter influences the agencies concerned, such as the family, the schools, the voluntary bodies in general), but rewards and penalties are the concern of 'authority' in the polity, and the co-ordination of the members of society into a real group is in large part the result of action from within the polity. The new nations provide an outstanding example of this.[16]

Unlike Easton, and, to a lesser extent, Almond, Mitchell devotes considerable attention to the *internal structure of the polity* ('inside the box'), through which, demands, resources and supports are 'processed', so that they emerge as authoritative decisions. The structure as a whole, and the relationships of the component parts, are important. Basic to a consideration of these structures is the concept of roles and the sets of norms governing them, bearing in mind that there are both formal and informal structures and relationships. Roles and norms are particularly important in relation to Power, more specifically, to what Dahl calls 'offices'; and also in relation to the capacity of citizens to control the power structures or offices. More broadly, there is the influence of political culture, its beliefs and symbols. Formal 'institutional' enquiries as to the numbers, characteristics, and tenure of role-incumbents may, of course, tell us little. Note, for example, in Britain, that the 'constitutional superiority' of the Minister tells us little about his actual relationships with his top level civil service advisers.

We can only indicate briefly here the kinds of questions which Mitchell suggests must be asked. Is the polity functionally specialised?; perhaps more accurately, to what degree? To what extent is the internal structure differentiated, and along what lines? How visible is the power structure? How open is the power structure? This involves consideration of the nature and extent of the 'circulation' of power-holders; the extent and the basis of their accessibility to demands. How concentrated or diffuse is the power structure? How are authoritative roles acquired and controlled? How are the norms enforced? What effect does the structure have on the functions of goal-attainment, allocation, tension-management, and integration? For the application of these questions and, indeed, of the whole conceptual and theoretical framework, to an empirical political system, Mitchell's own analysis of 'The American Polity' should be consulted as a means of assessing the extent to which this approach provides new insights.

Finally, reference must be made to some further observations on *inputs* and *outputs*. The latter may be dismissed rather more briefly, since they have already been examined in some detail in the general analysis of the functions of the polity—goal-attainment, allocation of values and costs, controls. *Inputs* require a little more elaboration. First, we note that when we speak of *demands* being made on the polity, they are, in fact, being made *through* the political system on *other members of society*—hence the need for the polity not only to select goals, but to allocate values and costs and, in the last resort, to exercise the necessary controls. Mitchell makes some suggestions as to how the input of demands might be 'operationalised'; they include, for example the number of bills introduced into the legislature (more valid when private members' bills are relatively easy to introduce e.g. in the U.S. in contrast to the U.K.); the proliferation of interest groups and the number of group resolutions; demands made in newspapers etc; the size of government budgets; the number and types of government employees; the work-loads of officials. More generally, in relation to demands, we need to enquire, as already noted, about their types, the number of people affected, their costs, and their intensities.

Expectations, which Mitchell has added to Easton's *demands*, are a more amorphous group of beliefs about what governments *ought* to do, and about the way in which its officials and other citizens *ought* to behave. These will differ in different political systems.

Resources have been adequately considered above. We need note only that they appear on the input side, since the polity must draw them from society, but their actual 'requisitioning' and allocation is an 'authoritative' decision of the polity.

Finally, *supports* are concerned with the willingness of citizens to give support to the polity, whether through positive feelings, indifference, habit, or compulsion. Support among citizens exists in various forms and degrees, and for different objects. The objects of support, Mitchell suggests, in a scheme similar to that of Easton's and to the analysis of political orientations by Almond and Verba, can be considered in the form of a hierarchy of levels, ranging from the most generalised political values, through structures and laws, to leaders and policies. While it remains true that societies can tolerate a great deal of conflict or disagreement—there is 'a great deal of ruin in a nation'—this is the truer the lower down the level of the hierarchy one goes. But support must be generated, and by all available methods ranging from socialisation, through the use symbols, rewards and sanctions, to commands.

This account may be rounded off with the reminder that there is an important feedback in the political system, mentioned by Easton and emphasised by Mitchell, in the sense that *outputs* influence the *inputs* of demands, resources, and supports. Outputs are the 'price' paid for inputs, and the whole process may be regarded as one of a 'circular flow' of decisions, action, demands etc., leading to further decisions and actions.

Mitchell's references to the notion of the *equilibrium* of the system, adds little to our account from Bredemeier and Stephenson. The system is in equilibrium, he says, whenever the expectations of members have been met, or they have nothing else to gain by further exchanges. There are, of course, 'varying degrees of stability' which may, broadly, be measured by the nature of the demands being made on the polity and, alternatively, by the emergence of rebellion or civil war. Political change may occur either in the system itself, or in the persons within the system, though the latter may lead to structural revisions. In between these two, there may be changes in the power structure, in ideologies, in symbols, or in the bases of authority. Changes of any kind may be induced either by internal (endo-genetic) or external (exo-genetic) influences. Although the system operates within a political culture—a system of beliefs (values and norms), symbols, and authority ('legitimate' power), it is always to be regarded as a system of structures and processes—the 'polity in motion'—the latter consisting of the transformation of the three inputs of demand, resources, and supports, into the output of system goals and the means of their implementation.

We discuss further in a later section the problem of including 'change' in our structural-functional approach (below, pp. 212 ff).

VI: ANOTHER VIEW OF THE POLITICAL SYSTEM

In his study of 'The Political Systems of the Historical Bureaucratic Empires', Eisenstadt offers a general analysis of 'the political system' with which we deal here, both because it has intrinsic merit as a useful approach, and because, in many ways it provides a link between Mitchell's schema just dealt with, and that of Almond which follows.

The political system, says Eisenstadt, is a basic part of the organisation of any society. We must examine its place within the social structure, and its relation to the other parts of that structure. Different types of political systems develop and function under specific social systems, and the continuity of any political system is related to such specific conditions. There are three basic functions which are performed by any political system:

1. The Political System is the organisation of a territorial society having a legitimate monopoly over the authorised use and regulation of force in society.

2. It has defined responsibilities for *maintaining* the system of which it is a part. To recall Apter, if the minimal structures of government fail to operate, it must undergo drastic modifications, and/or the system itself (society) will also do so. It will be noted that Eisenstadt's specific citing of 'maintenance' relates the political system to the functions of pattern-maintenance and tension-management, integration and control.

3. Its organisation imposes severe secular sanctions in order to implement the main collective goals of society, to maintain its internal order, and to regulate its foreign relations.

All the social roles and groups fulfilling these distinct functions in a society, regardless of what other tasks they perform, constitute the political system of the society. Specific political roles may not be clearly distinguishable, but there must be a *legitimate pattern of interactions* for goal-achievement and order-maintenance. As Almond says, 'if the functions are there the structures must be'.

The question of the extent to which political activities and organisations can be discerned and differentiated is of key significance in both the analysis of any one political system, and in comparison between more than one such system.

Eisenstadt next examines in more detail the functions of the polity which follow from the broad functions described above. First, there is *legislative decision-making or 'ultimate ruling' activity*. This is concerned with the determination of the primary goals of the society, and the formulation of general rules for maintaining (or changing) the existing order in society.

Secondly, there is *administrative activity*. This involves the execution of the basic rules in the different social spheres, and the organisation of the technical activities necessary for the efficient execution of services to groups. This activity also regulates and assures the provision of resources to the political system by the different strata and groups in society.

Thirdly (and altering Eisenstadt's order, since these first three functions appear to be closely connected as *outputs*), there is *judicial activity*. This involves testing and authorising the validity of the basic rules in relation to particular concrete cases arising in society.

Although expressed differently, these are Almond's rule-making, rule-application, and rule-adjudicating functions.

Fourthly, there is *party-political activity*, which is concerned with mobilising *support* for different political measures and rules, and for the holders of different political positions. It should, perhaps, be added that it is also concerned with recruitment *to* political roles. This is, of course, an *input* function performed within the political system, but penetrating the output function also.

The *Rulers*, who may be in greater or lesser degree subject to the ruled, play an active part in the political process; they define goals, formulate and execute rules, adjudicate, and contend for political support.

The *Ruled* are subject to the rules, *demand* adjudications, and wish to *influence* legislators. Rulers and ruled may at times be interchangeable.

The degree to which each type of political activity is *differentiated* varies greatly from one society to another, but in all there will be a differentiation between *inputs* i.e. types of supports and resources which the political system needs to fulfil its functions, and *outputs* i.e. the major contributions of the political system to society as a whole.

Political sociology has an important contribution to make to the understanding of the inter-relations between political and other institutions as a feature of the working of political systems. The specific output of the polity to other institutional spheres consists of the various *authoritative decisions*, as both Eisenstadt and Easton emphasise. Eisenstadt's further analysis of this general output (and of inputs, below) is similar to Mitchell's. It includes (1) the definition of major collective goals, and the priority to be assigned to them (2) the allocation of prestige, influence and the authorised use of power and facilities, and (3) the distribution of various facilities, benefits, and rights to groups and individuals.

In the other direction, the polity is dependent upon the other sub-systems of society for a continuous inflow of resources, services, and support for the implementation of collective goals, the maintenance of the polity's position in society, and the fulfilment of the regulative and integrative functions. From the economic sphere come manpower, labour, material, and money. From the cultural sphere come basic support, identification with the symbols of the regime, the legitimisation of rules, and the motivation for the performance of political roles. From the social stratification system come organisation, support for different policies, and the willingness of different groups and individuals to engage in political activities. These contributions are articulated through the *demands which the political institutions make* on the different groups and strata in society, and through the *transmission of political decisions* from rulers to ruled. Those who occupy political roles must make continuous demands on the other institutional spheres.

But these demands are closely connected with, and largely contingent on, the *demands made on the polity* by different groups that various types of decisions should be implemented. These demands derive from the political orientations and activities of groups, and mainly through the *articulation* of their interests in *political terms*, together with the *aggregation* of those interests in the frameworks of some *political organisations*. We shall examine these last points in greater detail in our consideration of Almond's conceptual framework in the next chapter.

The continuous interaction between the polity and the other institutional spheres in terms of their specific contributions and demands, constitutes the dynamics of the political process in society.

NOTES

[1] Much of the ensuing section is taken from the author's *Inaugural Lecture*, noted on p. 46.

[2] B. de Jouvenel, *The Pure Theory of Politics*, C.U.P., 1963.

[3] G. E. Catlin, *Systematic Politics*, Allen and Unwin, 1962.

[4] A. de Grazia, *Politics and Government*, Vol. I. '*Political Behaviour*', Collier Books, N.Y., 1962.

[5] Latham, 'The Group Basis of Politics' *in* Eulau etc., eds., *op. cit.* pp. 232–45.

[6] D. Easton, 'An approach to an analysis of political systems', *World Politics*, April, 1957.

[7] This is a bare summary of an excellent section of W. G. Runciman, *Social Science and Political Theory*, C.U.P., 1963, espec. pp. 22–34.

[8] Robert E. Dahl, *Modern Political Analysis*, Prentice-Hall, 1963, p. 12.

[9] J. D. B. Miller, *The Nature of Politics*, Duckworth, 1962.

[10] *The Analysis of Social Systems*, Hart, Rinehart, Winston, 1962.

[11] Parsons, 'Voting and the Equilibrium of the American Political System', *in* Burdick and Brodbeck, eds. *American Voting Behaviour*, Free Press of Glencoe, 1959, pp. 91–92.

[12] cf. David Apter, *The Gold Coast in Transition*, Princeton U.P., 1955, especially p. 309.

[13] David E. Apter, 'A comparative method for the study of politics', *Am. Journal of Sociology*, Vol. LXIV, No. 3, Nov. 1958, pp. 221–237, reprinted in Eulau etc. ed. *op. cit.* pp. 82–94.

[14] David Easton, 'Analysis of Political Systems', *World Politics*, Vol. 9, No. 3, April, 1957; reprinted in Macridis and Brown eds. *A Reader in Comparative Politics*, Dorsey Press, 1961, pp. 81–94.

[15] W. R. Mitchell, *The American Polity*, Free Press of Glencoe, 1962 pp. 2–25.

[16] cf. Karl W. Deutsch and William J. Foltz eds. *Nation Building*, Atherton Press, 1963.

Note:—Two books by David Easton appeared too late for consideration here. They are:—

    1. *A Framework for Political Analysis*, Prentice-Hall, 1965.
    2. *A Systems Analysis of Political Life*, Wiley, 1965.

5

The Political System—2

PERHAPS the best-known sociological approach to a study of 'the political system' is that of Gabriel Almond in his Introduction to 'The Politics of the Developing Areas'.[1] We have already discussed Almond's general definition of 'the political system' (above, pp. 23–4). From this, he proceeds to examine 'the universe of political systems', and concludes that there are four characteristics which all political systems have in common, and in terms of which they may be compared. Firstly, all political systems have *political structure* i.e. legitimate patterns of interaction. Secondly, the same general *functions* are performed in all political systems, though with different frequencies, and by different kinds of structures and in different 'styles' (which may be compared on the basis of pattern-variable analysis). Thirdly, all *political structure*, no matter how specialised, is *multi-functional*, though in different degrees in different systems. Finally, all political systems are *'mixed'* in the cultural sense, containing elements both of modern (rational) and primitive (traditional) cultures and structures, though in varying degrees. We now take up each of these points in more detail.

1. As to the first point, Almond holds that there is no such thing as a society which maintains internal and external order, which has no *political structure* i.e. legitimate patterns of interaction by means of which this order is maintained. Further, all the types of political structures to be found in modern systems are to be found in non-Western and primitive ones, though they may be occasional or intermittent, and not clearly visible. We may just note, at this point, a useful modification suggested

by Hoselitz.[2] He argues that there is more than a 'quantitative' difference between the *structures* in simple non-complex societies, and the allegedly analogous structures in more modern 'rationalised' societies. The difference is one of kind. The *action systems* may have analogies, but the *institutions* differ profoundly. If, he says, Almond means by 'structures' merely a set of actions (which does, we think, appear to be the case), this is all right. But if he means what Hoselitz calls an *institution*, then they differ. Hoselitz contends that there may be 'a conscious organisational change in the society' e.g. the establishment of new administrative structures, and that it is useful to make the distinction between *action systems* and *institutions*, since this permits a more extensive characterisation and analysis of the various functional dimensions of each structural complex. However this may be, Almond insists that his approach has the advantage that 'the classic distinction between primitive societies which are states, and those which are not [becomes] a distinction between those in which the political structure is quite differentiated and clearly visible, and those in which it is less visible and intermittent'. To repeat, 'if the functions are there, then the structures must be'.

2. Almond's second point means that in order to understand the political system and its structures, we must ask *functional questions* in addition to describing the specialised structures. Functions may be performed by other than such structures. It is sometimes overlooked that Almond has emphasised that his functional categories were developed for the specific purpose of comparing political systems as whole systems (and, in particular, Western and non-Western systems), and that the functional categories employed must be adapted to the particular aspect of the political system with which the researcher is concerned (cf. Coleman and Rosberg, below, pp. 151–52). Moreover, the emphasis on *input* functions, and the relative lack of sophistication in designating the *output* functions, derived from a belief that the former were more important for characterising non-Western systems. We refer later to the question of more precise categorisation of the output functions. But, in our view, the 'seven-function' schema is none-the-less useful as an approach to the analysis of *any* political system. The schema is outlined below; a detailed examination of it follows, after we have

considered the last two of Almond's four general points. The
schema is:

A. *Input Functions* (political)
    1. Political socialisation and recruitment.
    2. Interest articulation.
    3. Interest aggregation.
    4. Political Communication.

B. *Output Functions* (governmental)
    5. Rule-making.
    6. Rule-application.
    7. Rule-adjudication.

3. Almond's third general point concerned the *multi-functionality* of political structure. It is important to repeat that
this applies in Western as well as in non-Western systems. In
the former, certain structures have emerged which have a
functional distinctiveness, and which play a 'regulatory' role in
relation to that function. For example, the recruitment function
of other structures—interest groups, media of communication—
tend to pass through and be processed by the party system.
Interests developed by informal status and lineage groups, and
such institutions as churches and corporations, tend to pass
through and be articulated by associational interest groups. The
legislative body must pass acts of interest aggregation performed by political parties and other structures, before they
become acts of rule-making. These specialised regulatory
structures create the *modern* political system and its peculiar
pattern of *boundary-maintenance* between the polity and the
society or its other sub-systems. Thus there is a relatively high
degree of *structural differentiation* between legislatures, political
executives, bureaucracies, courts, electoral systems, parties,
interest groups, and media of communication—with each
structure *tending* to perform a regulatory role for that function
within the political system as a whole.

But even in modern systems, courts adjudicate and legislate;
the bureaucracy legislates; legislative bodies affect administration and adjudication; pressure groups initiate legislation and
participate in administration; the media of communication

represent interests and sometimes initiate legislation. Conversely, there are varying *degrees* of structural differentiation in more primitive and traditional and transitional systems, and their comparative compactness and lack of differentiation should not be exaggerated. On the other hand, traditional and intermittent structures continue to operate inside and outside other structures; they are not *completely* regulated by the latter. The specialised structures of interest articulation (interest groups), aggregation (political parties) and communication (the mass media) exist in relation to persisting non-specialised structures, which are *modified* by the specialist ones, but not assimilated to them. Boundary-maintenance is less clear. However, some of these features persist in modern systems. Diffuse and primary structures perform governmental and political functions; other social systems and structures in society—the family, the church, the educational system, the economy—are parts of the political system as *intermittent* political socialisers, recruiters, interest articulators, and communicators. 'No political system, however modern, ever fully eliminates intermittency and traditionality.'

4. Almond's last general point referred to 'mixed' political cultures. We have already examined this point in some detail in connection with his analysis of 'political culture', and his examination of various kinds of political culture (above, pp. 23–33). No further consideration is necessary here. The more detailed examination of the seven 'functions' to which we now turn will throw light on this, and on the other three general points which we have discussed.

Political Socialisation and Recruitment. This is, broadly, the function of citizenship training, and recruitment into political roles. All political systems tend to perpetuate their cultures and structures, mainly by the socialising influences of the primary and secondary structures through which the young pass, though the process continues through adult life. These structures include the family, the church, the school, the work group, voluntary associations, and media of communications, political parties, and governmental institutions. Political socialisation, the 'process of induction into the political culture', which may be either latent or manifest, results in a set of attitudes or orientations towards the political system. The style of political socialisation may be specific or diffuse; it may combine particularistic and universalistic elements i.e. kinship, lineage, village, caste, or religious sect influence, as well as that of 'citizenship'. Membership of the political system may be 'constituent' i.e. through a group, or individual. 'Modern' political systems tend to penetrate and affect the socialisation process of other social systems, by providing a 'general citizenship content'. There will also be different combinations of the affective and instrumental elements. In all systems also, the 'latent' elements are at work; in modern systems the manifest ones operate more strongly, but the latent never wholly disappear.

> 'If political socialisation produces the basic attitudes in a society towards the political system, its various roles, and public policy, then by studying political culture and political socialisation we can gain understanding of one of the essential conditions which affect the way in which these roles are performed, and the kinds of political inputs and outputs which these roles produce.' (*Loc. cit.* p. 31.)

Political recruitment takes up where general socialisation leaves off. It is concerned with the recruitment of citizens into the specialised roles of the political system. Again, it is necessary to examine the role of family, kinship, and lineage, as well as the structures affecting specific induction patterns, such as political parties, election systems, bureaucratic recruitment systems, and other governmental structures. 'The recruitment function . . . consists of the special political role socialisations which occur in a society "on top of" the general political socialisation.' (*Loc. cit.* p. 32.) Styles of political recruitment may be compared according to the way in which ascriptive and particularistic criteria are combined with achievement (or performance) and universalistic criteria.

Interest articulation is concerned with the formulation and expression of interest claims, and demands for political action. Since it occurs at the boundary of the political system, the structures which perform this function, and the style of their performance determine the character of the boundary between dolity and society. Almond distinguishes four main types of interest articulation structures. They are: (1) institutional interest groups; (2) non-associational interest groups; (3) anomic interest groups, and (4) associational interest groups.

The first category includes legislatures, political executives, bureaucracies, armies, churches etc. These, or blocs within them, may articulate their own interests, or represent the interests of other groups in the society. The second category includes kinship and lineage groups, ethnic, regional, religious, status, and class groups. These often perform the articulation function intermittently and informally. The third category is concerned with 'spontaneous break-throughs into the political system from society'—riots, demonstrations, and the like. We recall that such activities, however, may be 'stirred up' *by* existing incumbents of political roles rather than *against* them. Although anomic groups articulate interests, they may end up by transferring power (recruitment), changing the Constitution (rule-making), freeing political prisoners (rule-application), lynching (rule-adjudication) or 'communicating' (to enlist support). The last category, of associational interest groups, includes specialised structures like trade unions, business-men's organisations, professional, civic, educational associations etc. They are formed to represent explicitly the interests of a group, to formulate procedures for expressing demands and channelling them to the other political structures, parties, legislators, bureaucracies.

Some general comments may be made on these categories of groups. The style of performance of the function of interest articulation may be manifest or latent, specific or diffuse, general or particular, instrumental or affective. A high incidence of anomic interest articulation, or of non-associational interest articulation, or of institutional interest articulation, will tend to affect boundary-maintenance both within the political system and between the political system and the society or its other sub-systems. Contrariwise, a high incidence of associational interest articulation may indicate good boundary-maintenance between society and polity, and may contribute to such maintenance within and between the sub-systems of the political system. Associational interest groups exercise a regulatory role in processing raw claims or interest articulations, and by diverting them in an orderly way through political parties into the authoritative decision-making system.

The more latent, diffuse, particularistic, and affective the pattern of interest articulation, the more difficult is it to *aggregate* interests and to translate them into public policy. The more manifest, specific, general, and instrumental the pattern of interest articulation, the easier is it to maintain the boundary between polity and society, and the better the circulation of needs, claims, and demands from society, in an *aggregable* form, into the political system.

The applicability of this conceptional approach to empirical political systems may be illustrated from Almond's own account of the British and the French (to 1958) political systems. As we saw in his earlier analysis of political culture, Britain has a homogeneous, fusional, political culture; the members of society and the political elites are homogeneously oriented towards the polity, and combine 'civility' and 'deference'—the 'civic culture'. There are institutional, non-associational, and (rarely, nowadays) anomic interest groups. But there is a thoroughly elaborated system of associational interest groups which regulates the impact of other interest structures, mitigates their particularistic, diffuse, ascriptive, and affective impacts, translates these into explicit, general, and bargaining demands for public policies, and works out strategies of influence and access. They may also provide a link between society and polity, through the vast array of Advisory Committees etc.

The functions of interest groups and political parties are sharply differentiated. Interest groups articulate political demands in society, seek support in other groups, attempt to influence the choice of political personnel, and the various processes of public policy-making and enforcement. Political parties tend to be free of ideological ridigity, and are 'aggregative' i.e. they seek to form the largest possible interest-group coalitions. Both interest-group systems and political-party systems are differentiated, bureaucratic, and autonomous. (The affiliation of the Trade Unions to the Labour Party does not alter this general picture. The former exist also as an autonomous pressure group; the latter is an independent political group and is no more influenced by affiliated Trade Unions than the Conservative Party is by non-affiliated employers' organisations etc.) The party system stands between the interest-group system and the authoritative policy-making agencies, and screens the latter from the particularistic and disintegrative effects of special interest. The choice between general policies can be made in cabinet and parliament, while the bureaucracy functions as a neutral instrument of the political agencies. (In the U.S. some agencies tend to represent their clients. The Ministry of Agriculture in the U.K. is frequently said virtually to represent the National Farmers' Union.)

The French political systems of the Third and Fourth Republics operated in a political culture which was not homogeneous and fusional. Not only was there the division between traditional and rational; the latter tended to be of the 'absolute-value-rationality', rather than of the 'bargaining-instrumental-rationality' variety; it was 'apocalyptic' rather than civil or pragmatic. Against this background, institutional and anomic interest groups were of far greater importance than in the United Kingdom. Their significance was directly related to the uneven effectiveness of associational groups, the absence of an effectively aggregative party system, and the fragmented or isolative political culture. Parties and interest groups did not constitute differentiated, autonomous political sub-systems; they inter-penetrated one another. Some parties more or less controlled interest groups (e.g. the Communist Party and the Communist-dominated Trade Unions and, to a lesser extent, the Socialist Party and the Socialist Trade Unions). The most powerful institutional interest group, the Catholic Church, controlled other interest groups (e.g. the Christian Trade Unions), and strongly influenced political parties (e.g. the M.R.P.).

When parties control interest groups, they inhibit the capacity of interest groups to formulate pragmatic, specific demands; they impart a political-ideological content to interest-group activity. When interest groups control parties, they inhibit the capacity of parties to combine specific interests into programmes with a wider appeal. 'Raw', unaggregated demands reach the legisative process, or, alternatively, the legislature is faced with the diffuse, uncompromising, or revolutionary and reactionary tendencies of the Church, and the movements of right or left. No interest group is large enough to have a majority; the party system cannot aggregate the different interests into a stable majority and a coherent opposition; the electoral and legislative processes fail to provide alternative effective choices.

The legislature is penetrated by relatively narrow interests, and uncompromising ideological tendencies. It is used as an arena for propaganda, or for the protection of special interests by veto or otherwise, but not for the effective and timely formulation, and the support, of large policy decisions. Without a strong legislature, special interests and ideological tendencies penetrate the bureaucracy, and undermine its neutral, instrumental character.

There is poor boundary-maintenance between society and the political system, and among the various parts of the political system. The high incidence of anomie (e.g. Poujadism) reflects the incapacity of the associational interest groups to receive demands from society, assimilate them, transform them into aggregable claims, and transmit them to the party system, the legislature, the cabinet, and the bureaucracy, from which they may emerge as impacts upon public policy and regulation.[3]

Interest Aggregation, to which reference has been made in the preceding section, is achieved either by the formulation of general policies in which interests which have been articulated may be combined, accommodated, and compromised; or by the recruitment of political personnel who are more or less committed to a particular pattern of policy. Articulation and aggregation overlap, as do aggregation, recruitment, and rule-making; though the boundaries are well preserved, for example, in the Anglo-American mass democracies.

To obtain the maximum flow of inputs of raw claims from the society, a 'low level of processing into a common language' of such claims is required. This is best performed by associational interest groups. To assimilate and transform these interests—these claims thus processed—into a relatively small number of alternatives of policy and personnel, a 'middle range of processing' is necessary. If *both* these two functions are substantially performed before the claims reach the authoritative government-structures, then the *output* functions of rule-making and rule-application will be facilitated. The political and governmental processes will become more calculable and responsible. The outputs will be related to, and controlled by, the inputs, and circulation—Mitchell's 'circular flow'—within the political system, and between it and society, will be relatively free.

Aggregation, then, refers to the more inclusive levels of the combinatory process. Pressure groups and parties in developed modern systems have distinctive and regulative functions, the first for articulation, the second for aggregation. In some systems, however, the aggregative function may be performed by the legislature, the executive, the bureaucracy, the media of communication, the interest group—especially of the 'general' or 'civic' type—as well as by the political parties. But the party system is the distinctively modern structure of political aggregation; without it, aggregation may be performed corvetly, diffusely, and particularistically, as, for example, in Spain.

Almond turns from these generalisations to an examination of different kinds of party systems (*loc. cit.* pp. 40–45). We merely summarise his schema here. He distinguishes four broad types of party system:

1. The *authoritarian.* This may be subdivided into: (i) the *totalitarian,* in which there is a high rate of 'coercive social mobilisation', although there *is* an upward flow of significance; (ii) the *authoritarian* e.g. the Republican People's Party in Turkey after the Ataturk Revolution; in this there is more upward flow, but also alternative policies *within* the party.

2. The *dominant non-authoritarian* (which, in Shils's categories of *political system* may be compared to the 'tutelary democracy'). In this, a nationalist movement unites, or attempts to unite, all interests. As a result, cohesion is difficult to maintain, and diffuse programmes are formulated.

3. *Competitive two-party systems,* in which an effective and autonomous system of associational interest groups introduces claims into the party system, legislature, political executive, and bureaucracy, which claims are combinable into responsive, alternative public policies. Boundary-maintenance between society and polity, and among the articulative, aggregative, and rule-making structures is good. The whole process tends to be overt and calculable, and results in an 'open circulatory' flow of inputs and outputs. The U.S., the U.K., and the 'old' Commonwealth members are examples.

4. *Competitive multi-party systems.* These may be subdivided into (i) the *working system,* in which some parties are broadly aggregative e.g. the Socialist Parties; in which there is a more homogeneous political culture, and stable majority and opposition coalitions are possible. Not only some parties, but also the coalitions are aggregative. The Scandinavian countries provide examples here; (ii) the *immobiliste system,* as in France. In a

143

fragmented, isolative culture, aggregation by the parties is relatively narrow; coalitions are fragile; certain groups remain continuously alienated from the system. In Laski's phrase, there is 'a politics of manoeuvre, not of policy'.

Parties also differ in the *style* of their performance. Three broad types may be distinguished: (1) secular, 'pragmatic', bargaining parties (Lipset's 'parties of representation'); (2) absolute-value-oriented ideological parties (Lipset's 'parties of integration'); (3) particularistic or traditional parties. Parties may also be broad- or narrow-based in their activities. For example, many Latin-American parties are 'broad' at elections only. They may be revolutionary, reactionary, or oriented towards national independence or power; such parties may be narrow-based at first, and later become parties of total integration. Many examples of this may be found in the new African states. Finally, they may be identified with ethnic or religious groups, and may be more like interest groups, although they present candidates.

Almond applies this conceptual framework for illustrative purposes to Britain and India. In Britain, the aggregative function is distinctively performed by the party system. Interest aggregations in the bureaucracy are controlled and to some extent assimilated into the aggregative processes of the party system. Parties are broad-based and can aggregate interests into general policy. There is a high degree of interest aggregation prior to the performance of the authoritative governmental functions, and the responsibility for outputs is clear. There is a free movement of interest groups among parties (although some, of course, tend to look to one party more than another, and in some cases to be closely associated with it, though unable to bend it entirely to their own sectional purposes; even these groups, however, will turn to the other party when it becomes the government). In India, there is a relatively low degree of interest aggregation through the party system. The boundaries between party, legislature, and bureaucracy are poorly maintained, and the last-named of these performs much of the aggregative function. Communal movements, ethnic and linguistic groups, traditional groups, sectarian socialist movements, also perform this function, or prevent its effective performance by other structures. There is a low mobility of the interest groups in the party system, and a relatively low potential for stable coalitions among parties. Of course, interest groups are less likely to 'move', and parties less likely to be concerned with coalitions, in view of the dominance of the broadly-integrative Congress Party. The situation might well alter if the Congress Party were to disintegrate after the removal of Mr Nehru's controlling influence; it has never prevailed as strongly at State level, in any case. As Professor Morris Jones has put it, in India there are 'two levels of politics and political styles'.

The last of the four political or input functions is that of *Political Communication*. All functions, of course, are performed by means of communication. But Almond holds that it is of great importance that in modern systems some media of communication have developed a 'vocational ethic' of 'neutral' or objective communication, and perform their function separately from the other political functions. Those political systems with homogeneous political cultures, and autonomous and differentiated structures of interest articulation and aggregation (e.g. the U.K., the U.S., and the 'old' Commonwealth) have to the greatest extent developed autonomous and differentiated media of communication. Those with fragmented political cultures, and relatively undifferentiated structures of interest articulation and aggregation (e.g. France and Italy) have a press which tends to be dominated by interest groups and political parties.

Political communication, Almond contends, is the *crucial boundary-maintenance function*. With an autonomous system of communication, covert communications in the bureaucracy, interest groups, and political parties (and overt but government-controlled communications through public relations officers and central offices of information etc.) may to some extent be regulated by critical publicity. Latent interests may be made explicit by neutral media of communication. Autonomy in these media makes for a free flow of information from society to polity, and from one political structure to another, as well as an open feedback from output to input again. The communication function can regulate the interest articulation function independently of the associational interest groups. It can communicate the articulations of interest emanating from political parties, legislatures, and bureaucracies which themselves can correct the actions of interest groups. The communication function also limits the regulatory power of political parties in the aggregative function; of the legislative and political executive in rule-making; and of the bureaucracy in rule-application. It 'regulates the regulators', and preserves the autonomies and freedoms of the democratic polity. The crucial control in the totalitarian political system is, conversely, the monopoly of the media of communication, since even in such a system coercion has a strictly limited role.

Almond further holds that an autonomous, neutral, and thoroughly penetrative system of communication is essential to the development and the maintenance of an active and effective electorate and citizenship. More specifically, it creates an informed stratum of citizens, public-policy oriented rather than interest-oriented; they form 'general-policy pressure groups', and help to sustain the regulatory role of the media of communication in the polity. In the modern political system, the specialised communication structure is even more elaborate; it penetrates the unspecialised and intermittent structures of political communisation—kinship, lineage, status, and village groups. The problem posed by the need to penetrate such centres of communication is well illustrated by the new African and Asian states, with their attempts to achieve 'grass-roots' contacts. The paradox here is that to achieve such nation-wide penetration it is frequently considered necessary for the government to control *all* media of communication; in any case the modern specialised media, directed primarily to the urban, modernised sector of the community, even if left alone, are seldom as effective in traditional centres as the government itself.

Styles of political communication also differ. They may be manifest or latent, specific or diffuse, particularistic or generalistic, affectively-neutral or affective. There is a mixture of these styles, even in modern systems, but in them latent, diffuse, particularistic and affective 'messages' tend to get translated into manifest, specific, generalistic, and affectively-neutral ones, and to get 'placed in envelopes with the correct political address'.

In applying this analysis, Almond contrasts the United States and India. In the former, there is firstly, homogeneity of political information; there are widely distributed 'interpreters' of political information, which penetrate the primary cells and connect them with the secondary media of communication. In the latter, the messages are heterogeneous, the impact of the specialised media is relatively limited, and there is a greater gap between the literate modern sector and the illiterate traditional sector, due largely to difference of language and of cognitive maps. In the U.S. there is mobility of information; in India there are many obstacles. There are great differences in the volume of information, and in the extent of informed, animated, and controversial discussion. Finally, as regards the direction of the flow of information, the output of messages from the authoritative governmental structures tends to be far larger in India, and other traditional systems, than the input of messages from society.

As we have seen, Mitchell's analysis of functions was followed by an account of the working of the decision-making process within the authoritative governmental structures ('inside the box'). Almond pays little attention to these, except indirectly in relation to output functions. Moreover, in his discussion of the latter, his division into *rule-making*, *rule-application*, and *rule-adjudication* is much less sophisticated than his analysis of the input functions. He justifies this partly, as we saw, by suggesting that for an understanding of non-Western systems, the input functions are more important; but partly by emphasising the 'indeterminacy' of formal government structures in such systems, and the gross deviations in the performance of output functions from the constitutional and legal forms.

His account of the output functions is prefaced by an analysis of various types of political systems. This is entirely based on Shils's categories, which we have already discussed in detail (above, pp. 70–86). Here we are concerned only with repeating briefly the consequences of these political systems (excluding political democracies and totalitarian oligarchies, the features of which are sufficiently well known, as extremes at each end of a continuum) for the political structures. The tutelary democracy tends to concentrate the rule-making and rule-application functions in the executive and the bureaucracy.

Moreover, since there are only rudimentary party, interest-group, and communication systems, the executive and the bureaucracy also tend to be far more dominant in the performance of political functions than they are in political democracies. In modernising oligarchies, there is an even greater concentration of functions in the ruling clique, and in the bureaucracy. There is no competitive party system; associational interest groups are limited in number and influence, and there is an overt pluralistic system of interest articulation by local communities, informal status and lineage groups and institutional groups. In traditionalistic oligarchies the development of modern structures is a defensive move; it affects only the army, the police, and parts of the civil bureaucracy; otherwise, the elite aims to control or prevent modernising tendencies in society. The aggregative, articulative, and communication functions are usually performed by the bureaucracy and/or the army, as well as by kinship and tribal units, status groups, and local units.

In characterising the governmental functions of rule-making, rule-application, and rule-adjudication, Almond states that it is necessary to specify the structures which perform the functions, the style of their performances, and the way in which the problem of cultural dualism is solved. (Almond suggests that 'rule-making' may be an inadequately precise category, which should e.g. be broken down into 'initiation', 'modification', and 'vetoing'—p. 55. We refer below, p. 152, to a further possible breakdown of the output functions.) For example, there is the division in the U.S. between the executive, the legislature, and the courts; in the U.K. between Cabinet, Parliament, and the courts, with the last-named less influential. (Almond also distinguishes Federal, Confederal, and Unitary systems and, in the latter, the degree of autonomy of local government structures. We note only that Federalism differs from particularistic, pluralistic systems in that there is a *formal* constitutional division of powers.) Boundary maintenance tends to be good in these modern Western democratic systems (though there is controversy over delegated legislation and administrative adjudication), and relatively poor in transitional systems. In the U.S., Congress and the Presidency in its legislative role tend to regulate the rule-making activities delegated to and performed by the bureaucracy; the latter operates under grants of power which may be rescinded or modified. In the U.K. the boundaries are drawn somewhat differently, but there is a similar regulatory control by Parliament and Cabinet over rule-making by the bureaucracy. The boundary between the courts and other governmental structures is effectively maintained in both the U.S. and the U.K., and the courts exercise a regulatory control over other rule-adjudicating structures. There is however, in the U.K., doubt as to the effectiveness of such control. The most striking difference between the U.S. and the U.K. is that in the former there is judicial review of the rule-making, as well as of the rule-application and rule-adjudicating functions, by other federal structures, and, in addition, a regulation of the division of power between the central government and the state governments. In both countries there are informal primary structures within the formal ones, but these tend to be penetrated by and acculturated to the formal primary and secondary structures. In the American Congress, however, party control over informal groups is less effective than in the British House of Commons.

In transitional political systems, boundary-maintenance between governmental structures tends to be less effective. For example, legislatures are not as powerful in regulating rule-making by bureaucracies, and the rule-making function tends to be performed by the executive and the bureaucracy. Primary groups within the governmental structures are of the 'communal kind, and operate with equal legitimacy. There is also a serious problem of continuity between the central government structures and the local ones, in which e.g. the mayor may be a chief, or the courts may be subverted by the traditional system of adjudication. This is one of the reasons for the appointment of 'political' regional and district commissioners, and for the extension of government party control of local structures.

Almond concludes his introduction with a section entitled, 'Towards a probabilistic theory of the polity' (pp. 58–64). To many, this is the least persuasive part of his work; in any case, a detailed critical consideration of his ideas would take us far beyond the introductory purpose of this book. We do, however, present some brief comments on the general significance of his 'seven-function' schema. Firstly, the basis of the approach is the separation of political function from political structure. The schema specifies the elements of two sets, one of functions and one of structure. 'Political systems may be compared in terms of the probabilities of performance of the specified functions by the specified structures.' It also specifies styles of performance of function by structure. (At this point Almond refers to the possibility of making precise comparisons, relating the elements of the three sets—functions, structures, and styles—in the form of a 'series of probability statements'. As preliminary indications of this possibility he cites Robert A. Dahl's *A Preface to Democratic Theory*, David Truman's, *The Governmental Process*, and V. O. Key Jr., *Politics, Parties and Pressure Groups*. The reader is referred to these, and to Almond's own discussion.) To repeat, 'political systems may be compared with one another in terms of the frequency and style of *political functions by political structures* (*loc. cit.* p. 61). But as Almond consistently warns us, his set of political functions is most preliminary, while the structural categories are even more tentative. He has 'simply used the nomenclature of political and social institutions without pretending to have arrived at clearly defined, universally applicable categories of structure' (*loc. cit.* p. 62). Further, in comparing styles of performance of function by structure, he admits to having made no significant advance on the pattern-variable concepts. This problem of categorisation of function, structure, and style, clearly needs to be 'solved' before quantification becomes feasible. Moreover, there is the complication that 'all political structure is multi-functional, and all political culture is dualistic' (*loc. cit.* p. 63). There is, as yet, no set of 'reliable indicators' for Almond's concepts of functional regulation by one specialised structure of the performance of particular functions by other structures; nor for the penetration of traditional styles by 'rational' styles. Indeed, he admits that our knowledge of the performance of *modern Western politics* needs to progress from beyond its present state. Nevertheless, the author has found Almond's schema useful as providing new insights into individual political systems, and as a basis for more illuminating comparisons between different political systems in a *much larger universe* than the traditional one of most political scientists. He can, as yet, however, see no basis for more far-reaching claims. Indeed, as we shall see, the approach has been criticised even in relation to the first, more limited, purpose.

Meanwhile, an interesting example of the way in which the concept of function may be used to examine the role of the polity in new states is provided by Coleman and Rosberg in a study of Tropical Africa.[4] They refer to the 'heavy functional load' which is thrown upon the new polity, and the extensive and many-sided role of the political party in the performance of the relevant functions. They make it clear, however, that, there is no implication that if these functions are only intermittently or inefficiently performed, or even not performed at all, the new states will necessarily disintegrate 'although such a development is not impossible'. One reason for this modified optimism is the existence of large segments of population who 'are not yet exclusively dependent upon central government or the modern sector. In their interstices, the rich pluralism and the persisting family pattern, there are still important dimensions of functional performance'. Nor is it postulated that the single party is a structural requisite in new African political systems. 'Simply for analytical purposes, we consider it useful to postulate the *existence of certain minimal political functions which are performed in all polities*, although with varying degrees of explicitness and emphasis, and with wide structural variation'. (Our italics.)

The 'functional load of the polity' is described as follows:

Interest articulation and aggregation: The unaggregable character of most interests, and the non-existence, weakness, or ethnicity of interest associations, dispose the governing party generally to identify and to determine interest satisfactions in terms of its concept of the national interest, as well as the state of public opinion.

Political recruitment: The monopoly over the political arena and hostility to alternative structures or channels of recruitment dispose the governing party to develop, routinise, and regulate recruitment processes within all the authoritative and non-authoritative structures in society.

Political socialisation: The widespread persistence and pervasiveness of parochial ties dispose the party to perform the dual function of (1) facilitating the extinction of old psychological commitments to subcultures viewed as terminal communities, and (2) politically socialising both present and upcoming citizenry into (i.e. inculcating respect for and loyalty to) the new national political culture, new authority structures, and new bases of legitimacy.

Political communication: The absence or weakness of mass communication media and the underdevelopment and discontinuities in the communication network increase the need for the governing party to develop a penetrative communication process both within the party structure and between party and population, as well as to ensure high informational output regarding government plans and programmes and expected commitments from the population.

National integration: Ethnic, regional, and other parochialisms, not transcended or contained by a sense of national community or by habituation to national institutions, and the elite–mass gap, dispose the party to serve as the main instrument, singly, or through the auxiliary instrumentalities which it controls, for both territorial and political integration.

We may add that it is made clear that the above functions were meant to be only illustrative. 'Neither the number nor the formulation of the functions of the polity is immutable; they are no more than *ad hoc* heuristic devices.' (cf. Almond, above, p. 135.) Moreover, dominant parties may contribute to the performance of a variety of *authoritative functions* e.g. rule-making and rule-application, the mobilisation and allocation of resources; as well as to the constitutive and legitimating functions of formal institutions of government.

ADDENDUM TO SECTION I

We have seen that Almond has admitted the rudimentary nature of his categorisation of the output functions. As an alternative, he refers briefly (*loc. cit.* pp. 15 and 56) to a scheme devised by Harold D. Lasswell.[5] Lasswell suggests a 'problem-solving frame of reference' for the consideration of the political system, and would examine problem-solving in relation to goals, trends, conditions, projections, and alternatives. It is necessary to clarify the legitimate aims of the body politic; to determine whether the trend of events has been toward or away from a realisation of preferred events; to ascertain which factors condition one another, and determine developments; to project the course of future events, on the preliminary assumption that we do not ourselves influence the future; and examine what policy alternatives promise to bring all the preferred goals to their optimum fulfilment. For all these purposes, the existence of authority and effective control is essential within the political system. Lasswell then proceeds to his seven categories of functional analysis. These are:

1. *Intelligence*, which includes information, prediction, and planning.
2. *Recommendation* or *promotion*, which includes all activities designed to influence the outcome, and to promote policy alternatives.
3. *Prescription*, which includes the articulation of norms, and the enactment of general rules.
4. *Invocation*, which involves a preliminary characterisation of the set of concrete circumstances affecting—
5. the *Application*, in final form, of decisions, in such a way as to characterise conduct according to the prescriptions.
6. *Appraisal*, which characterises the relationship between policy goals and strategies, and the results achieved—the assessment of the success or failure of the policy.
7. *Termination*, the handling of expectations (rights) established when a prescription was in force, or the ending of prescriptions and of arrangements entered into within their framework—with a view to possible changes, leading us back to intelligence etc.

At each stage it is necessary to ask, who are the significant participants, official or unofficial, and including such 'aggregates' as class etc?; what are their perspectives of the outcome (the values) which they seek, their prospects of success, the groups they identify with, etc?; what arenas are specialised in the task e.g. situations which are relatively specialised in power groups?; what assets (base values) are at the disposal of the participants?; what strategies do they employ?; what are the immediate and the long-term results—the outcomes and effects? The decision process will take into account (1) pre-arena events—all the interactions that precede the involvement of the authoritative or controlling decision-makers in the context, (2) arena-events—all the interactions in which the decision-makers are involved, and (3) post-arena events—all the inter-actions that are influenced by the outcome.

Almond points out that these categories were clearly designed primarily for governmental, and particularly for judicial, comparisons. The *input functions* are handled in two rather formal categories, *intelligence* and *recommendation*, 'gentle concepts which hardly do justice to the vigour of politics'. (*Loc. cit.* p. 15.) (Though Lasswell's 'pre-arena events' suggest a somewhat more detailed empirical application.) *Prescription* and *termination* are divisions of the *rule-making function. Invocation* and *application* are subdivisions of the *rule-application function. Application* also, to-gether with *appraisal*, forms part of the *rule-adjudication function.* Almond adds (*loc. cit.* p. 56) that this approach to functional cate-gorisation does not satisfy 'our need for a set of conceptual tools which can bring out the differences in the performance of governmental functions in different kinds of political systems'. (Nor, he admits, does the division into 'initiation', 'modifica-tion', and 'vetoing', used by himself and Cohen in a series of studies of foreign policy-making in the U.S.) It is suggested, however, that this approach might, again, provide new insights into the working of any given political system.

II: DEVELOPMENT AND POLITICAL SYSTEMS

Almond has recently[6] elaborated his concept of the political system in ways which, he considers, make more possible an examination of the processes of change. We need not discuss his restatement of functional-system theory and its three implied conditions: functional requisites, interdependence, and equili-brium, nor his general reply to certain general criticisms of functional theory. But it is important briefly to state the 'need to think of systems as functioning at different *levels*'. One level involves the unit as a whole in its environment, including other social systems. Another is internal to the system and is con-cerned with 'conversion processes', the transformation of inputs into outputs. In regard to political systems Almond speaks of the performance of the system in its environment as its 'capabili-ties', and of the internal working as its 'conversion functions'.

Finally, he speaks of 'system-maintenance and adaptation functions'; such functions as recruitment and socialisation do not directly enter into the conversion process but affect its internal efficiency and therefore the performance of the system. Political systems may be compared in terms of *capabilities*, *conversion functions*, and *system-maintenance* and *adaptation functions*. Political development may be discussed in terms of the inter-relations of these three kinds of political functions.

'The theory of the political system will consist of the discovery of the relations among these different levels of functioning . . . and of the inter-relations of the functions at each level. The theory of political change deals with those transactions between the political system and its environment that affect changes in general system performance, or capabilities that in turn are associated with changes in the performance of the system-adaptation functions and the conversion functions.'

Almond next repeats his argument that the special identity of the political system is provided by its association with the use of legitimate physical coersion in societies. He refers to Easton's 'authoritative allocation of values', Lasswell's and Kaplan's 'severe deprivations', and Dahl's 'power, rule, and authority'—as all associating politics with 'legitimate heavy sanctions'. Inputs are all related in some ways to claims for the employment of legitimate physical compulsion; outputs to its actual employment (or threat thereof). This is to be understood subject to two provisos. Political elites may be concerned with other matters e.g. peace, social welfare, individual freedom. Other systems may also make rules and enforce them. But in the first case the other matters are somehow related to compulsory actions e.g. taxation; in the second case only the rules of the *political* system go 'all the way' in compulsion. At this stage Almond's elaboration of the political system, with Easton's inputs (demands and supports) as the starting point, begins.

Demands he classifies under four headings:

1. Demands for goods and services e.g. wage and hour laws, education, roads etc.
2. Demands for the regulation of behaviour e.g. public safety, labour relations etc.
3. Demands for participation in the political system e.g. the franchise, the right to associate etc.

4. Symbolic inputs e.g. demands for the display of 'majesty and power', or communication of policy intent etc.

Supports he also classifies under four headings:

    1. Material supports e.g. payment of taxes.
    2. Obedience to laws and regulations.
    3. Participation e.g. voting, associating etc.
    4. Manifestation of deference to public authority etc.

As regards *outputs*, there are 'four classes of transactions initiated by the political system that tend to match up with the supports . . . and may or may not be responsive to demands, depending on the kind of political system that is involved'. These are:

    1. Extractions e.g. tribute, taxes etc.
    2. Regulations of behaviour.
    3. Allocations or distributions of goods and services, honours status etc.
    4. Symbolic outputs e.g. displays of political symbols, policy statements etc.

'. . . The inputs of demands and supports are *converted* into extractive, regulative, distributive, and symbolic outputs.' When demands can be handled without unbearable strains and with no basic change in structure or culture; when outputs are responsive to demands in expected ways and supports are similarly responsive to outputs . . .' the political system may be said to be in a state of equilibrium both internally (in the performance of conversion functions by political structures) and in its relations with its environments. It should be noted that inputs do not necessarily come *only* from the society of which the political system is a part. There are transactions between the political system and components of both its domestic and foreign environments. Inputs may come from the domestic society, the political elites, and the international environment. Demands (from wherever) affect the policies or goals of the system; supports provide the resources avaliable to the system to attain goals.

Almond then turns to the events which occur in the political system i.e. *conversion functions*. He adds little to his earlier discussions of political structures, institutions, and roles; nor to the functions of articulation, aggregation, policy-making, rule-making etc. He does, however, emphasise that his list of political conversion functions 'is not derived from generic system theory, or from concepts in use in sociological theory', but from 'the observation of political systems'. In complex political systems specialised structures perform distinctive tasks. The functional categories can be used 'to compare complex political systems with one another, and these with less differentiated ones'. Political conversion functions are classified as:

1. The articulation of interests or demands.
2. The aggregation or combination of interests into policy proposals.
3. The conversion of policy proposals into authoritative rules.
4. The application of general rules to particular cases.
5. The adjudication of rules in individual cases.
6. The transmission of information about these events within the political system from structure to structure and between the political system and its social and international environment.

It will at once be observed that this analysis does not take us very much further towards an examination of what we earlier called 'the contents of the box'. However, the further analysis of the *capabilities of political systems* does appear more fruitful. This concept, Almond suggests, adds two more questions to the traditional ones of 'who makes decisions?' and 'how are decisions made?' They are (1) 'what impact does the political system have, what does it do, in its domestic and international environments?' and (2) 'what impact does society and the international environment have on the political system?' Answers to such questions involve breaking down into their components the broad concepts of 'goal-attainment', 'integration', and 'representation' and treating such elements as *continua*. Almond suggests five categories of capability, derived from the earlier classification of inputs and outputs, which may be regarded as *functional requisites*. They are:

1. *Extractive capability* i.e. the range of performance of the political system in drawing material and human resources from the domestic and international environment. Some systems e.g. the Mongol Empire, the warlords in China, guerilla chieftains in Mexico have little more than an extractive capability but it is found in all political systems.

2. *Regulative capability* i.e. the flow of control over behaviour and of individual and group relations stemming from the political system. We are concerned with the objects of regulation, the frequency and intensity of regulation, and the limits of tolerance of regulation. By the use of these first two concepts it is possible to distinguish between primary extractive systems and extractive-regulative ones, such as Eisenstadt's historic bureaucratic empires. We can also 'chart the developmental process from the one to the other'.

3. *Distributive capability* i.e. the allocation of goods, services, honours, statuses etc. Just as an extractive capability implies some regulation and distribution (albeit unintended) so a regulative capability implies an extractive capability; so, again, a regulative capability must in some way affect distribution. These capabilities 'are not only logically related. They suggest an order of development'.

4. *Symbolic capability* i.e. the rate of effective symbol flow from the political system into the society and the international environment. Displays, ceremonies, affirmations of values, policy statements, may all serve to facilitate other kinds of system capability. We may note that symbolic output is not the same as symbolic capability—effectiveness is the test. One example of the application of this concept is in new nations where 'central symbolic output' may compete with symbols of local authority.

The four above capabilities are ways of describing the pattern of *outputs* of the political system. The fifth is a relationship between inputs and outputs. It is:

5. *Responsive capability* i.e. the degree to which outgoing activity is the consequence of demands arising in the environments of the political system.

We do not pursue here Almond's applications of this scheme to the international interaction of political systems, nor his analysis of the relations between internal and international capabilities. But it is useful to summarise his 'aims of research on political systems'. They are:

1. To discover and compare capabilities profiles summarising the flows of inputs and outputs between political systems and their domestic and international environments.

2. To discover and compare the structures and processes which convert inputs into outputs.

3. To discover and compare the recruitment and socialisation processes which maintain political systems in equilibrium or enable them to adapt to environmental or self-initiated changes.

We note, further, that it is necessary to examine the capabilities of other social systems since 'the flow of inputs into political systems, the kinds of problems they confront, and the pressures on them to develop capabilities will vary with the performance patterns or the capabilities of these other social systems'.

A consideration of *supports* in relation to capabilities is of great importance. For example, extractive capability is affected by such things as tax evasion, willingness to co-operate etc. French and Italian *incivisme*, involves e.g. a tendency to non-performance, evasion, unresponsiveness, desertion. 'We need some way of estimating social performance in response to the outputs of the political system.' Here we are concerned not only with actual but *potential* support; we probe 'the political culture in order to ascertain what the support possibilities are . . .' Nor will such support necessarily be the same for all kinds of outputs.

At this point it is useful to summarise Almond's views of the contribution to political enquiry so far made by his scheme. It 'is more than a classification of variables and less than a theory of political systems. It is more than a taxonomy, since it suggests inter-relations among capabilities, and between capabilities, the structure and culture of the political system, and the performance of the system-maintenance and adaptation functions. These relations, derived at least in part deductively, may be formulated as hypotheses for empirical testing against historical data. It is less than a theory, since prior to systematic study it is an open question whether these particular categories of capability and of converison and maintenance functions will help us to discriminate the variables we need to know about in order to construct a good theory. They may be viewed as a proposed first step towards constructing a theory of the political system and of the development of political systems . . .' (cf. especially pp. 205–206 *loc. cit.*)

Most important, perhaps, is that the 'analysis of the capabilities of a political system . . . does not tell us what factors affect political change or development, what produces change in cababilities'. These changes result from the interaction of *certain kinds* of inputs with the political system. When the flows of demands, supports, and outputs 'have a particular range of content and level of magnitude, such that the existing structures and culture of the political system can cope with them, we may speak of the political system as being in equilibrium'. But change in content or magnitude e.g. depression and unemployment, or war, or new schemes for large-scale development, or any other fundamentally new demand by the political elites, may be innovative, *dysfunctional* i.e. 'they may require significant changes in the magnitude and kind of performance of the political system'. Dysfunctional input flows *cause* changes in the capabilities of political systems, in the conversion patterns and structures of the political system, and in the performance of the socialisation and recruitment functions. How do these dysfunctional flows affect political development and what kinds of dysfunctional flows affect what kinds of capability problems?

The flow of inputs may vary in any of five dimensions. They are:

1. *Quantitative* i.e. dysfunctional inputs may be incremental; demands for participation may start in the middle classes and spread to others. Or they may come all at once. These two examples are designated 'incremental' and of 'high magnitude', respectively. The one may need only a small adjustment in attitude and a limited set of structural adaptations; the other may require fundamental cultural reorientation and a new complex political infrastructure.

2. *Substance or content* i.e. inputs may refer to particular subject-matter areas such as the franchise, educational opportunities, eligibility for public office etc. Different political structures and cultures may show different degrees of toleration for different kinds of demands e.g. they may be more responsive to demands for what Joseph Chamberlain called the 'ransom' (social services) than to demands for redistributory taxation.

3. *Intensity* i.e. the contrast between orderly petitions and violent demonstrations. Low-intensity demands may produce

no system adaptation; high-intensity demands may cause either a change in the responsive capability of the system e.g. extension of the franchise, or in the regulative capability e.g. repressive action.

4. *Source* i.e. demands may come from the international political system, from the political elite, or from the domestic society; in the last case they may come from different strata or sub-systems. Demands from political elites may be more immediately translated into changes in political capabilities; those from the upper strata may involve less structural or cultural change than those from the lower strata.

5. *Number of kinds* of dysfunctional inputs at any one time. Simultaneous or cumulative demands clearly affect the political system more fundamentally. (This point may be compared with Lipset's analysis of the historical emergence of certain basic issues, cf. pp. 191–8.)

There may be *dysfunctional outputs*, since outputs may initiate social change, which then affects inputs or produces capabilities in other social systems which affect the flow of demands and supports. 'But the relation of dysfunctional outputs to political development are indirect, through *input feedbacks*.' The welfare state, for example, may produce changes in social structure and attitudes which increase support inputs of some elements in society and demand inputs of others.

Dysfunctionality can also result from fluctuations in the flow of *supports* e.g. loss of morale, disobedience etc. Fluctuations in support will, of course, be affected by the kinds of demands made on the society by the political elites and by the latter's responsiveness to demands from the society.

We may note, without developing the point at length, that 'the extent to which the political system is loaded by dysfunctional flows will vary with the capabilities of other social systems in the domestic society and international system'. For example, there may be developments in the economy or in United Nations technical assistance etc. which affect the political system.

One extremely important variable to be considered is '*the reaction pattern of political elites*, the behaviour of important role incumbents in the political system as they are exposed to dysfunctional demands or supports'. (Our italics.) 'Reaction' must not obscure the 'originative and creative activities of political elites', which will also have consequences for the society and for the international system—and for the political system itself. We listed above the dimensional varieties of dysfunctional inputs. The reaction of political elites to such inputs may affect the dimensions e.g. as between low and high magnitude, low and high intensity, simple and multi-issue flow, single and many sources. 'This interaction between dysfunctional pressures and elite reaction is on the same level of importance as is the response patterns of other social systems from the point of view of the development of political system capabilities.'

A political elite may react in different ways to dysfunctional flows of demands. It may react *adaptively* e.g. by accepting changes involved in an extension of the franchise or in welfare programmes. Or it may react *rejectively* i.e. explicitly refuse to accept demands for innovation or suppress such demands. Such reaction may increase the pressure for innovation to the point where the elite must either act adaptively or repressively. A third possible response is *substitutive* e.g. the provision of 'circuses' rather than 'bread', or war instead of welfare. Such reaction may 'absorb' the dysfunctional demands, at least for a time e.g. Germany under Hitler. Or it may merely postpone the issue. Or it may produce a mixture of both.

Finally, Almond considers system adaptation, recruitment, and socialisation. 'New roles and new attitudes are the essence of system change. New capabilities or levels of capability, new political institutions and processes, call for new elites, changes in elite training and indoctrination, and changes in expectation, commitment, values and beliefs among the various strata of the population. *The socialisation and recruitment processes of a political system have a special relation to political change.*' (Our italics.)

Recruitment and socialisation patterns affect political development through changes in other systems. The process of industrialisation affords one example of this for its effects may spill over into political orientations e.g. by stimulating new demands for participation and welfare. New elites may be recruited and these may demand structural change in the political system. There may be 'a sequence in which industrialisation affects general socialisation, role differentiation, and recruitment, which affects political socialisation and recruitment, which in turn builds up innovative pressure on the political system'. Changes in the religious system may also affect the political system, witness the effect of the Reformation.

Recruitment and socialisation may also affect political change through actions of the political elites. The processes may be manipulated, as in totalitarian countries and some 'control' will exist in most political systems.

Again, elite reaction to innovative pressures may affect socialisation and recruitment indirectly, since such reaction may affect society through the media of political changes. Adaptive reaction may produce support, rejective reaction, alienation. It is clear that foreign policy and warfare may also affect the processes. Almond discusses illustrations of this to be found in France and Germany (pp. 213–214).

To summarise, 'what we have been suggesting here is that the performance of a political system (e.g. its "immobilism" or "mobilism"), its conversion characteristics, (e.g. the congruence or incongruence of its structures, the cohesion or fragmentation of its culture), the operation of its recruitment and socialisation processes, are explainable in terms of a particular history of interaction between the political system and its social and international environments'. Political development may be approached by way of systematic comparative history. For this, we need 'a common coding scheme, a set of categories, and hypotheses about their inter-relation'. Readers will judge for themselves, both by a study of the scheme and, perhaps, by attempts to apply it, whether 'the adaptation of political systems theory proposed here may serve as a starting point'.

III: APPLICATIONS OF THE SEVEN-FUNCTION SCHEMA

Almond's introduction, which we have analysed in the previous section, was written for a study of the politics of a large number of countries in South-East Asia, South Asia, Sub-Saharan Africa, the Near East, and Latin America. In the conclusion to this book (*op. cit.* pp. 532–576), James Coleman sums up 'the modal characteristics of the political systems' covered in the survey. In our summary we shall attempt to indicate to what extent the 'seven-function' schema was found useful in the study of these systems. It is, perhaps, significant that Coleman found it necessary to go somewhat outside the schema in order adequately to sum up his conclusions about the political systems concerned. In particular, this is true of his consideration of the degree of 'political modernity' in the systems, and of the degree of 'competitiveness', an 'essential aspect of political modernity'. Since we are not concerned here to pursue in detail a comparative study of these particular political systems, we shall simply sum up Coleman's broad conclusions, based on a table (*loc. cit.* p. 534) which lists the countries concerned according to the degree of competitiveness (competitive, semi-competitive, and authoritarian), and the degree of political modernity (modern, mixed, and traditional). Three features stand out. First, the 'mixed' character of the social, economic, and political processes. Secondly, their lack of integration. Thirdly, the wide gap between the traditional mass and the essentially modern sub-society of the Westernised elite.

Coleman then proceeds to a consideration of further general characteristics, which are related (*a*) to the processes of change in the countries concerned, and their political implications, (*b*) to the *functions of the political system.* The first of these groups is predominantly concerned with the relationships between economic development on the one hand, and political development on the other (*loc. cit.* pp. 536–544). This aspect has also been considered by Lipset, and we devote a separate section to a consideration of it (below, Chap. 6). The second of these groups, however, is directly relevant to the application of Almond's schema to empirical political systems. Coleman takes each of the seven functional categories, and relates it to the countries covered by the detailed studies.

Political socialisation, the process of induction into the political system, is affected by the fact that the political cultures of the countries concerned are almost all fragmented. There is the gap between the predominantly urban, modern sub-society of the Westernised elite, and the traditional societies into whose political cultures a large segment of the population continues to be socialised. There are also horizontal divisions between the 'melange of indigenous cultures' within the national boundaries. The governing elites are concerned to develop and strengthen system-wide secondary structures which will impinge directly on individuals, and penetrate the primary socialising structures. But they are resisted by particularistic forces. It follows from this that there is a wide variety of patterns of *political recruitment*, based on varying admixtures of the traditional and the modern, and varying rates of recruitment, not merely in different countries but in areas of the same country at different stages of development. A nationalist movement tends to increase rapidly the rate of upward mobility into political roles. In the post-independence period there is a decline in recruitment to authoritative and bureaucratic roles, and, perhaps, a cleavage between the older generation (not always 'old' in fact), already occupying such roles, and the younger generation. Moreover, independence frequently leads to the emergence of rural or 'provincial' elites, which do not necessarily work harmoniously with the Westernised elites.

To turn to *interest articulation*, ascriptive, communal, and similar groups persist, while economic and occupational interests are mainly latent, and are not articulated by functionally specific associations. Institutional groups (armies, religious groups, bureaucracies) play a predominant role. Again, the effort to achieve independence tends to develop national movements which absorb all specific interests, and such movements desire to maintain this 'creative unity' after independence. On the other hand, functionally diffuse groups of all kinds may become activated *after* independence, while the functionally specific groups tend to greater autonomy in the articulation of their interests.

As regards *interest aggregation*, there are varying party systems, but most frequently the system has *either* a number of parties which are narrow-based and which 'serve essentially as vehicles for competition between different elements drawn from the modern sector', especially for strong personal leaders; *or*, alternatively there is a one-party system, ranging from comprehensive nationalist movements, through broadly aggregative non-dictatorial parties, to narrow-based dictatorial systems. Dominant parties are, of course, the more likely to develop where they are faced with unreconciled tribal, communal, or regional groups, or with new parties organised by more ideological younger leaders determined to 'complete the revolution'.

In relation to both interest articulation and interest aggregation, the phenomenon of anomic movements in most of these countries must be noted. Weiner, in his studies of India, has suggested that 'their appearance is probably the result of the fact that more discontent exists in the society than has been articulated through organised groups'.

In most of the countries concerned, there are gross discontinuities in *political communication*, which coincide with the fragmentation in political cultures. Near-autonomous communications systems may develop from linguistic differences, but there is always the problem of how mass media can penetrate into the rural, predominantly traditional sectors. These discontinuities may be overcome to the extent to which modernisation has spread; the extent to which political organisation, recruitment, and participation are national in scope; the extent to which vernacular languages persist; and the extent to which transportation and mass communication media have developed. Modernisation may assist in 'nationalising' the media of communication, but it may, of course, exaggerate the discontinuities.

The authoritative functions, *rule-making, rule-application, and rule-adjudication,* are as scantily discussed by Coleman as by Almond. The generalisation that the Western impact has been felt to the greatest degree at the level of formal structure is broadly true. But the 'imported' formal structures differ in the degree to which they constitute 'innovations'. 'Central representative parliaments endowed with a determinative role in the rule-making function, and secular independent judicial structures through which rules are authoritatively adjudicated', represent the most drastic innovations. Executive-bureaucratic government, either through traditional or colonial structures, has long been a feature of the systems with which the study under reference is concerned. One result is the 'under-participation of parliament in the rule-making function, the fragility of the independent judiciary, and executive-bureaucratic predominance'. The degree to which an independent civil service continues to operate depends in part on the nature of the colonial experience undergone, and in part on developments after independence. In any case, there is a tendency towards the centralisation of decision-making, which is, in part, a

166

reaction to the strong centrifugal forces pressing for greater local autonomy, or even for secession.

The last section of Coleman's concluding chapter (*loc. cit.* pp. 559–576) contains an attempt to draw up 'functional profiles of type political systems'. It cannot be fully appreciated without careful reading and study of the charts provided. All we can state here is that it is based on the degree of *differentiation* of spheres, and *functional specificity of structures* in the political systems covered. Such degree is measured against the model of a modern political system whose characteristics have already been sufficiently described. The detailed examination of the political systems indicates the striking predominance of certain structures in the performance of both governmental and political functions e.g. the army in Latin-American systems, the bureaucracy in Afro-Asian systems, and the executive in both. There is also a multiplicity of structures involved in the performance of the several functions.

Of particular interest, though it is impossible to discuss it in detail here, is Coleman's attempt to group the African and Asian countries according to Shils's classificatory scheme—to which, however, he adds 'terminal colonial democracy' and 'colonial or racial oligarchy'. We note, however, that many of the countries discussed could be regarded as marginal in the category to which they have been assigned. In addition, many of them have moved to another category since Coleman wrote, and one interesting exercise would be to attempt to re-assign them on the basis of the changes which have occured since that date. It should be added, further, that Coleman also discusses in greater detail the political systems of the Philippines (political democracy); Indonesia (tutelary democracy—but here we should query the classification at present); Tanganyika (terminal colonial democracy, but now probably to be classified as a 'tutelary democracy' if President Nyerere's pronouncements are accepted, and provided conditions do not change to produce a change towards 'modernising oligarchy'); and Ethiopia (a traditional oligarchy, but now, perhaps, more accurately 'traditionalistic').

Coleman concludes with the proposition that the 'seven-function' schema has greatly improved 'our capacity to order the phenomena of non-Western political systems, and to compare them with the Western ones, and with one another'. With the claim, expressed with somewhat more reservation, that the schema also contributes to a better understanding of the processes of political change or modernisation we are not here concerned. We do, however, at a later stage (below, Chap. 6) examine more closely the problem of modernisation, and, in particular, the question whether a distinction ought not to be made between 'economic' and 'political' modernisation, in order the better to understand the connection between the two. Meanwhile, we turn to some criticisms of the general approach to a study of 'total political systems', and to a consideration of suggested alternative approaches.

IV: A CRITIQUE OF THE SEVEN-FUNCTION SCHEMA

One of the most detailed criticisms of the seven-function approach is contained in Leonard Binder's introduction to his study of Iran. We discuss Binder's alternative approach later, and deal now only with his general criticisms of Almond's schema.[7] Even this section of his work is relevant also to our general discussion of structural functional analysis, (below, Chap. 7) but it is so directly concerned with the material presented in the two previous sections that it seemed more useful to examine it at this point.

Binder begins by suggesting that Almond has simply generalised the broad classes of political activity—derived, he asserts, neither logically nor empirically—to be found in Western political systems. The result is 'several descriptive generalisations but few theoretical hypotheses'. Even these generalisations, are not derived from the logical relationship of the functional categories. 'The more systematic effort to draw conclusions'—and here Binder refers especially to Coleman's conclusion—'went off into uncharted territory the original categories do not include.'

The most important claim of the seven-function schema is that it lends itself to an analysis of whole political systems. This, however, postulates the need for some conception of the nature of *the political system*. Almond's analysis, according to Binder's view, merely involves some *implicit* assumptions. First, a *system* is any collection of elements which the observer decides to relate in terms of his own analytic purpose. Such systems *may or may not* have a *product* e.g. integration, adaptation, decisions, stability etc. *Action* going on within the system *need not* be *purposefully* directed at maintaining the system, or at producing anything. Nor can it be assumed that *changes in any part* of the system will necessarily cause changes in all or any of the *other parts* of the system. A more specific sub-category of the concept *system* is 'one for which the existence of *inputs and outputs* is postulated; this also involves a distinction between the *system* and its *environment*, and the notion of *boundaries*. In organic systems, the tolerance for change is limited; the interaction of its components easily leads to description as *adaptive* or *directed at maintaining the system in being*.' (Our italics.)

The possible relationship between the action of the components of the system and the continued existence of the system, poses the problem of *functionalism*. Activity necessary for the maintenance of the system is functional activity. In sociology, Binder continues, this means functional for *any* social system, or for the *total social system*. In anthropology, this involves concern with particular practices or customs in their (functional) effect for a *concrete* social or cultural system. Some writers, like Merton, have neglected the idea of *system*, while retaining the principle of functionality.[8] They classify diverse social activities in terms of their impact on concrete social structures (groups, classes, demographic categories, societies) and, as well as studying their *functional role*, they admit the possibility of *dysfunctionalism*. Functionality (or otherwise) must be determined empirically.

Political scientists, and especially comparative government specialists, Binder goes on, have denied the utility of formal, institutional categories, and have sought other categories in which to describe what governments do, or what happens in politics. The *polity*, the social sphere of political activity, is often described as a *system*, but the use of the concept of functionality is not related therewith. The emphasis is on what is *done* in a political system i.e. on *political functions*. (If the implication here is that the functions of the polity *for* the society, or the functions of the sub-systems of the polity *for* the polity, are not discussed, this comment seems unfair to e.g. Mitchell, Sutton, Eisenstadt, Hoselitz, Johnson etc., even if not to Almond.) Almond's system, Binder declares, is clearly of the

169

latter type. It represents, in different terms, merely the older concept of political functionalism as contained, for example, in the Federalist Papers, if such terms as executive, legislative, and judicial, are rejected on empirical rather than on conceptual grounds. (Binder is, perhaps, a little unfair in concentrating on the analysis of 'output' functions, which, it is admitted, is the least developed part of Almond's schema.)

The functionalist approach is also, Binder suggests, described as a *behavioural* orientation. This further substantiates the view that its emphasis is on devising *descriptive categories* rather than on classifying behaviour in terms of the *analytically* defined or *empirically* discovered processes of a system; or in terms of the maintenance of the system in more or less unchanged form; or in terms of the impact of behaviour on the various structures or components of the system. (cf. below, pp. 242–9 for Apter's, attempt to distinguish the functional and the behavioural approaches.)

The only relevance that the term *system* can have in Almond's framework is with reference to the supposition that a limited number of functions i.e. types of behaviour, comprise the political system. But it is empirically unfeasidle, if not logically impossible, to limit the variety of categories into which such behaviour may be classified, without the aid of the analytical limitations and synthetic facilities of *a priori* theory. Almond's seven-function system ('really neither functionalist nor a system'), despite its advance over institutional description, may be praised as 'interesting' or 'perceptive', without compelling further attention. It is useful to those who seek a better way to *define the problems* they want to study, but it cannot serve as a foundation for the study of whole political systems. Binder again emphasises the 'relative lack of use' of Almond's categories in Coleman's conclusions.

What is needed, in order to study whole political systems, is a statement of what the political system is, even if unaccompanied by an elaborate set of descriptive categories. There is need for a general theory of comparative categories for widely divergent systems. In our next section we examine Binder's own attempt to develop such theory.

V: THE POLITICAL SYSTEM—ANOTHER APPROACH

In order to analyse whole political systems, Binder postulates the necessity of categorising not only the *component parts of the political system*, but also *types of system*. The distinguishing factor among diverse political systems will be the differential operation of the various components, which will depend in turn on the differences in the structures on which the functional components depend. In concrete structures, we may assume that structures and functions may exhibit a greater or lesser degree of unity or integration—between thought and action, ideal and practice, legitimate and actual. (This kind of problem is briefly referred to by Riggs in relation to *formalistic* systems, above, pp. 58–62.) 'Integration is the goal of social and psychological engineering, its definition and measurement is the goal of social science.' The starting point, is the existence of diverse ethical systems standing in juxtaposition to diverse patterns of political behaviour. (There appears to be some similarity between this notion, and that of Almond and Verba in their discussion of dedrees of *congruence* between culture and structure.)

There then follows a discussion of Beliefs and Political Behaviour, which can be only briefly summarised here. Together, Binder asserts, 'they comprise an analytical system which is, by definition, always in equilidrium'. But when we refer to specific beliefs and specific behaviour 'in the perceptible world of continuous change', we must focus our attention on *degrees of malintegration* of ideas, of political behaviour, and of each with the other. In human affairs there is a constant conscious effort to bring about greater integration, but we discern only greater or lesser degrees of integration upon each discrete observation. 'Assuming that *beliefs* about the legitimacy of the social order are of "the same material stuff" as our *analytical abstractions of behaviour*, and that they are more amenable to rational understanding than our limited *perception* of behaviour, we *construct abstract models* of the static configuration of beliefs and acts against which concrete systems may be compared.' (Our italics.)

So, Binder would characterise system types by the dominant conceptions of *legitimacy*, but (bearing in mind that beliefs and acts are essentially different and not logically transferable to one another) he assumes a certain degree of *malintegration*. It is then pertinent to enquire, how much and of what sort? The two basic elements of the political system, beliefs and acts, inter- act with one another, but it is a partial and discontinuous interaction in which only certain types of behaviour call forth ideologically malintegrative consequences—or formal re- affirmations of existing legitimacy. These types of behaviour, organised and institutionalised in political processes, challen- ging or maintaining the legitimacy of an existing distribution of values, comprise the *political system*. (Influencing factors must be distinguished as 'environmental' e.g. a rise in the cost of living, and 'systematic' e.g. a teachers' strike.) *The study of politics is the study of the legitimisation of social power in situations of social interaction.*

Binder notes, further, that for the theory of the social system, the question of whether the respective responses of the units of social interaction are qualitatively and quantitatively equal is relatively unimportant. But for political science, this difference is crucial, since it determines the power relationship between two actors. (cf. further on this, Bernard, below, pp. 224–242.) Moreover, not all kinds of social power are of interest to the political scientist: only that social power which has relevance to the action of persons in *governmental roles* i.e. political power. In some passages which appear to owe something to Almond, or at least to Almond's application of Talcott Parsons's concepts, Binder goes on to state that in a highly developed society it is not difficult to discern which is and which is not a governmental role. The institutions, or institutionalised roles, are often described in a constitutional document, while other subordinate institutions are established through their agency. In under- developed societies, on the other hand, the division of labour or role specification has not reached an advanced level. It is necessary to define governmental roles in terms of the actual functions performed by persons, either in their diffuse capacities as individuals, or in one of their special capacities e.g. making or interpreting the law, applying or enforcing the law. These roles or functions have an ultimately decisive effect on the allocation of authority, security, wealth, prestige; and also on the defini- tion of the social and territorial limits of the polity.

Political power is characterised by its potential effect, through governmental roles, on the authoritative allocation of values, to use Easton's terminology.[9] But the behaviour involved is not limited to such things as voting or making speeches; it includes all forms of social relationships which affect influence, control, inhibition, or support—'the stuff of social psychology, reference group behaviour, the theory of socialisation, and the impact of primordial sentiments'. A relationship of any kind may be relevant, though certain kinds of relationships are more significant than others in regard to the allocation of values. Binder then refers to pattern-variable analysis as an approach to the consideration of these relationships. The latter, of course, are abstractions; they concern only certain characteristics of real persons e.g. their membership of social classes or occupational groups, or their behaviour as *actors performing particular roles.*

Returning to the point that the elementary power relationship involves qualitative and quantitative differences in the respective responses of the participants, we may look briefly at Binder's further analysis. *Qualitatively,* the important distinction is between a direct or indirect impact. If *indirect,* the resultant situation is regarded as part of the *environment* of the political system. When the resultant has a *direct* impact on government, it may be differentiated in four ways according to whether (1) two actors have combined for a common goal, (2) two actors co-operate for complementary goals, (3) two actors have hindered one another in the pursuit of situationally conflicting goals, or (4) two actors have opposed one another in pursuit of mutually exclusive goals. *Quantitatively,* we are concerned with time, intensity, and number of objects; above all, with the question of whose power is greater.

To recapitulate so far, the argument is that we should attempt to analyse whole systems; that it is valid to treat systems as more or less integrated units in terms of their dominant pattern of legitimacy; that it is necessary to understand the nature of the political act in its most elementary and least-structured form. It is then possible to work back from the elementary power relationship to the global concept of the political system. The basis of such attempt is to seek the nexus between power and legitimacy; but it includes also the marking out of the components of the system i.e. the sort of things which ought to concern anyone engaged in an analysis of whole political systems. (In passing, Binder remarks that cultural and moral considerations, on the one hand, and notions of political legitimacy, on the other, are not necessarily the same things, although they are related.)

What is required in order to move back from the smallest unit of the political system to its largest and most comprehensive characterisation is an *analytical means*. Everybody is part of the political system, but 'in order to better grasp the [individual's] problem of living in civil society', some *unit of analysis* larger than the individual is required; one which will enable us to 'treat large numbers of personal relationships as constant and theoretically manipulable units'. Such unit of analysis, Binder suggests, may be either *the class* or *the group*. We provide only a brief summary of his consideration of these concepts.

Class may mean either (1) any collection of persons having some single common characteristic, or (2) persons having certain characteristics in sufficient measure to *objectively* justify the application to them of a commonly accepted idea of social class. The first of these is so broad as to comprehend the second, as well as 'categoric' or 'demographic' groups, interest associations, and institutional groups such as the military, the bureaucracy, or the clergy. But the use of the second depends on agreement about the nature of a social class in theory, or on devising an empirical definition. In attempting an economical description of power relationships in a political system, Binder considers that the political analyst is free to choose between classifying persons in terms of the *types of power relationships*, or attempting to discover the types of power relationships most frequently appearing among those who are part of an 'objective' social class. He opts for the latter. This concept of social class is useful as a descriptive category. But he also includes *categoric groups*, whose definition is justified either on the assumption that for certain purposes all members of the category have a single interest and are capable of working together to serve that interest; or that, in a passive sense, they limit the formation of other groups, or limit the construction of an ideological consensus. The dividing line between 'categoric groups' and social classes is not a sharp one.

As for the second possible unit of analysis, organised primary, secondary, and party *groups* are less important in traditional political systems than in modern. Nor do all their members control the same base-values or have identical interests; membership is not continuous and members may have other affiliations. But 'the formal continuity and legitimacy of the group as a political actor actually renders the group a more significant category than the class'—*if* it is continuous, and not subordinate to a traditional leader, and *if* it is legitimate, and not dominated by a primary group. (cf. Riggs's 'clects', above, p. 59.)

There is an important distinction between power relationships *within* groups, and those *between* groups. We do not propose to elaborate Binder's consideration of the first of these (*loc. cit.* pp. 25-27), but cite only his conclusions. Firstly, the power structure of politically oriented groups is not merely the sum of a random collection of elementary power relationships; the essential character of a group lies in 'the very persistence of the power relationship which it connotes'. Secondly, in any group which persists over a period of time, there is a strong tendency towards the formation of a stable hierarchy, towards the institutionalisation of a number of leadership, administrative, and communicational roles, and towards the emergence of a concrete oligarchical leadership of real persons.

As for the *power relationship between groups*, there is a dynamic relationship of great importance to a concrete power system. There is a 'relational situation' even between groups which do not seem to be either co-operating or in conflict, because the political values which each seeks will be either compatible or incompatible with those sought by the others. The latter fact arises from the limited availability of values in any concrete system. 'Every individual and group engaging in purposeful action aimed at the maximisation of political value is intersecting with all others in a *single power system*, the limits of which are defined by a *government*. True, governmental action is not always required to resolve differences between group and group leader. Moreover, in some cases it merely confirms the existing power relationships. Systems may combine direct bargaining, or direct dominance-submission relationships, in which the government acts to resolve the issues according to established values.

In this case the power relationship is conventionalised. Such a procedure involves accepting power to move a *government* as the equivalent of power to control the behaviour of an *opposing group* or even of the *whole society*, at least for a time. But even where such 'conventionalisation' exists, certain relationships are more or less known and permanent, while others may be evidenced from time to time in specific events. Power relationships between groups (as, indeed, within them) tend to become *institutionalised*. But such institutionalisation is most importantly accomplished by what we commonly call *government*. 'The structure, personnel, and legal procedures of what are usually known as governmental institutions lend permanence to certain aspects of the existing pattern of power relationships in any polity. This permanence, or institutionalisation, is what we shall call *legitimisation*. The function of government, then, is the legitimisation of power in a political system, and the limits of such a system are set by the effective performance of this function. A power relationship which one seeks to make permanent through the action of a government is a *political* power relationship, the classification of the actions which may lead to such legitimisation being a *classification of the political processes and techniques* prevalent in any concrete system.' (Our italics.)

As Binder points out, the government may not be the only legitimising institution. (cf. Almond's 'more or less legitimate . . .') Family, tribe, firm, party etc. may legitimise power relationships. But none of these relationships have conferred upon them legitimacy throughout the *whole* political society unless they are recognised by the government. There are two kinds of power in the political system, legitimate and non-legitimate. *Legitimate power* may be further analysed in terms of whether the *form* of its legitimisation accords with its *objective* character. *Non-legitimate power* may further be classified according to whether it has (1) *no* bearing on legitimate power or the working of government, (2) an *indirect* bearing, in the sense that it tends to widen the gap between real and legitimate power i.e. it is an 'environmental' factor, or (3) a *direct* bearing, in which case it seeks legitimisation to alter a non-legitimate relationship, or to bring the form of a particular legitimisation into closer conformity with the real relationship i.e. an *issue* is created.

Law-making and enforcement actions are not the only means of legitimisation in the hands of the government. The *kinds of legitimising actions* may vary from system to system; this is one of the bases for differentiating types of systems. The means, for example, may include consultation with bureaucratic or legislative organisations; the delegation of quasi-legal powers; inclusion in ceremonies; granting of audiences; informal meetings with the Head of State; the granting of honours, or key posts—or the holding of referenda. The specific means may in part be designated in a constitutional document, or depend entirely on the institutionalisation of cultural values. (Binder notes at this point that his view is in 'moderate conflict' with two others. *Easton* states that politics is concerned only with the 'authoritative allocation of values for a whole society'. In so far as 'authoritative' is stressed, this approaches the notion of 'legitimacy'. But it fails to note that not only is the 'authoritative statement' a product of political interaction, its *effectiveness* is, also. With Easton, 'legitimisation' is psychological rather than symbolic, and he fails to distinguish the legitimisation from its *implementation*. Lasswell's analysis does not differentiate between value allocations that are *politically relevant* and those that are not. (cf. Lasswell and Kaplan, *Power and Society*, New Haven, 1956.)

It must now be noted that the legitimisation of certain power relationships does not exhaust all the functions of government. Leaving aside foreign affairs, some governmental activities are akin to those of private associations. Governments themselves also engage in activities calculated to maintain their own existence, and the existence of the structure of power relationships which they, as governments, legitimise. So, governments may perform *political* as well as legitimisation functions. Political scientists may, of course, investigate any kind of power, 'but for the study of the political system, its relevance to legitimisation is of crucial importance'.

The political system is composed of two elements, closely integrated in mutual causality—power relationships and legitimising actions backed by the dominant control of coercive force. The two elements may be seen in an *input–output relationship*. Power relationships are the *input* that create the legitimising act. The acts in turn, as *outputs*, tend to reinforce existing power

177

relations or to change them. We may proceed from this to see the political system in action. Many power relationships are continually resulting in many legitimising acts, not all of which may be compatible with the rest. It also is impossible accurately to describe a power relationship in a legitimising act; the common tendency of such acts to exaggerate leads to the transformation rather than to the rigidification of power relationships. Further, new power relationships are continually emerging at the political level from the geographical, economic, social and cultural background which is constantly setting limits to the possibility of actually transforming power relationships into the form in which they have been legitimised. All these are 'systematic inefficiencies'. They result in repeated reviews of the legitimacy of power relationships and, more generally, in *system-maintenance* activities on the part of governments, which do not seem to be directly related to group conflicts. This means, if the political system is to be maintained, either an attempt must be made to bring the real power relationships into conformity with existing legitimisations, or to revise the legitimisations in terms of the existing or of some preferred power relationships.

It is out of this system-maintenance activity that the institutions known as *government* tend to acquire a *functional autonomy*, independent of the legitimisation of power relationships. The government is much more sensitively oriented to external forces; it is more immediately concerned with the physical and administrative problems of the effective enforcement of a formalised power relationship. Various governmental organisations are engaged in activity calculated to increase the efficiency of legitimisations, and such activity will affect power relationships. The government may even be accorded—or claim—the right to consider something called the 'public interest'.

> 'Action directed at achieving the legitimisation of a particular power relationship, or that which is directed at manipulating power structures with a view to future legitimisation is *politically functional activity*.'

Such activity may have as a consequence the allocation of security, wealth, or prestige. But 'its allocative character does not make it functional'. (Presumably, 'for the political system'?) In simple systems, Binder suggests, it may be difficult—even if

178

worthwhile—to distinguish between legitimising activity and allocative activity. But 'within any system having differentiated institutions of government, and, of course, well-articulated cultural values, the performance of political functions becomes highly stylised; in some cases it even approaches a sort of ritual'. (The allocative consequences of legitimising action may surely affect the 'legitimacy' of the regime in so far as it is judged by its results. Such consequences therefore, it seems, *may* be functional or dysfunctional for the system.)

One of the major political activities of groups is the restatement of a power relationship in a manner in which it can be acted upon by the government i.e. presenting a 'formal demand' to government, whether by informal approaches, petition, or legislative proposals. There will follow the more concrete form of political activity-votes, membership drives, protest meetings, strikes, coalitions, bribes, or bargains. The political function involves not only an adjustment to established patterns of legitimisation, but a resourceful exploitation of the complex and diffuse power structures, the prevailing culture-based ideologies, and of the attitudes, social relationships, and interests of persons occupying governmental roles (and of other interests capable of influencing such role-incumbents). The pattern of effective legitimisation is dependent on politically functional activity and the relative inflexibility of power relationships. Conversely, and by a 'feedback' process, the environmentally rooted power relationships are altered to some extent by the flow of legitimisations and by the canalising tendencies of the established forms of political activity. Politically functional activity is limited by the power relationships and purposefully adjusted to the character of the legitimising function.

Stylised political processes are the specific forms in which the *political function* has been institutionalised in a particular system. Even where these processes have not been legitimised, there is usually a set of empirically discoverable practices that are engaged in with a high degree of regularity. At this point Binder remarks that these procedures do not correspond to Almond's fourfold classification of political (input) functions, though they may involve elements of each. Attention to specific processes helps us to distinguish between THE *political function* systematically conceived, and broad classifications of *political activity*. In a footnote (*loc. cit.* p. 35), Binder adds that 'politically functional activity' is essentially a behavioural definition of the political system. The behaviour is 'functional' only in the sense that it is an observable representation of the analytical construct, 'political system'. In so far as 'function' implies 'purpose', the purpose of such activity is analytically defined by the definition of the political system. The term 'dysfunctional' is used to refer to the impact of concrete or objectively defined behaviour on a specific system or type of system. (*Sed quaere*: cannot 'functional' also be used in this sense if the context and interpretation are made clear, and not merely as meaning 'having to do with politics'.) We need merely add that, throughout, 'a distinction between *the* system and *a* system must be maintained'.

The combination of various classes of political activity to be found in any political system will depend on the actors concerned, their value-oriented techniques, the nature of the issues at stake, the extent to which the processes have become formalised by previous legitimisations, and the general level of the economic, communications, and bureaucratic development of the system. At this point, Binder turns to his typology of political systems (discussed in detail, above, pp. 65–9). We refer briefly to one general point only. On the basis of his threefold classification of political systems into traditional, conventional, and rational, he then suggests that corresponding to each there is a predominant, though not exclusive, type of *process*. These he characterises as (1) bargaining, or control of leaders by leaders, (2) polyarchical, or control of leaders by non-leaders, and (3) rational, or hierarchical control of non-leaders by leaders. (The term 'bargaining', although taken from Dahl and Lindblom, *Politics, Economics, and Welfare*, New York, 1963, is more usually applied e.g. by Almond and Coleman, to Western political systems e.g. 'secular, pragmatic, bargaining parties'. The term 'bazaar-canteen', used by Riggs, is, perhaps, more distinctive.) He then goes on to suggest that once the existence of stable processes can be discerned in a system, it will also appear that these are themselves carried forward through patterns of discrete political acts, which vary from system to system to a greater extent than do the political processes, which are fairly consistent for any political system.

To sum up, the political system is compromised of power

relationships which are exploited in a limited number of ways, in order that legitimisations may be won. A *perfectly efficient system* is one in which all power relationships are immediately and accurately translated into legitimisations. But (1) power relationships are expressed only in limited ways in order to win legitimisations, (2) any particular array of legitimisations limits the kind of power relationships which may be recognised, and (3) since the legitimisation is a verbal and at least somewhat rationalised statement of the power relationship it cannot match the flexibility of a power relationship. There may also be a discrepancy between the statement of legitimacy and its administrative application. There are behavioural consequences of importance to the working of the political system which arise from the cognition of the discrepancy between power relationships and legitimisations. These consequences and their causes clearly provide a possible starting point for a study of the dynamics of the political system, since the discrepancy exists everywhere to a greater or lesser extent. Readers who turn to Binder's account of the political system of Iran will be able to judge in more detail the practical value of his theoretical approach.

VI: SOCIAL CONFLICT, LEGITIMACY, AND DEMOCRACY

Our preceding approach to 'the political system' was based primarily on the notion of 'legitimacy' and the 'legitimisation' of power relationships. It seems to us useful to add to this a summary of Lipset's study[10] of this problem with specific reference to democracy, partly as a supplement to Binder's analysis, partly so that it may be read in conjunction with Lipset's study of economic development and democracy (below, pp. 191–8). Lipset is concerned here with both effectiveness and legitimacy. The former means actual performance; the extent to which the political system provides for the performance of the basic functions of government as the people and powerful groups in society perceive them; the degree of goal-attainment. The second means the capacity of the system to engender and maintain the belief that the existing political institutions are the most appropriate for the society. 'Effectiveness is primarily instrumental, legitimacy is evaluative.'

Groups will regard a political system as legitimate or otherwise as its views fit theirs; for example, there was the rejection of the Weimar Republic of Germany by large segments of the army, civil service, and aristocratic classes. Legitimacy, of course, may be accorded to many types of political system; indeed, 'crises of legitimacy' are a recent historical phenomenon linked with the emergence of sharp group cleavages and the ability of rival groups, through mass communications, to obtain support for new 'values'.

Such crises occur during the transition to a new social structure if (1) the *status* of major conservative institutions is threatened, and (2) the major groups in society do not have access to the political system. (cf. Binder's 'claims for the legitimisation of new power relationships.) On the other hand, if the new regime, when established, is ineffective i.e. fails to sustain the expectations of major groups for long enough to establish a new 'legitimacy', another crisis may occur.

But if the *status* of the major conservative groups is not threatened during the transitional period, even though most of their *power* may be lost, democracy may be the more secure. (There is some similarity here with the features of the civic culture, as seen by Almond and Verba.) Lipset notes the stability of democracies which are also monarchies. Loyalties which might otherwise be turned against democracy are retained. Moreover, the old institutions and 'symbols' enlist the loyalty of the 'new citizens'. The French Third Republic and the Italian constitutional monarchy were both threatened by the existence of alienated 'older' groups which regarded the regime as 'illegitimate'.

> 'Thus one main source of legitimacy lies in the continuity of important traditional integrative institutions during a transitional period in which new institutions are emerging.'

The role of the King in Morocco seems to be a recent case in point.[11]

Another factor affecting the loss of legitimacy is the way in which societies handle the 'entry into politics' i.e. react to the demands of new social groups for access to the political system. When new groups become politically active e.g. the bourgeoisie in the *ancien régime*, the industrial workers in the 19th century, the colonial elites in the 20th century, 'easy access to the *legitimate* political institutions tends to win the loyalty of the new groups', while allowing the 'old' groups to maintain their status. The denial of access to power also encourages 'millennial' hopes and utopian projects. When these hopes are not fulfilled and the utopias turn to 1984s after *eventual* granting of access, the new groups do not remain loyal to the system; yet, at the same time, the system has been altered in such a way as to alienate the conservative groups—witness right- and left-wing opposition to the centre in France, but not the possibility of a 'peaceful' alternative. In the new nations, it may be difficult to keep the loyalty of the masses, deprived of traditional bases of authority, to democracy, when it fails 'to produce the goods' promised by the nationalist leaders during the struggle for independence. Under any circumstances, ineffectiveness in goal-achievement may undermine legitimacy, but differences of opinion about the legitimacy of any regime may, conversely lessen its effectiveness.

Lipset suggests that 'a major test of legitimacy is the extent to which given nations have developed a *common secular political culture*'. Part of this is attachment to 'national rituals and holidays'. The United States, for example, has such common culture; France, for example, has not.

Clearly it is important to ascertain the relative degree of legitimacy in a system if we are to assess its stability when faced with a 'crisis of ineffectiveness'. This may be approached diagrammatically, thus (*loc. cit.* p. 81):

Effectiveness

	+	—
Legitimacy +	A	B
—	C	D

Box A (high legitimacy and effectiveness) denotes stable political systems e.g. U.S., Sweden, U.K. Box D (ineffective and illegitimate regimes) denotes unstable political systems, unless they are maintained by force. The other combinations may be illustrated by specific examples. In the late 1920s large and powerful segments of society regarded both the republics of Germany and Austria as illegitimate. But they remained reasonably effective for a period (Box C). When their effectiveness broke down they shifted to Box D and the system collapsed. Countries in Box A, however, managed to cope with similar, even if less catastrophic, problems e.g. unemployment and economic crises, and survived; they moved to Box B.

In the short run, a highly effective but illegitimate system (e.g. a colonial regime) is more unstable than a regime which is relatively low in effectiveness but high in legitimacy. But prolonged effectiveness over a number of generations may give legitimacy to a political system. Conversely, even a high degree of legitimacy cannot forever stave off the consequences of gross ineffectiveness. Today, there is a very close connection between 'effectiveness' and economic development. 'Those nations which have adapted most successfully to the requirements of an industrial system have the fewest internal political strains, and have either preserved their traditional legitimacy or developed strong new symbols.' (This does not necessarily mean that they have *democratic* political systems. cf. below, pp. 200.)

In all democratic systems, group conflict may develop so as to threaten the system, unless conditions exist which moderate the intensity of the conflict. This is almost the same thing as saying that the system must have a high degree of legitimacy, if we include not only generalised values but specific norms, including legitimate patterns of interaction. So far as the concrete causes of crisis are concerned, 'the character and content of the major changes affecting the political stability of a society are largely determined by historical factors which have affected the way in which major issues dividing society have been resolved or left unresolved over time'. The three major issues of modern times in Western nations have been (1) the role of the church and religion, (2) the admission of the 'lower strata' to political and economic citizenship, and (3) the distribution of the national income. The key question is whether these issues emerged and were dealt with one by one, or whether they accumulated. (On this cf. also Spiro, *op. cit.*) Resolving tensions one at a time contributes to the stability of the system; carrying them over from one historical period to another produces bitterness and frustration, and threatens the stability of the regime. The possibility of victory for the opposing forces is seen as a 'moral threat'; the whole system lacks 'value-integration'. We briefly consider these three issues.

In most Protestant nations the church issue was resolved during the 18th and 19th centuries; and even where religion is state-supported it has ceased to be a major source of controversy. But in countries like France, Italy, Spain, and Austria, there has remained a division between right-wing conservative groups, largely supported by the Catholic Church, and left-wing movements which are largely anti-clerical. The battle is not merely an economic one, but an 'absolute-value' one—Almond's 'isolative political culture'. Democracy requires a universalistic belief system which accepts various ideologies as legitimate. The Roman Catholic Church, in particular, does not assist in legitimising a regime which accepts that the 'good' can be discovered by conflict between opposing beliefs.

The citizenship issue has also affected different political systems in different ways. In countries like the U.K. and the U.S., the workers obtained the suffrage in reasonable time and without too serious opposition, at least relatively speaking. In Sweden, stronger resistance to their claims linked the struggle for citizenship rights more closely with socialism as a political movement; but the problem was resolved.[12] The longer the denial of political rights, the more ideological the workers' movement. We may thus explain the strength of the Communist Parties in France and Italy.

The struggle over the just distribution of the national income —of which one aspect is the problem of industrial relations—is, of course, still going on, and needs no elaboration.

The importance of all this to the problem of legitimacy is simply that when one division is piled upon another, settlement becomes more difficult. 'Where a number of historic cleavages intermix, and create the basis for ideological politics, democracy will be unstable and weak, for by definition such politics does not include the concept of tolerance.' One result, as we have seen earlier, is the existence of 'parties of integration' which question the whole system and not merely its decisions, as opposed to 'parties of representation' which are concerned only to assert their claims—aggregated and moderated—through the existing system. The Catholics and the Socialists (later the Communists) in Europe have been outstanding examples of the former type. Each has tried to create 'a network of social and economic organisations within which their followers could live their entire lives'.

One of the most important practical effects of this is to isolate members of political parties from those 'cross-pressures' which encourage the shifts of support from one election to another, and the gradual resolving of issues between parties over a period of time—both requisites of a stable democracy. 'The necessary rules of democratic politics assume that conversion both ways, into and out of a party', is possible and proper, and parties which hope to gain a majority by democratic methods must ultimately give up their integrationist emphasis'. It must be added, however, that the social structure itself may hinder such cross-pressures and conversions, particularly when whole groups are geographically and economically isolated. People in such communities are more likely to be strongly committed politically than those whose membership of a number of different groups, or whose personal contacts, are mixed, and who are more likely to be subject to cross-pressures. 'Multiple and politically inconsistent affiliations, loyalties, and stimuli reduce the emotion and aggressiveness involved in political choice.' Moreover, people thus influenced are more likely to be aware of the need to safeguard minorities.

To return specifically to the question of basic issues, 'a stable democracy requires relatively moderate tension among its contending forces'. Such moderation is facilitated by the resolving of existing basic issues before new ones arise. Lipset links this with his examination of the relation between economic development and democracy, by suggesting that the best condition for the 'political cosmopolitanism' which assists in the resolution of basic issues in a pragmatic, bargaining manner, are those produced by the development of urbanisation, education, communications media, and wealth. We quote his next paragraph *in extenso*.

'Thus the factors involved in modernisation and economic development are linked to those which establish legitimacy and tolerance. But it should always be remembered that correla-

186

tions are only statements about relative degrees of congruence, and that another condition for political action is that the correlation never be so clear-cut that men feel they cannot change the direction of affairs by their actions. And this lack of high correlation means that for analytic purposes the variables should be kept distinct even if they intercorrelate. For example, the analysis of cleavage presented here suggests specific ways in which different electoral and constitutional arrangements may affect the chances for democracy.'

This, of course, is to recognise, as Binder pointed out, that the political system may have a degree of autonomy. Lipset proceeds briefly to examine some of the procedures of the political system which, in his view, may be conducive to democracy. He emphasises, however, that, in his opinion, the variations in *systems of government* which he discusses are much less important than basic differences in social structure. Nevertheless, he expresses a preference for two-party rather than multi-party systems; elections on a territorial rather than a proportional representation basis; and federal rather than unitary states.

The preference for a two-party system rests upon the assertion that in complex societies parties need to be broad-based coalitions, not serving merely the interests of one major group, and that they must seek to win support from opposition groups. Parties of integration, or small splinter parties turn elections not into occasions for seeking the broadest possible basis of support, but for stressing cleavages. Lipset links his preference for a territorial rather than a proportional representation basis with that for a two-party system on the (arguable) ground that proportional representation either maintains or encourages a multi-party system. Moreover, territorial constituencies compel the various groups to press their claims through aggregative, compromising parties. To quote Talcott Parsons, it is desirable that mechanisms be found to assist the 'involvement of voting with the ramified solidary structure of the society in such a way that, though there is a correlation, there is no *exact* correspondence between political polarisation and other bases of differentiation'. (*Op. cit.* Voting etc. pp. 92–93.)

As to Federalism, it increases the opportunity for multiple sources of cleavage by providing for the expression of regional interests and values, as well as others which also cut across the social structure. Lipset, however, sees the danger of federal arrangements which in fact reinforce existing cleavages based on ethnic, religious, or linguistic factors as e.g. in India and Canada. Otherwise, federal divisions of power supplement those based on voluntary associations, help to prevent over-centralisation of power, train political leaders, and provide an opportunity for national parties which fail to win federal elections to prove their worth at state or provincial level.

In the end, however, Lipset reasserts his belief that none of these political structures are *essential* for democratic systems. When the underlying social conditions facilitate democracy e.g. as in Sweden, then such factors as many parties, proportional representation, and a unitary state do not necessarily weaken democracy. The reverse, however, would appear to be true e.g. in the Weimar Republic and the Third and Fourth Republics of France.

Finally, what of the new states and what Lipset calls the 'contemporary challenges of communism and nationalism'? He considers that the stable Western democracies are now in a 'post-politics' phase, and that there is relatively little difference between the political parties. The 'citizenship' issue has been settled with the incorporation of the workers and their parties into the legitimate political system, and issues such as collective bargaining and the distribution of the national income do not encourage extremism.

But in most of Latin and Eastern Europe, the integration of the workers into the system was not complete before the emergence of communist parties, which have not been absorbed into the system and, according to Lipset, 'cannot possibly be accorded the right of access to actual political power by a democratic society'. In so far as this is the case, the sense of alienation from the system on the part of communists is enhanced. It cannot be assumed that economic development will stabilise democracy (or lead to its emergence) in such countries.

In new Asian and African states, conservatism has been associated with subservience to colonial rulers, left-wing attitudes with nationalism. Trade unions and workers' parties, therefore, have been a legitimate part of the political process

188

from the start. This is a reversal of the European situation, in which workers' movements developed *during* industrialisation and largely as a consequence of it. In the new countries the 'left-wing' regimes have all the problems of economic modernisation to face, and must accept responsibility for the effectiveness of their policies. This is happening at a time when the legitimacy of the regime may not be firmly established. 'Given the existence of poverty-stricken masses, low levels of education, an elongated-pyramid class structure, and the "premature" triumph of the democratic left, the prognosis for political democracy in Asia and Africa is bleak.' Countries like Israel, Japan, Lebanon, and perhaps Turkey, may succeed in maintaining something like a stable democracy in view of their high educational level (except Turkey), the substantial and growing middle class, and the retention of political legitimacy by conservative groups. Other regimes, if they avoid Communist and military dictatorship, are likely to develop along the lines of Ghana, Guinea, Tunisia, and Mexico, with 'an educated minority using a mass movement and leftist slogans to exercise effective control, and holding elections as a gesture towards ultimate democracy, and as a means of estimating public opinion, rather than as effective instruments for a legitimate turnover in office. (Reference should be made to Shils's typology of political systems, above, pp. 70–86.) There is also the danger that many Latin-American countries may follow this path, despite the fact that they have enjoyed independence for much longer. The conservative elements are still strongly entrenched, left-wing movements tend to take a Marxist direction, and the growing middle class may be alienated from democracy.

This account of some of the problems facing political systems, particularly in relation to the 'prospects for democracy', has been in part sociological, in part historical. It does not provide the sort of 'theory' which Binder, among others, has deemed essential, though it does call upon some of the concepts developed by such as Almond and Shils. Readers who wish to pursue further Lipset's approach to a study of political systems are referred again to his *First New Nation*.

NOTES

[1] Almond and Coleman, eds. *The Politics of the Developing Areas*, Princeton U.P., 1960. pp. 3–64.

[2] Bert Hoselitz, 'Levels of Economic Performances and Bureaucratic Structures' *in* La Palombara ed. *op. cit.* p. 179.

[3] cf. further, Almond, 'Interest Groups and the Political Process', *Am. Pol. Science Review*, Vol. LII, No. 1, Mar. 1958, reprinted in Macridis and Brown, *Comparative Politics*, pp. 128–156.

[4] James S. Coleman and Carl G. Rosberg, Jr. eds. *Political Parties and National Integration in Tropical Africa*, Univ. of California Press, 1964, pp. 656–658.

[5] *The Decision Process*, Bureau of Governmental Research, Univ. of Maryland, 1956. This has been further elaborated in Lasswell, *The Future of Political Science*, Atherton Press, 1964, from which our references are taken.

[6] *World Politics*, XVII, No. 2, 1962 'A developmental approach to political systems', pp. 183–214.

[7] L. Binder, *Iran: political development in a changing society*, University of California Press, 1962. For this section cf. especially pp. 7–11.

[8] cf. especially, R. K. Merton, *Social Theory and Social Structure*, Free Press of Gleneve, 1957.

[9] D. Easton, *The Political System*, New York, 1953.

[10] Lipset, *Political Man*, Heinemann, 1960, Chapter III.

[11] cf. Douglas E. Ashford, *Political Change in Morocco*, Princeton U.P., 1961.

[12] cf. Dankwart A. Rustow, *The Politics of Compromise*, Princeton U.P., 1955.

6

Economic and Social Development and the Political System

I: ECONOMIC AND SOCIAL CONDITIONS OF DEMOCRACY

'RECENTLY Western observers have begun to realise that social and economic change does not necessarily contribute to free or even effective political development, although our analysis has often displayed the same absurd deterministic assumptions of our largest ideological competitor.'

So Ashford concludes his study of political change in Morocco (*op. cit.* p. 418).

It is not intended to discuss in this book the general problem of the relationship between economic and political systems as it is dealt with in Marxist terms. The literature of the subject is too well known, and its thesis is not a new one to political sociology. The more specific recent interest in the relationship between economic development and political systems, arising largely out of the problem of 'political modernisation' in developing countries, does, however, justify some attention. We shall be concerned mainly with Lipset's contribution to the discussion[1] and with the application of Lipset's approach to the developing areas by Coleman.[2] The general question as to whether *economic* modernisation must automatically lead to *political* modernisation in the limited sense of Western-type democracy has already been considered briefly (La Palombara, above, pp. 61–2). Here a more detailed attempt is made to see the connection between economic and social changes, on the one hand, and political changes, on the other.

Lipset is primarily concerned with the connection between the former changes and the emergence of a *democratic* political system. The latter he defines as 'a political system which supplies regular constitutional opportunities for changing the government officials, and a social mechanism which permits the largest possible part of the population to influence major decisions by choosing among contenders for political office'. In more detail, this implies first, a 'political formula', a body of beliefs specifying which institutions are legitimate; secondly, one set of political leaders in office; and thirdly, one or more sets of recognised leaders attempting to gain office. If the political system has no value system permitting the peaceful distribution of power, including the peaceful change of leaders, the result will be the chaos typical of many Latin-American states. If effective authority cannot from time to time be conferred on one group of leaders, the result will be unstable and irresponsible government such as existed in pre-Fascist Italy and during much of the Third and Fourth Republics in France. If an effective opposition cannot be maintained, governmental authority will become too great, if not too irresponsible, and popular influence on policy will be at a minimum—the conditions which exist in one-party states.

Weber suggested that modern democracy can operate effectively only under capitalist industrialisation (though he also saw no *necessary* connection between capitalism and democracy). Lipset, however, suggests that even on theoretical grounds we should not expect a high correlation between such factors as income, education, and religion, on the one hand, and democracy, on the other, in any given society, because 'to the extent that the political sub-system of the society operates autonomously one of two things may result. A political form may *persist* under conditions normally adverse to the *emergence* of that form. Or a political form may develop because of a syndrome of unique historical factors even though the major characteristics of the society favour another form.' Further, key historical events may account for *either* the persistence *or* the failure of democracy, by starting a process which either increases or decreases the likelihood that at the *next critical point* in the history of the society democracy will again 'win out'. An established democratic political system has a validity of its own, with institutions which support its continuance. A 'premature' democracy may survive by facilitating the growth of conditions such as literacy or autonomous centres of power and influence. On the other hand, democracy may endanger economic development through public pressure for consumption rather than investment, and may lose out in the conflict between the drive for industrialisation and the popular demand for welfare. Lipset's primary concern, he emphasises, is with the *social conditions* which serve to *support* democratic systems, not with the 'specific rules of the political game' which serve to *maintain* them.

His starting point is an attempt to classify the countries with which he is concerned into general categories, with a somewhat imprecise line between 'more democratic' and 'less democratic' (democracy being defined as 'a complex of characteristics' which may be ranked in many different ways). He then concentrates on differences among countries within the same 'political culture' areas. His choice here for such internal comparisons are (1) Latin America and (2) Europe and the English-speaking countries, with more limited comparisons between the Asian and Arab States. But the criteria within each of the first two groups differ. In the first, the test of 'democracy' is whether a country has had a history of more or less free elections for most of the post-World War I period. In the second, the test is uninterrupted continuation of political democracy since World War I, and the absence of a major totalitarian movement gaining as many as 20 per cent of the votes at any election. In the first case we are looking for '*no* fairly constant dictatorial rule'; in the second, 'stable democracy'.

The most common generalisation about political democracy and other aspects of society, according to Lipset, is that democracy is related to the state of economic development. This thesis, which has the traditional authority of Aristotle to support it—though he would speak of 'polity' rather than 'democracy'—simply maintains that only a society with reasonably high standards of living, and with a minimum amount of real poverty, can provide the conditions for intelligent participation in democratic processes on the part of the vast majority of people and for effective resistance to populist demagoguery. Where there is a large impoverished mass, and a small favoured elite, the political system will be based either on oligarchy or tyranny. Lipset has tested this hypothesis empirically by using various indices of economic development, e.g. wealth, industrialisation, urbanisation and education; and then computing means for the countries classified (as above) as *more* or *less* democratic. 'In each case, the average wealth, degree of industrialisation and urbanisation, and level of education, is much higher for the more democratic countries.' (*Loc. cit.* Table II, pp. 51–54. In a footnote Lipset refers to the work of Lyle W. Shannon, who has correlated indices of economic development with whether a country is *self-governing* or not. Presumably all of Lipset's countries would fall into Shannon's category of 'self-governing'. Shannon shows that under-development is related to lack of self-government; my data indicate that once self-government is attained, development is still related to the character of the political system.)

We examine Lipset's indices in a little more detail, although it is not possible to do justice to his elaborate argument here. The main indices for *wealth* used are *per capita* income; number of persons per motor vehicle; thousands of persons per physician; and the number of radios, telephones, and newspapers per thousand persons. 'The differences are striking on every score', both for the 'more democratic' European countries and the 'less-dictatorial Latin-American countries. *Industrialisation* is measured by the percentage of employed workers in agriculture; and the *per capita* commercially produced 'energy' being used in the country. 'Both of these show equally consistent results.' The degree of *urbanisation* is also related to the existence of democracy, a phenomenon which had earlier been noted by Laski and Weber. Degree was measured by the percentage of people in communities of over 20,000. and of over 100,000, and, also, in standard metropolitan areas. The comparative data also support the generalisation that the higher the kind of *education*, the better the chances for democracy, whether the criterion is literacy rates or enrolments per thousand population in primary, post-primary, and higher educational institutions.

Lipset expands this last factor at some length, quoting from Lord Bryce to the effect that 'education, if it does not make good citizens, makes it a lot easier for them to become so'. The suggestion is that education broadens a man's outlook, makes him aware of the need for tolerance, renders him allergic to extremism, and increases his capacity for rational choice. Within countries, Lipset states, this emerges more clearly even than *between* countries. On the basis of a number of surveys, it appears that 'the higher one's education, the more likely one is to believe in democratic values and support democratic practices'. Education appears to be more significant in this context than either income or occupation. On the other hand, in countries like France and Germany a high level of education has not served to stabilise their democracies. 'It may be, however, that their education level has served to inhibit other anti-democratic forces.' Generally, however, even if a high level of education is not a *sufficient* condition for democracy, it comes close to being a *necessary* condition.

A most significant point, again deduced from various surveys,[3] is that all the above aspects of economic development are so closely inter-related as to form *one major factor which has the political correlate of democracy*. Further, as Lerner emphasises, important effects result from 'disproportionate development, in one area or another, for overall stability'; there is 'need for co-ordinated changes in all of these variables'.

Lerner introduces 'one important theoretical addition—the suggestion that these key variables in the modernisation process may be viewed as historical phases, with democracy part of later developments. Urbanisation comes first, then, within the urban sector, the growth of literacy and the media of communication. With the growth of an elaborate technology of industrial development, both the latter are speeded up. Lipset holds that the functional interdependence of these elements of modernisation has not been established by the data, but that further research is now possible to test the hypothesis.

A more specific aspect of the relationship between economic development and democracy is the effect of the former on the nature of the 'class struggle'. 'A belief in secular reformist gradualism', says Lipset, 'can be the ideology of only a relatively well-to-do lower class.' The correlation between the patterns of working-class political action and the national income in different classes is 'almost startling in view of the many other cultural, historical, and juridical factors which affect the political

195

life of nations'. We shall not attempt to summarise the evidence for this (*loc. cit.* pp. 61–63). But it must be observed that the correlation does not mean that economic hardship or poverty *per se* is the main cause of radicalism. Indeed, stable poverty in a situation where individuals are not aware of the possibility of change may breed conservatism. 'The dynamic in the situation would seem to be exposure to the possibility of a better way of life rather than poverty as such.' 'Keeping up with the Jones's' is an aspect of this, and it is important that the way in which the Jones's live in any part of the world is now common knowledge everywhere else in the world—hence the 'revolution of rising expectations'. Stable poverty and conservatism are likely to be found now only in tradition-dominated societies.

Where political activity is possible, these facts explain why the classes low down in the stratification system generally support political parties and other organisations which advocate some form of redistribution. When, on the other hand, no remedy seems to exist (at least in the minds of those concerned) for poverty, the phenomenon of the working-class conservative (as, for example, in Britain) appears. The 'redistributive' parties take a more extremist and radical viewpoint in countries where there is a greater degree of inequality. On the other hand, as the size of the national income increases, the distribution of consumption goods tends to become more equitable, so that there is *relatively* less difference between the classes in their consumption patterns. Moreover, 'increased wealth and education serve democracy by increasing the lower classes' exposure to cross-pressures', thus making them less receptive to extremist appeals. They become involved 'in an integrated national culture as distinct from an isolated lower-class one'. Again, increased wealth affects the political role of the middle class; the larger and more secure it is the more it 'tempers conflict by rewarding moderate and democratic parties, and penalising extreme groups'. Even the upper classes, as general standards rise, will become less likely to regard political rights for the lower strata as 'essentially absurd and immoral'.

More generally, the higher national income means that some redistribution of wealth is more acceptable and can be achieved through democratic processes. In a very specific way, it also makes more possible the recruitment of a competent civil service and an efficient bureaucracy, which seems essential to a modern democratic state. Further, increasing wealth would seem to go with the emergence of a large number of relatively independent voluntary organisations, which inhibit the State, or any single centre of private power, from dominating all political resources, help to communicate ideas and develop political skills, and generally increase tolerance and acceptance of democratic norms.

On the basis of all this we may reconsider the question of what association there is between rapid economic development and the development of democratic political systems. This involves consideration of the general thesis which has already been referred to—that industrialisation and high productivity can 'defeat the major threat to newly established democracies, their domestic communists'. As Lipset points out, this apparent 'victory of economic determinism or vulgar Marxism within democratic political thought', is not supported by the facts. Political extremism based on the lower classes is not to be found only in low-income countries but also in newly industrialising nations. On the basis of studies of leftist politics particularly in northern Europe, Lipset formulates the following statement. 'Whenever industrialisation occurred *rapidly*, introducing *sharp discontinuities* between the pre-industrial and industrial situation, more rather than less extremist working-class movements emerged.' The evidence of this must be sought in Lipset's own analysis, but it is worthy of note that in Russia an increase in the strike ratio and in union militancy paralleled the growth of industry between 1897 and 1913. When the transition to large-scale industry is *more or less complete*, and the improved conditions of the working class are stabilised, the situation may be different. But it is significant that where no industrialisation has taken place, or where it has *failed to build an efficient high-level economy*, the conditions for extremism continue to exist.

Lipset concludes his survey by emphasising that the conditions related to stable democracy which he has discussed are most readily found in the countries of north-west Europe, in America, and in Australasia. He refers to Weber's suggestion that a historically unique concentration of elements produced both democracy and capitalism in this area. 'Men may question whether any aspect of this inter-related cluster of economic development, protestantism, monarchy, gradual political change, legitimacy, and democracy is *primary*, but the fact remains that the cluster does hang together.' It will be noted that we are thus brought back to a combination of historical events and general causal explanations. It is worth recording that in doing this, Lipset claims that he is 'following a good sociological and even functional tradition'. He quotes Radcliffe-Brown to the effect that 'one explanation' of a social system will be its history, where we know it—the detailed account of how it came to be what it is and where it is. Another 'explanation' of the same system is obtained by showing . . . 'that it is a special exemplification of laws of social psychology or social functioning. The two kinds of explanation do not conflict but supplement one another.'

ADDENDUM TO SECTION I

Lipset has a 'methodological appendix' to the chapter we have just summarised, which is of considerable interest to those concerned with sociological approaches to problems of political science. He states that complex characteristics of a social system, such as democracy, degree of bureaucratisation, type of stratification system etc. have usually been handled by either (1) a *reductionist* or (2) an *ideal-type* approach.

The first dismisses the possibility of considering these characteristics as system-attributes as such, maintaining that the qualities of *individual actions* are the sum and substance of sociological categories. This approach regards the *extent* of democratic attitudes, or bureaucratic behaviour, or the *numbers and types* of prestige or power ratings, as constituting the essence of the meaning of the attributes of democracy, bureaucracy or class.

The second 'starts from a similar assumption but reaches an opposite conclusion'. Like the first, it regards societies as a complex order of phenomena, exhibiting such degree of internal contradictions that generalisations about them as a whole must necessarily constitute a constructed representation of selected elements, based on the particular concerns and perspectives of the researcher. But the second approach then goes further. In it, *abstractions* of the order of 'democracy' or 'bureaucracy' have no necessary connection with states or qualities of complex social systems which actually exist, but comprise *collections of attributes which are logically inter-related but characteristic of no existing society*; (e.g. Weber's concept of 'bureaucracy' and the common definition of 'democracy', which 'postulates individual political decisions based on rational knowledge of one's own ends and of the factual political situation'.)

Lipset suggests that criticism of such ideal-types solely on the grounds that they do not correspond to reality is irrelevant; they are not intended to describe reality but to provide *a basis for comparing different aspects of reality with the consistently logical case*. It is not, he says, his intention to substitute another approach for this one, but merely to present 'another possible way' of *conceptualising* complex characteristics of social systems on the basis of *multi-variate analysis*.

'The point at which this approach differs is on the issue of whether generalised theoretical categories can be considered to have a valid relationship to characteristics of total social systems.'

His statistical data, and his account of the reations between democracy, economic development, and political legitimacy, rest upon the assumption that there are *aspects of total social systems which exist*, which can be stated in *theoretical terms*, which can be *compared with similar aspects of other systems* AND which are '*derivable from empirical data* which can be checked by other researchers'. (Our italics.) Situations contradicting the general relationship may exist, or at lower levels of social organisation quite different characteristics may exist. (e.g. in the U.S. secondary organisations may not be 'democratic'.) But in making comparisons on a *certain level of generalisation*, referring to the functioning of a *total system*, generalisations about *society* are as valid as those applicable to other systems. Further, complex characteristics of a total system (e.g. society) have *multi-variate causation and consequences*, in so far as the characteristic has *some degree of autonomy within the system*.

In discussing certain conditions in society it is necessary not only to examine their possible initial consequences for democracy, but also the additional *consequences for other conditions in society* (e.g. the diagram in Lipset, *op. cit.* p. 74). A factor such as 'open class system', or 'egalitarian value system', or 'literacy', may appear both as an *initial condition* of democracy, but also one which is *sustained* by democracy, once the latter has been established. Contrariwise, some of the initial consequences of democracy e.g. 'bureaucracy' may have the effect of *undermining* democracy. However, it must be noted that democracy does not *cause* bureaucracy; it is merely an initial condition which favours its appearance. Nor does the fact that bureaucracy appears as one of the consequences of democracy imply that democracy is the *sole cause*, but merely an '*encouragement*', given other conditions. (Our italics.) Further development of this argument, Lipset holds, does not constitute a new theory of democracy, but merely the 'formalising and empirical listing of certain sets of relationships implied by traditional theories of democracy'.

II: ECONOMIC AND SOCIAL CHANGE AND DEMOCRACY

In his conclusion already referred to (above, p. 163–8), Coleman has attempted to apply Lipset's type of analysis to the countries covered by the book in question. Indeed, he supports Lerner's further thesis that modernisation has a distinctive quality of its own, and that its various elements 'do not occur in haphazard and unrelated fashion', a thesis, which, as we saw, Lipset considered not deducible from Lerner's own data. Before looking in detail at Coleman's data, it is necessary, first, to consider his general comments on the 'significant political consequences' of the changes observed in his societies.

First, national politics tend to be primarily if not exclusively, centred in urban areas and are a phenomenon of capital cities in which the modern elite sub-society is concentrated. Secondly, the gap between this modern-oriented, urban sub-society and the larger national society is not bridged, despite the close ties maintained by some urban dwellers with their rural homelands, which leads to intermittent participation in national politics by rural dwellers. Thirdly, the disparity between rural and urban living standards has accelerated the movement into the urban areas, but because of unemployment and under-employment this may produce not only 'modern' political activity but also anomic. Fourthly, the development of commercial and industrial activities has not always contributed to social and political integration, or to the emergence of a politically relevant middle class, because so much of this activity remains in the hands of alien groups. Fifthly, the changes in the social structure brought by 'modernity' have frequently intensified inter-group tensions. Indeed, where education and economic wealth *coincide* with ethnic or regional divisions, the tensions may be doubled in intensity. In any case, 'there is not a positive connection between economic development and greater social and political integration'. Finally, the modernisation process has contributed to 'secularisation', but religion remains a factor of great significance in the political process; indeed, the new secular elites often feel it necessary to use religion as a political force.

Having established these generalisations, Coleman proceeds to examine, on the basis of Lipset's approach, the relation between economic development and *political competitiveness*—'an essential attribute of democracy'. His 'major working hypothesis is that there is a positive correlation between economic develop-mant and political competitiveness'. (For the details of his data cf. *op. cit.* Tables 2, 3, 4 and Appendix I.) Eleven indices of economic development are used: *per capita* gross national product; the number of persons per doctor per vehicle, per telephone, per radio, per newspaper copy; *per capita* energy consumption; per cent of population in labour unions; per cent of population in cities over 100,000; *per capita* population literate; primary school enrolment.

There are substantial differences between the countries of Latin America and those of Africa-Asia. In each of the eleven indices the average level of economic development in the former group is higher than that of the latter group. In five out of the eleven indices Latin-American countries, irrespective of the degree of political competitiveness, consistently rank higher as a group than those of Africa-Asia. In five indices (wealth, doctors, vehicles, telephones or *per capita* energy consumption), *authoritarian* Latin-American countries rank higher than *competitive* countries of Africa-Asia. On the other hand, in all indices other than those relating to wealth (urbanisation, education, and labour unionisation), the average of *competitive* countries in Africa-Asia is higher than the average of all Latin-Americal countries in one or more of the three categories of competitiveness (i.e. competitive, semi-competitive, authoritarian).

More important, however, from our point of view, than inter-area comparison is the degree of consistency between the level of economic development and the degree of competitiveness of political systems. In both major areas, on ten out of eleven indices, the competitive countries have the highest average score, the semi-competitive the next highest, and authoritarian countries the lowest.

To move from the general to the particular, the question arises as to whether the positive relationship between economic development and political competitiveness continues to exist in the scores of *individual* countries. There are, in fact, several striking deviations. One type is represented by a cluster of semi-competitive systems which rank very low on the side of economic development (e.g. Tanganyika). These are all 'terminal colonial democracies', whose political competitiveness is a reflection of colonial policies aimed to achieve such competitiveness. (In considering these cases, Coleman is clearly combining 'historical' with 'social law' explanations, above, pp. 198ff. All countries are as at *circa*. 1958–9.) Another type of deviation arises in the two countries where economic development is very high, but the political system is only semi-competitive (e.g. Algeria and Southern Rhodesia). This is explained by the existence of a substantial settled European population. A third type of deviation is represented by the Belgian Congo, where Belgian policy fostered economic development but not parallel development in political participation.

Another set of deviations comprises those countries which 'fall significantly far outside the cell in which they would fall were economic development and competitiveness correlated'. Certain *authoritarian* countries rank very high in economic development. Again, special factors (e.g. Cuba's proximity to the U.S. and Venezuela's oil wealth), account for this. 'Nevertheless, such deviations tend to weaken the major hypothesis.' There are also certain *competitive* systems (e.g. Brazil, Ceylon, India, the Philippines) which operate in conditions of relatively low economic development. Historical conditions are again held to account for these deviations e.g. the effect of Western colonialism in developing competitive political systems.

Finally, there is a set of deviations where the relative economic rank of countries falling within a single category of competitiveness correlates *negatively* with the relative competitiveness of those same countries. For example, Costa Rica is more competitive than Argentina, Cambodia less authoritarian than Saudi Arabia. In each case the former country has a much lower level of economic development.

The general weakness of this analysis, as Coleman admits, is that 'for the majority of countries the inadequate state of our knowledge makes it impossible for us to differentiate more finely the degree of competitiveness within the three [broad] categories'. To sum up, 'the major hypothesis that economic development and competitiveness are positively correlated is validated when countries are grouped into major differentiating categories of competitiveness and when mean scores of economic development are employed'. But when the individual countries are examined, the hypothesis is weakened by negative correlations between economic scores and degrees of competitiveness.

Finally, Coleman adds that 'economic modernisation contributes only one dimension of the ensemble of determinants shaping political institutions and behaviour in the countries with which we are concerned'. Clearly, on the evidence, it is impossible to confirm the generalisation that industrialisation is a *certain* way of ensuring the emergence of democracy.

In this connection, some observations of La Palombara are in point (*op. cit.* pp. 34ff). He has criticised the linking of the notion of 'modernity' with 'democracy' on three grounds. Firstly the use of the term 'modernity' itself; in most accounts there seems to be a free substitution of 'society' or 'economic system', or 'social system', for 'political system'. But if 'modernity' means 'economic modernity', then a 'modern political system is simply one in a highly industrial society'. This conclusion, however, introduces a second objection. If it appears to put the U.S. and the U.S.S.R. in the same category then to introduce the notion of 'democracy' it becomes necessary to add further criteria such as 'the structural and behavioural attitudes of Anglo-American democracy'. These would include achievement rather than ascription; maximum role-differentiation; the articulation of group interests by associations, and their aggregation by more than one party; ultimate control by citizens over governmental institutions; universal suffrage and popular participation; particularism moderated by pragmatism and secular rationality. La Palombara points out that the addition of such criteria 'often implicitly and perhaps unintentionally' is *normative*. Provided this is clear, of course, there is no objection to using such a political system as a *model*, and then raising the question as to *how* political development might or might not move in the desired direction.

The third objection is more general; the use of 'modernity' in this way, and the inclusion of a 'model political system', suggests one single final state of affairs—a 'deterministic, unilinear theory of political evolution'. Are the total set of Anglo-American political institutions and behaviour a necessary condition of modernity in the economic sense? Might such institutions not, in fact, be a hindrance to growth? (We have already noted this, and cf. F. W. Riggs in La Palombara etc. *op. cit.* where he argues for a *conscious adoption* of certain political forms to achieve political democracy but admits that these might slow up economic development. A choice has to be made.) In any case, widely varying structural arrangements are likely to emerge from differing total conditions of development.

Binder has also criticised the Lipset-Coleman approach from a theoretical point of view. Attempts to relate economic and social conditions (*op. cit.* pp. 11–13) to political systems can be useful, he considers, only if we are clear about what precisely we mean by 'political system'. Binder would be content neither with Lipset's general description of 'democracy', nor with Coleman's limited notion of 'political competitiveness', nor with the wider description of 'Anglo-American' democracy referred to by La Palombara. Such attempts at definition 'lead us rather quickly to ask for a *theory* which will more clearly indicate the connection between particular environmental conditions and the behaviour of particular components of the political system'. He raises the important question as to 'whether the [political] system itself must always be seen as the dependent variable'. (But n.b. Lipset etc. do refer to the 'autonomy' of the political system, and cf. also Bernard, below, pp. 224–42.) in relation to each and every aspect of society or its other sub-systems which we may care to select from the information contained in such statistical questionnaires as those sent out by the various United Nations organisations. So far, in his view, regularities have either not been found, or else they are based on such broad generalities about whole groups of systems as to require greater precision in describing 'whole systems' (within the group), and in classifying them. The most important point is that if economic development is to become the independent variable *par excellence* then it is essential to seek at least equally reliable information about dependent political change.

The mere existence of data on economic development, demographic change, communications etc., points to some of the uses to which similar information about political behaviour might be put. Lipset, Coleman, Deutsch,[4] and the rest have really emphasised the need for political scientists to look in the *political system* also for a group of factors which must be considered together before any understanding of the system can be achieved. But before they can compare phenomena of the same class, they must first make certain qualitative judgments about the relevance of observed phenomena to the whole system. 'First let us understand the system as a whole, and then weigh the import of those factors which are given to empirical measurement.'

III: SOME FURTHER OBSERVATIONS ON INDUSTRIALISATION AND DEMOCRACY

Binder's advice has been followed by few researchers into the problem of economic development and democracy. This is not to say, however, that no useful work has been done. We illustrate this by an examination of a penetrating study by Karl de Schweinitz, Jr.[5] He examines the thesis that 'the emergence of political democracy in the western world was intimately, even causally related to industrialisation'. Having discussed in general the process of change, he proceeds to examine the evidence for this thesis in relation to Britain, the United States, Germany, and Russia, and then considers the problem of industrialisation and 'the prospects for democracy' in the developing countries. The skilled application of historical investigation and general theory can be appreciated fully only by a study of the book itself. We attempt merely to summarise his argument, and, in particular, his summing up in the last chapter of his book.

He argues first, on *a priori* grounds, that while democracy was not compatible with economies at early stages of development, it might be with economies at later stages. His next stage is to analyse the process of industrialisation in the 19th century in order 'to raise the possibility that a unique configuration of historical conditions . . . accounted for the emergence of the democratic political order'.

Western experience in the 19th century shows 'that the emergence of democratic political institutions represented a victory of society over the state'. Resources and demands from autonomous individuals and groups, taking advantage of the philosophy or ideology of the times and the limited powers of control of governments, created a set of democratic political institutions. But such institutions, for the most part, left alone 'the expanding realm of private economic activity'. In the 20th century, however, de Schweinitz argues, 'negative freedom' is insufficient; societies are regarded as existing for the welfare of people and the 'age of the common man' means the end of *laissez-faire*. Governments can no longer 'callously disregard the condition of man', and there is also 'a greater realisation of the potential benefits of economic development' which, it is felt, cannot be left to the unco-ordinated decisions of private individuals and groups. The new countries cannot afford to be patient when faced with the Western example of 'modernity'. 'Positive programmes for achieving [development] . . . rather than negative action in deference to the autonomy' of the individual, are the order of the day. Individuals must be encouraged, perhaps compelled, to accept these programmes in their own interest. The facts are simple and clear; 'in the underdeveloped economy today government is playing a much more important role than it did in the 19th century'. Moreover, such activity is taking place in the context of one-party political systems embodying no effective opposition. One alleged justification of this is the need to restrain consumptionist demands in the interests of economic growth. The key question then becomes, 'can one expect a state which has taken society in hand to devolve voluntarily some of its collective powers upon society in democratic reforms?'

To Western nations, and especially to the United States, any divergence from the 'Western model' is, of course, regarded at best as an unfortunate aberration, at worst a form of moral delinquency. But if principles are measured against reality, it is clear that if the developing countries 'are to grow economically, they must limit democratic participation in political affairs and perhaps some kinds of economic freedom as well'. We have pointed out that in the 19th century the sacrifices demanded to ensure economic development were imposed by private entrepreneurs. The individual was no more free to choose than he is today but for different reasons.

> 'Though free of the restrictions imposed by a purposeful state seeking to accelerate the rate of economic growth, he frequently found himself in circumstances when he suffered from the exercise of private power.'

Freedom and democracy cannot be considered apart from the growth of *income*.

> 'To make free elections and majority rule the measure of a nation's moral worth when it scarcely produces enough income to subsist is to reveal one's ignorance of the historical genesis of democracy in the West. That is to say, it is to apply tests to non-Western nations that the Western nations did not pass when they were at a comparable stage of economic development.'

The general conclusions derived from the detailed examination which, we repeat, must be looked at in the book itself, may may be stated briefly. They do not, de Schweinitz emphasises, suggest that democracy is impossible in the 20th century, but rather that the 'macrocosmic conditions' are less favourable for its emergence. For any particular nation, the outcome will depend on the 'microcosmic conditions'. *Conscious* decisions, as Riggs has suggested, will have to be taken not only in relation to economic growth but 'in forming the political community'. If this diagnosis reduces the possibility of formulating general laws about the relationship between economic development and types of political systems, it by no means renders useless the search for them. This search has important results, even if, with George Bernard Shaw, we conclude finally that 'the golden rule is that there is no golden rule'.

NOTES

[1] S. M. Lipset, *Political Man*, Heinemann, 1960, Chapter II, 'Economic development and democracy'.

[2] Almond and Coleman, *op. cit.* especially pp. 536–44.

[3] Especially David Lerner, *The Passing of Traditional Society*, Free Press of Glencoe, 1958.

[4] cf. Karl. W. Deutsch, 'Social Mobilisation and Political Development' *in American Political Science Review*, Vol. LV, No. 3, Sept. 1961, pp. 493–514.

[5] *Industrialisation and Democracy*, Free Press of Glencoe, 1964.

7

Structural-Functional Analysis

I: A RESTATEMENT

WE have referred earlier to the standard work of Bredemeier
and Stephenson. At this point we examine their general account
of 'functional analysis of social systems' (*op. cit.*, pp. 39–47). To
study how any system operates is to study the objective consequences of any one part of the system for another part, or
parts, or for the system as a whole. Clearly it is not possible to
take account of *all* the consequences of any particular action,
rule, or structure. The first limitation applied in functional
analysis is to ascertain the consequences which are *directly
relevant* to the system being analysed. Secondly, a distinction is
made between those consequences which are 'helpful' or 'useful'
to the system ('eufunctional' in some texts, in others simply
'functional'), and those which are 'harmful' (dysfunctional).
In social systems the 'parts' with which the sociologist is concerned are social structures—cognitive, cathectic, and normative definitions; statuses; roles, status-sequences etc.

The biologist usually deduces some *necessary* condition or
requirement of the organic system and proceeds to enquire how
the parts contribute to these requirements. Such necessary
conditions are termed 'functional requirements' or *functional
requisites*. In a social group, similarly, it is generally held that
there must be some division of labour (i.e. some social system)
whereby each member can get from the other members what
he needs to perform his roles in the group, and so that the
group itself can adapt in some degree to its environment. The
group must thus be provided with some degree of *integration*,
defined as the extent to which group members get *from one*

another the attitudes, services, and goods they have learned to need; and of *adaptation*, defined as the extent to which the group as a whole gets *from other groups* the attitudes, services, and goods its members have learned to need, and also the extent to which the group gets from its physical environment the things it needs.

> 'As far as we can deduce, integration and adaptation would be two basic and essential requirements for the operation of any social system.'

It is once more emphasised that to indicate the function of a structure is not to indicate why it 'exists'. Nor does it tell us what motivates people to act in terms of the structure. Further, we repeat that structures may not merely contribute to the integration or adaptation of a system i.e. be (eu)functional; they may also impede or hinder integration or adaptation i.e. be dysfunctional. There may also be, as we have seen, structures which have no consequence either for integration or for adaptation.

Next, we must also repeat the distinction between an objective analysis of how certain structures or actions contribute to, or are functional for, or impede, or are dysfunctional for, adaptation or integration, on the one hand, and the subjective motives and ideas of the actors, on the other. Further, the *consequences* of an act may be understood by actors, or they may not. If they *are*, the *functionality* or *dysfunctionality* of such consequences may or may not be understood. Yet again, even if they *are* understood, they may or may not have been the reasons or motives of the actors in acting that way. So, there is a distinction between consequences that are recognised and those that are not recognised by the actors. Still further, there is a distinction between the consequences that actors *want* to produce and those that they actually *do* produce. Empirically determined consequences are not always those intended or anticipated by the persons acting in a system. When a structure has positive i.e. contributory consequences for a system that are *unintended and unanticipated*, they are called *latent functions*. If a structure is formulated in anticipation of certain consequences we speak of its *manifest function*. There may, of course, be both *latent and manifest dysfunctions*.

Finally, many different structures may perform the same

function, just as any structure may perform more than one function. It is the *function* which is a requisite of the system, not a particular structure (unless it can be demonstrated, which is unlikely, that no other structure can perform the essential function). In other words, we may speak of *structural alternatives*. In addition, because a particular structure performs a necessary function, it does not follow that that structure must necessarily be practised. There may be *functional alternatives*, better serving the needs of a group. A simple example of all this will illustrate the point. In primitive societies the rain dance may be expected to produce rain. In fact, it has nothing to do with this natural phenomenon. Yet it may brind together the scattered groups of a tribe and assist integration. But the rain dance is not the only structure which can perform this integrative function. Any structure that would bring people together in the same way would serve. An alternative structure, additionally, might serve the tribe better than the rain dance, since the latter may prevent the discovery of the natural laws governing rain, and prevent man from controlling rain altogether.

We follow this relatively simple analysis of the functional approach with a somewhat elaborate analysis, which both expands the above account and also raises some of the aspects of the approach which are criticised in our next section. It is taken from Johnson's analysis (*op. cit.*, pp. 63–78). He begins with the simple proposition that any 'partial structure' (sub-group, role, norm, value etc.) has a *function* if it contributes to the fulfilment of one or more of the social needs of a social system or sub-system. It has a dysfunction if it hinders such fulfilment. He, too, distinguishes between (1) purpose, which is something subjective in the minds of the participants, and (2) function, the objective consequences of an action. (We take up later his point that the fact that a social phenomenon has a function does not account for its existence, below, p. 213.)

Next, a structure or pattern of action may have mixed consequences; it may have indirect functions or dysfunctions for other structures in the same system. What of the assertion that societies are functionally integrated to such an extent that every structure contributes to the maintenance of the social system? Here, Johnson refers to Merton. Firstly, it cannot be assumed that every partial structure is functional or dysfunctional—Gellner's 'functionless appendices' again. Secondly, it cannot be concluded that all the partial structures *reinforce* one another. Thirdly, a partial structure may sustain another that is functional, and yet another that is dysfunctional.

No mechanism, as we have already seen, is indispensable to a social system. We can always conceive of the system's achieving its goals and meeting its needs, without that particular mechanism; some other mechanism might have the same function. A simple example would be the alternative between an hereditary monarch and an elected head of state. (It is a matter for empirical enquiry as to whether they do, in fact, perform exactly the same function, and as efficiently.) There are 'functionally equivalent mechanisms', and the 'substitutability' of mechanisms is an important subject for study. Nevertheless, Johnson asserts, every social structure imposes *some* limits on the structural innovations that would be compatible with it. As we stated above, two different mechanisms might not fulfil the same need to the same degree. In addition to our example above, we may cite the question as to whether elected, as against appointed, judges fulfil the same function as effectively. Moreover, the substitute mechanism might provide a different combination of functions and dysfunctions, manifest or latent.

Johnson deals with one of the most serious charges brought against functional analysis—that it cannot account for social changes e.g. in the political system from parliamentary government to dictatorship, or from a two- to a one-party system. (See further, below, p. 214.) His general answer is that it is a question of degree and emphasis. It has been suggested that the functionalists emphasise equilibrium as a theoretical device for the delineation of the major features of society, and as an empirical observation that the dissolution of a society into a 'state of nature' is unknown in man's history. On the other hand, even societies which are ridden with tensions still have what Parsons and Shils call 'considerable zones of solidarity'. But no society is *completely* integrated. Johnson takes the answer somewhat further.

Firstly, since partial structures sometimes weaken other partial structures (e.g. bureaucracy and democratic structures). and sometimes change the distributional aspects of social systems (e.g. the ratio of family businesses to corporations); and since many of the *effects* of such weakening or change have both functions and dysfunctions for the social system, therefore, 'functional analysis is far from being static'. But few changes affect the *total* system; different groups are differently affected, and there are also both short-term and long-term effects. Secondly, a change in the *setting* of the social system necessitates a fresh assessment of the functional consequences of some partial structures. Consider, for example, the discussion of the possible effect of Britain's entry into the European Economic Community on her monarchy, parliament, laws etc. It must be mentioned also, that for a sub-system, changes within society may also be regarded as environmental. Thirdly, a reassessment of the goals of a system may produce changes e.g. a decision for 'collective' rather than 'separate' defence arrangements, or one to concentrate upon the area 'East of Suez'.

We need say little of Johnson's consideration of 'functional analysis and causal analysis' here. He repeats that it cannot be assumed that a given partial structure was established *because* of its function, and for three reasons. Firstly, some functions are latent i.e. unintended and unrecognised. Secondly, many structures are the result of historical events 'working more or less blindly', while the functions and dysfunctions of partial structures change over time. Thirdly, many social systems lack certain partial structures which would be functional. Nevertheless, some structures or mechanisms with manifest functions may be consciously motivated.

Finally, we touch briefly on the problem of 'attributing functions and dysfunctions' i.e. of making such statements as 'if the social system in question did not have that partial structure (or some alternative), then some need or needs of the system would not be so well fulfilled'; or, 'without certain partial structures the system would work better', i.e. they are dysfunctional. Johnson suggests three broad ways in which we may arrive at knowledge concerning functions and dysfunctions. Firstly, that of mental experiment i.e. we 'think away' the partial structure. Secondly, that of comparative analysis i.e. we examine cases that are similar but for the particular structure in question. Thirdly, we may analyse what happens when the partial structure is not adhered to i.e. the problem of deviance.

It remains to add, in reply to the charge that value-judgments may be implicit in functional analysis, that 'functional' does not mean 'good', or 'dysfunctional' 'bad'; the consequences of a structure are assessed only in relation to the *particular social system* under consideration.

II: FUNCTIONALISM—SOME CRITICISMS

In this section we examine two general criticisms of the structural-functional approach offered by a sociologist and a political scientist concerned with the uses of political sociology. T. B. Bottomore (*op. cit.*, pp. 37–42; 51–53), begins his critique by suggesting that there are two broad types of 'explanation', *causal* explanation, which states that 'because of' . . . x . . . 'therefore' . . . y, and *teleological* explanation, which states 'in order that' . . . x result . . . y . . . is done . . . The latter may be subdivided into explanations in terms of *purpose*, in the sense of 'intent', and those concerned with 'end-states'—it being assumed, apparently, that such end-states are *intended* (but n.b. the distinction between 'manifest' and 'latent'). Between 'social causal' and 'individual-purposive' explanations therefore Bottomore holds, we may locate these last-named explanations in terms of *end-states of society*. Functionalist theory purports to explain social phenomena in terms of the part they play in *maintaining the existence of society*.

We are not concerned to examine in detail the validity of Bottomore's criticism of particular functionalists, but it is necessary to state briefly the basis of such criticism, since it provides the foundation of his subsequent analysis. Of Malinowski, for example, Bottomore states that he purported to explain social phenomena by referring them to biological needs and 'derived cultural needs'; this mixture of description and psychological explanation is now 'discredited'. Durkheim, particularly in his 'Elementary Forms of the Religious Life', presented 'two incompatible kinds of explanation'—the causal and the functional—and 'never resolved the question of which was the more appropriate in sociology or how they were related', although in his earlier work he observed that functional explanation did not *account for the existence* of a given phenomenon. Radcliffe-Brown 'followed Durkheim in simply explaining social phenomena by their functions', but he reformulated the concept of social function. 'The function of any recurrent activity . . . is the part it plays in the social life as a whole and *therefore* the contribution it makes to the maintenance of the structural continuity' of a society. One basic question arises here in relation to the word 'therefore': does the part actually played by a social phenomenon *necessarily* make such a contribution? We return to this point later. Meanwhile, we note that whatever approach is used, there are three problems to be considered (1) what kinds of structure are there? (2) how do social structures function?, and (3) how do new types of social structure come into existence?

At this point, Bottomore raises the question whether functionalism is a theory at all. Firstly, he says, it is possible to argue that the postulation of end-states may *never* be explanatory and certainly not *always* explanatory. The functionalists give us merely a (re-)description. Secondly, the analogy between social life and organic life is not sufficiently close to provide valid explanations of social phenomena. Societies change their structures, while organisms do not. It is impossible to determine the health or sickness of societies as for organisms, or to speak precisely about the 'normal' and 'pathological' functioning of their organs, or about 'functions' and 'dysfunctions'. Value-judgments are inevitably involved in such attempts. Further, it is difficult to determine the functions of a social activity or an institution with precision, particularly since there is no one-to-one correspondence between organ and function—a point which, as we have seen, is not overlooked by the functionalists, although they argue that there are degrees of 'specialisation' despite, in Almond's terms, the 'multi-functionality of political structures'.

On the basis of the above reasoning, Bottomore argues that '*therefore*' (1) even if some functional explanations of social phenomena were valid, the range of explanation would be severely limited, since the important phenomenon of *social change* could not be so explained (but cf. Johnson, above, p. 212), (2) we cannot in fact decide in many cases the contribution which a social activity makes to the maintenance of the social system except in evaluative terms, and (3) we cannot easily assign a specific function to a particular social activity. Somewhat condescendingly, perhaps, he concludes that functionalism is no more than 'a useful approach or method'.

He does, however, consider certain modifications of the functionalist approach in more detail. Taking from Durkheim the broad statement that 'the function of a social institution is the correspondence between it and the needs of the social organism', and from Malinowski the 'dogmatic assertion' of the functional integration of every society (as opposed to 'the tentative formulation of a hypothesis about the inter-relation of institutions') he then examines the approach adopted by Merton, who has modified the functionalist approach and used it as 'one possible approach to the study of social behaviour'. In particular, he notes Merton's distinction between *'function'* and *'dysfunction'*, which 'allows for endogenous social change'. However, to Bottomore this is no more acceptable than Durkheim's 'normal' and 'pathological', since it claims to discriminate 'scientifically' between activities which, in most cases, are matters of 'moral evaluation' (but cf. Johnson, above, p. 214). Merton's distinction between *manifest and latent* functions, however, makes for 'more careful and imaginative study' and also indicates that institutions may have several functions (or, as we have seen, may be both functional and dysfunctional). Bottomore suggests that it might be better to speak of the 'working' of an institution, and of the 'way in which it is connected with other specific social institutions or activities'. What is most valuable in the functionalist approach, he concludes, is the greater emphasis and clarity given to the simple idea that in every particular society the different social activities are inter-connected. It is then a matter for empirical enquiry as to which are the various social activities and how they are related.

Runciman (*op. cit.*, pp. 39–41; 109–123) devotes considerable attention to the functionalist approach, and appears to find greater use for it in sociological analysis than does Bottomore. He begins by repeating Weber's warning against trying to define the state by what it *does*—or, as in the standard English version of his work, by its 'ends'. If the state is defined by what it does, it must cease to be a state if it fails to do anything which a state must do in order, by definition, to be a state! He also refers to

Almond's definition which, for convenience, we repeat here. 'The political system is that system of interactions to be found in all independent societies which performs the functions of integration and adaption . . . by means of the employment, or threat of employment, of more or less legitimate physical compulsion.' Suppose, says Runciman, that the state chooses to use its legitimate coercive means for functions that are not either integrative or adaptive, however defined: does it then cease to be a state? If so, the definition is a tautology. We shall return to this point later, but observe here that it must surely be possible to establish empirically that certain functions *are* performed, and then to compare by what structures and in what styles they are performed in different systems. It might, further, be possible to argue that certain functions *must* be performed if the political system (and the social system) is to continue.

But to return to the general argument, what is common to the functionalist approach in all its forms is that we ask, in studying any given social or political system, not how a pattern of behaviour may have originated so much as *what part it plays in maintaining the system as a whole*—Bottomore's 'end-states' approach. Malinowski argues that 'in every type of civilisation, every custom, material object, idea, or belief fulfils some *vital* function, has some task to accomplish, represents an *indispensable* part within a working whole'. But the question arises whether this is in fact always true—are there not 'functionless appendices?'

And also, to what *extent* it is true even where a function does exist—*how* vital, *how* indispensable, and are there no alternatives? Referring to the passage from Radcliffe-Brown quoted by Bottomore (above, p. 215), Runciman also suggests that we cannot assume that because an activity *plays a part* in any system that it *necessarily* ('therefore') helps to maintain structural continuity.

Moreover, it is a mistake to suppose that a behaviour-pattern which is shown to have an important effect on the social structure has thereby been *explained*. We are once more referred to Durkheim's point that to show how something is useful is not to explain how it originated, or why it is what it is. If there is a conscious purpose behind the behaviour-pattern, then its effect can explain its origin; but this kind of explanation (the

217

teleological) does not require the notion of functionalism. On
the other hand, the notion of 'functional requisite' is sometimes
so trivial e.g. that food is required in order to live, as not to
require a functional *theory*. Again, an institution may survive
its original purpose, in which case it is better explained in
historical terms. We may speak of the need for a religion, and
assert that Marxism is a 'substitute' for it, but we cannot
explain the spread of Marxism purely on the basis of the
'messianic' urges of mankind.

Runciman then raises the same question as Bottomore—
whether functionalism can provide an explanatory theory at
all. Any meaningful statement in terms of function, he claims,
can without loss of meaning be translated into an 'if . . . then'
statement of cause and effect. But the functional approach
may 'help in the search for an explanatory theory'. It directs
the investigator to particular statements of cause and effect
about 'self-regulation', or 'adaptation', or 'universal pre-
requisites'.[1] Indeed, it has been suggested that functional
analysis is synonymous with sociological analysis in general.[2]
The functionalists, however, claim that they have a distinctive
approach. Runciman then suggests that there are 'two types of
sociological cause and effect for which functionalist terminology
may be heuristically useful and logically defensible'. In what
follows, he certainly appears to be less dubious about its
validity than does Bottomore.

The first type is where the analogy from biology is important
—a possibility which seems likelier to Runciman than to
Bottomore, and which is asserted as generally valid by Bernard
(below, pp. 224ff). By this, Runciman means the situation
'where it is possible to specify the extreme permissible limits of
certain variables such that where these limits are exceeded the
system breaks down'. An analogy here is with the relationship
between the temperature of the human body and the homeostatic mechanisms which maintain acceptable limits (cf. Easton,
below, p. 221). It is, of course, more difficult to define the
acceptable limits in social systems. But if a system is defined as a
set of variables, then a sub-set of the possible values of the
variables may be designated as constituting the range of
acceptable states. Cybernetics may assist us here. For the
economic system, Runciman suggests that 'slump' may be

excluded; for the political system, 'anarchy' or 'civil war'. It is then possible to ask what aspects of the system's state or behaviour may be regarded as *functional* i.e. what serves to keep the essential variables of the system within their predefined acceptable limits. This can lead to explanations based on the notions of 'functional interdependence', 'reciprocal causality', 'dynamic equilibrium' etc. (cf., again, our discussion of Bernard's analysis, below, pp. 224ff.)

The second type of sociological cause and effect for which functional terminology is appropriate is when the *goals* of a system (*not* individual intentions) as such are considered. Two principal dangers must be avoided here. The first is that purposes cannot properly be spoken of when only observed results are meant. The second is that even where purposes are not being confused with results, it must be possible to specify the particular persons whose specific purposes are meant (cf. Eisenstadt, above, p. 129), again, *not* individual purposes. In this approach, we must give 'both a description of the mechanism by which a *goal* is pursued, and an *ascertained purpose* on the part of the designated person or set of persons'. We must be able to specify the values of the 'state co-ordinates' of the system which constitute the purpose of designated members (present or past) of that system. We must also know what sort of evidence would enable us to *reject* an assertion like that of 'the goal of system S is x', since 'only in this case can we assign an unambiguous meaning to assertions like that of 'A is functional for S'. Thus, for example, the main organisational objectives of bureaucratic agencies can in general be clearly defined; or we may say that 'the goal of any specific industry is to add value to its typical products'. With a *total society*, however, there may be ambiguity: do we mean the goals of the effective ruler, or the wishes of the majority of citizens, or the principles written into the constitution by the founders, or what? (Runciman suggests that Talcott Parsons, for example, never considers this point.)

Nevertheless, despite the necessity to overcome these ambiguities, Runciman's view is that it *is* possible to make functionalist statements about causes and effects related either (1) to the predefined acceptable states of the system concerned (cf. the author's suggestion that it may be postulated that

219

certain functions must be performed if the system is to be maintained: Runciman would add 'in a particular form or state', above, p. 218); or (2) to the designated purposes of the persons whom it is plausible in some sense to identify with the system. In both cases, a sense can be given to the *adaptation* or *adjustment* of the system which the observed *patterns of behaviour* are presumed by the functionalist to help to bring about, Nor, *pace* Bottomore, need this involve value-judgments. It is merely a 'particular statement of cause and effect'; a question of *whether a given pattern of behaviour tends to produce results tending to cause the system to change in a pre-defined direction.* (Runciman illustrates this by reference to Merton's analysis of the function of 'boss-politics' in the U.S. in *Social Theory and Social Structure*, Rev. ed., 1957. But he adds that Talcott Parsons's analysis of 'Voting and Equilibrium', *op. cit.*, shows a confusion between a theory and a conceptual scheme, between classification and analysis. It is not possible to answer the question why American politics follow a relatively stable pattern (if they do) by redescribing the findings of surveys in terms of pattern-maintenance or integration.) But, to conclude, 'the presupposition that social systems, of whatever kind, have a *built-in tendency to equilibrium* is as undemonstrable as Marxist assumptions' (cf. Easton, below, pp. 221–4).

Functionalism as a theory to Runciman, then, is not a set of causal laws, but an interpretation which places *a priori* emphasis and value on the normative elements of social systems, as Marxism does on conflicts. Parsons, for example, cannot *prove* that the factors in society which make for agreement and harmony are fundamentally more important than those making for disagreement and conflict. 'Functionalism is a conscious alternative to Marxism.' Nevertheless, it is useful; it has the virtue of presenting 'explanatory propositions to which it guides the investigator of a particular problem'. In view of the main theme of this book it is particularly worthy of note that Runciman argues that functionalism provides *a framework for a comparative discussion of different political systems*, for which purpose the vocabulary of traditional political theory is no longer adequate. It may direct attention to causes and effects that might otherwise pass unnoticed. It may also help in clarifying some of the problems of traditional political theory posed by such notions as 'collective purpose' or 'general will'.

III: EQUILIBRIUM AND THE SOCIAL SYSTEM

The equilibrium model is 'perhaps one of the few analytical orientations common to all social research'. Thus Easton, who, as we have seen, was one of the earliest political scientists to apply the input–output approach to a study of the political system. We attempt in this section to summarise his analysis of the 'limits of the equilibrium model in social research'.[3] In political science, he says, the concept usually appears as adjustment, accomodation, balance of power. This is in part the result of a widespread opinion that 'all scientific research . . . ultimately deals with determinate systems of behaviour . . . Since all systems are determinate, they must show the property of striving to achieve equilibrium, variously called steady state, homeostasis, adjustment, balance and the like'. But it is necessary to ask to what extent equilibrium analysis can be profitably employed at the present level of development in the social sciences. To anticipate Easton's conclusions we may state briefly (1) that it is useful to approach societies and their major segments as systems of social behaviour (2) that no prior commitment to the equilibrium approach is required, and (3) that equilibrium analysis is suitable only for throwing light on some limited aspects of behaviour.

We may postulate that all those variables essential to an understanding of a significant area of social behaviour constitute a determinant system. The interacting elements within a system are the variables; those elements outside the system are the parameters. At this point Easton emphasises that normally the social scientist does not intend to equate the equilibrium in a social system with one in thermodynamics. (Second law: every system is assumed to have a fixed quantity of energy. In the process of interaction among the elements, energy differences tend to disappear until the system approaches 'entropy death'. All forms of energy are transformed into heat, and heat differentials are reduced to a common level—Easton's own explanation.) They do not intend to suggest that a social system is characterised by entropy. There is a large store of energy available to any social system, and entropy cannot occur. In the most general sense, Easton considers that equilibrium implies the following: 'In every system the component variables will interact in such a way that if the interaction is allowed to continue without further disturbance, ultimately a state will be achieved in which no variable changes its position or relation with respect to the other variables. In this sense only is it meaningful to say that variables are in equilibrium, that they have adjusted to each other, that they have reached a steady or homeostatic state, or that they enjoy a condition of harmony, stability, or balance.'

But where human beings are concerned, activity does not cease even under equilibrium conditions. Nor need change cease. The pattern of interaction at the centre of attention becomes fixed. If in a given interval of time, the relationships among the variables remain fixed, the system is in equilibrium as regards these variables. To emphasise that activity does not cease in such conditions, it is useful to look at the two broadest categories of equilibrium.

Stationary equilibrium occurs when there is equilibrium and the parameters of the system are held constant over a given interval of time. All the groups in a political system compete for power; if a policy is achieved in which they all acquiesce, the political system may be described as being in equilibrium. If the environment is held constant—factors such as technology, preferences, social structure, size of population etc. do not change—this is a state of stationary equilibrium. But activity continues in the sense that each group continues to exert its available pressure.

In *dynamic equilibrium* change takes place as well. This concept is therefore adapted to the study of historical change in social systems. The parameters (or environment) of the system under discussion undergo constant change. The position of equilibrium of the system itself is always shifting. But if the *rate* of change is constant, or the change has a pattern that consistently repeats or maintains itself, the *process of change* has achieved a state of equilibrium e.g. if civilisations rise and fall in a fixed repetitive pattern over the ages.

There is also the concept of equilibrium which includes a condition in which, if the environment is held constant, and if any variable is disturbed and released, the system will display a tendency to return to the initial state. This is the condition of *stable equilibrium*, as contrasted with either *unstable* or *neutral* equilibrium. Doubtless most social science researchers agree that social systems are stable. But stability in the above sense is a characteristic of only one type of equilibrium, and 'in the light of the paucity of serious equilibrium research with regard to social systems, it is certainly premature to characterise all such systems as stable'.

One further meaning of equilibrium remains to be considered. This is the equilibrium found in the human organism and which is described as a *steady state*. This point of rest is independent of the path taken by the variables. It can be achieved from a variety of different initial states, regardless of the path followed. But this is not necessarily the case with all social systems. In economics, for example, only in certain circumstances is the final position independent of the route followed.

Whatever particular *kind* of equilibrium may be involved, however, Easton considers 'the human participants [in a social system] to be in equilibrium when no individual or group changes its position vis-a-vis the other participants'. Viewed thus, Easton claims that the equilibrium concept offers '*one* rewarding way of understanding the mutual relations among the elements of a system'. To obtain such reward, we must ask the appropriate questions. These are set out broadly in Easton's terms.

What are the conditions of equilibrium? What are the multiple relations among the variables if the system under study is to achieve equilibrium? If the conditions of equilibrium can be ascertained, 'we hold in our possession a set of generalisations from which a vast body of deductions may flow'. We may, for example, explore the way in which a disturbance of one of the variables influences the behaviour of the system. What effect has this on the state of equilibrium? Does the system return unimpaired to its initial state or is the subsequent equilibrium position changed? How quickly does the system move to its new state? To what extent does the position of equilibrium depend upon the route followed in the period of adjustment after the displacement? We are in a position 'to unearth invariant relations among the components of a system'.

In view of the theoretical orientation of these questions, it must be emphasised that we are also concerned with an empirical investigation into *whether* a social system *does* achieve

223

equilibrium. The parameters of any significant social system may be in constant and irregular flux. But 'it would still be valuable . . . to search for the invariances that abort equilibrium in a system'. If we 'specify the speculative conditions of equilibrium' i.e. how the variables would have to be related in order for equilibrium to occur, we then have a *norm* against which to check and compare actual systems'. The concept of equilibrium may become a purely *heuristic* device.

The fundamental question, of course, is whether in the social sciences it is possible to realise upon these potentialities. The basic need is *careful quantification* of the relevant variables. Even though this may be satisfactorily done by *ordinal scaling*, there are still difficulties. But without such measurement we should be unable to tell when an empirical system was, in fact, at a point of equilibrium, or, at least, unable to demonstrate this beyond reasonable doubt. An example would be the problem of achieving some measure of *power*. Yet without this, we cannot obtain more than impressionistic observations about group relations. As Easton says, 'political scientists have as yet developed no reliable measure for the amount of power held by pressure groups'.

This does not mean, however, that equilibrium analysis cannot be used at all. The existence of equilibrium may, in certain cases, be ascertained by inspection. Nevertheless, we have to hope that an increasing number of social variables will yield to precise identification and measurement. Otherwise we may get 'the impression that we have a useful general theory when in fact, lacking measurability, it is a mere pretence for knowlege'.[4]

IV: TOWARDS A STRUCTURAL-FUNCTIONAL THEORY OF THE POLITICAL SYSTEM

The following discussion is based upon a recent contribution to structural-functional analysis by Stephane Bernard.[5] With the sophisticated attempt to combine 'the method of biological explanation and of the concept of social function' with 'the method of logical mathematical explanation and of the notion of sociological law' we are not concerned in detail. Rather, we have tried to extract from the article concerned some pertinent ideas about the nature of 'the political system', and the structural-functional approach to its analysis. This certainly involves consideration of Bernard's attempt 'to distinguish the political system from other systems', without necessarily accepting his contention that structural-functional theory is the '*only* conceptual system of reference which permits political science to ensure its development . . .' (Our italics.)

We agree broadly with the general estimate of the advantages of the structural-functional approach. By examining the structural and functional aspects of life in society it is possible to develop an explanatory framework for the study of any social phenomenon, while being aware of 'the ambivalances which surround the concepts of structure and function'. But, first, it is necessary to attempt to establish a clear notion of what is meant by 'the political system'.

The notion of 'system' is 'a basic concept of modern scientific analysis', as Easton, too, asserted. Just as a 'given ensemble of material bodies establishes a mechanical system', or 'a given ensemble of organs and tissues . . . the nervous system'; so 'the sum of the factors taken into consideration by political economy constitutes the economic system', or '*the sum of the factors taken into consideration by political analysis forms . . . the political system*'. A society in which the political system functions badly, suffers, by analogy, as an individual whose nervous system is defective: both resolve their problems badly. The adoption of this notion of system involves discovering what separates the system under analysis from other systems with which it is in contact i.e. in our case, establishing the *factors which are peculiar to the political system*. This is a more difficult process in sociology than in biology, because while each cell of the organism belongs to one unique physiological system, each individual belongs to a large number of social systems. It is not the less difficult because our purpose is not to *define* the political system, but only to evolve a criterion by which its limits may be fixed in such a way as to distinguish it from other social systems. Even though in advanced societies the political system may be sufficiently recognised by the fact that its centres of decision are controlled by the political leaders of the global society, it still remains to discover how this system is to be distinguished from other social systems.

225

A first approach to our problem might be to establish whether an individual, collectivity, or other social factor raises political problems for the leaders of the society. But there are no individuals, groups, or social factors which are likely never to raise political problems relevant to the political system. Each may be linked to other systems but none can 'escape the influence of the political system, nor avoid supporting or running down by its attitudes, the political decisions taken by the governing bodies. Moreover, political phenomena are not just one group among other such social phenomena; they are 'phenomena of synthesis' which involve first principles, and therefore the study of all aspects of social life. As Talcott Parsons has remarked, 'the political reality cannot be studied according to a specific conceptual scheme . . . because . . . the political component of the social system is a centre of integration for all the aspects of this system which analysis can separate, and not the sociological scene of a particular class of social phenomena . . .'[6] Political science has a specific nucleus, not a specific field of action. One aspect of this has been expressed by Merriam in the statement that 'the types of institution or behaviour that we call political must be more rigorously defined . . . [yet] . . . in a sense any person or institution may become political or change its aspect at times'.[7] The field involved is that of the whole of sociological investigation. As March has said,

'the science of politics is the science of human behaviour. It concerns itself with a specific segment of the activity of humans—that which takes place in, or has a clearly discernible effect upon the formal government machinery of the community. The characteristic feature of a political scientist is not a unique theoretical framework, but his special empirical interest.'[8]

Nor is it sufficient to establish the limits of a system; the system itself must be analysed. Social systems are made up of factors whose variations are the object of sociological analysis. The comparison of these variations reveals the laws of the systems under observation, though these laws may be less stringent than those governing e.g. physics. In political systems, some of the principal factors to be considered are authority, force, collective attitudes, and social positions. 'The expression of the fluctuations of political authority in terms of the other factors on which it depends would be a law of that system.' The political system fulfils a social function. It consists of elements which act as support for definite social sub-functions.

The use of functionalism in sociology, Bernard claims, has been far too long established to be abandoned; from Malinowski to Merton 'a pleiade of research workers have distinguished themselves in this field'. But he quotes Almond to support his claim that there has been a lack of application of this approach in political science. 'Nothing has really been added to the functionalist theory of politics since the elaboration of the doctrine of the separation of powers.' (Almond, *op. cit.*, p. 13. The statement, it is suggested, is no longer as true since Almond's own work.) Three questions which we now state are then postulated by Bernard. First, how does the theory of the political system appear when it is considered as an element of collective structure invested with a specific social function? Secondly, how does the theory of the same system appear when it is perceived as an ensemble of functional links between variables? Thirdly, how and to what extent are the two functionalisms linked the one to the other in so far as they have for support a common structure? (The 'two functionalisms' are 'biological' and 'mathematical'. We repeat that we are primarily concerned with the first. But 'functionalists', as we have seen, have applied themselves to Bernard's second question without 'quantification'.)

The concept of social function is directly descended from biology. In its wider meaning in sociological functionalism it implies that any significant element of the objective or subjective structure or culture of a society tends to fulfil a social function. In political science, for example, 'the political ideology of a dominant social class justifies its situation with regard to the other classes by making it appear to conform to the order of things or to the existing moral attitude'. The political centres of society fulfil a function; the question is, what? The function of *political power*, Bernard holds, consists in resolving the social problems that the subjects, left on their own, would be unable to resolve, or could only try to resolve by putting the unity of the group in jeopardy.

Why then are certain social problems raised by governing bodies, while the solution to other problems, apparently quite as important, is left to the subjects? (cf. Binder's similar question about requests for 'legitimisation'.) The answer to this question involves a consideration of the *attitude of the subjects*. 'A social problem becomes a political one when the actual or potential disturbances brought by the situation which engenders it lead all or a section of subjects to turn to the national power to ask for its settlement.' Changes in attitudes would explain, for example, why many economic problems which were left to be settled by Adam Smith's 'invisible hand' in the nineteenth century, have to be dealt with by the state in the twentieth century (or in twentieth-century Africa or Asia, but not in twentieth-century America). If follows from this that, theoretically, there are no bounds assignable to the powers of governing bodies; their determination is not a question of principle but of social attitudes. (cf. the warning against defining the state by its functions.) There is *intrinsically* no political problem; a political problem exists by convention. The more a situation causes, or is likely to cause, serious disorders, the more likelihood is there that certain subjects and certain governing bodies will agree that such situation raises a political problem.

A political functionalist must thus consider the most widely diverse social situations to discern what political problems they present, or might present, to the governing bodies. 'Decisions' of such bodies are solutions, or elements of solutions, to such problems. Political centres must be studied in relation to their social functions; changes which might affect these functions; and to the transformations which are likely to result when, as society evolves, the nature of the problems which it puts to governing bodies becomes modified, thus calling for a modification of previous solutions.

One important result for the political scientist emerges from this approach. When he is concerned with the way in which governing bodies fulfil their social function by trying to resolve problems raised by subjects, he 'is led quite naturally to seeing matters from the same standpoint as the leaders'. Political functionalism, therefore, enables us to see the 'why' of phenomena as well as the 'how' (though the latter is also revealed, and perhaps more clearly, by 'analysis by variables' in the mathematical sense). Bernard holds that 'this partial annihilation of the distance which separates the observer from the object observed reveals to him what might be called the human aspects of political objectivity, since men's actions are never judged more objectively than when one puts one's self in their place'. We spoke of the result for the 'political scientist' of the functionalist approach. But it must be noted that the study of a 'political crisis' involves the whole range of the social sciences. However, the scope of study can be delimited. The notion of the *political problem* appears, to Bernard, the 'theoretical concept most capable of affecting the synthesis between the large mass of heterogeneous facts which the investigator must integrate to reveal the mechanism of a phenomenon of this nature. It allows him to isolate almost automatically the political from the non-political components of the phenomena under observation'.

In the course of his discussion of 'the method of logical mathematical explanation and the notion of sociological law', Bernard formulates certain concepts which he considers essential to a study of the political system. We examine these, without embarking upon mathematical refinements, because they lead into the important discussion of certain aspects of the political system. The concepts of 'power', 'authority', 'decision', and 'force', he considers to be the chief variables of 'objective political science'. Those of 'situation', 'attitude', 'motivation', and 'ideology' are the chief variables of 'political psychology'. The more general concepts of 'culture', 'structure', 'productivity', 'underdevelopment' etc. have no direct relevance for political science, but they become significant when it is necessary to try and reinstate the study of a political phenomenon in the 'wider sociological context of which it is a part'.

In order to set out the *fundamental principles of political sociology*, Bernard considers it necessary to use only the concepts of *factor, influence,* and *reaction.* Factors are the constitutive elements of social systems, the active or passive props of interchanging influences. They include power, beliefs, ideologies, attitudes, behaviour, techniques, etc. Actions are the *standard influences* which these factors exercise the one on the other. 'The reciprocated action exercised by an influenced on an influencing factor is called the *reaction* of the influenced on the influencing factor.' Influences and reactions are abstract or concrete according to whether the factors themselves are abstract or concrete. We may speak of the influence of a need on a technique, or of a technique on a belief, as well as of the influence of one individual on another. Bernard then proceeds to examine what he regards as four general principles in sociology. (The third and fourth of these have been elaborated by Bernard.)

First, there is the principle of the global interdependence of factors. Any sociological factor is at all times under the *potential* influence of all the other factors in the system of which it is a part. The question of knowing to what extent this network is set in motion by a given phenomenon is, however, purely a question of fact.

Second, there is the principle of reciprocity of influences, which is a corollary of the first. There are not, as a rule, one-way influences in social systems. Any influence exerted by factor A on factor B implies an influence in the opposite direction, of B on *A*.

Third, there is the principle of the inequality of influences. This asserts that the influences exchanged by sociological factors are not usually of equal force. The importance of an influence is measured by its effects. There are, in social systems, both strong and weak factors, strong and weak influences, and combinations of each. 'Any political analysis is likely to be distorted if the power of the influence exercised by society on the governing bodies is underestimated, or if the possibilities of influence by the governing bodies on society are overestimated.' (Binder, as we saw, makes this point in a somewhat different way.)

Fourthly, there is the principle of the dependence of reaction with reference to influence. In so far as factor A influences factor B, the reaction of B on A appears as depending on the influence which gives rise to it; it is as if A were influencing itself through the intermediary of B. We do not pursue the complications arising as the number of factors involved increases.

Bernard now embarks upon the application of these principles to the notion of the *political system*, and we shall follow his argument in some detail. *Society* (S) is governed by the political medium (p). The separation of these 'automatically reveals two complex sociological factors (S–p) and p'. The first principle (above) postulates that *all* the factors which make up the social system S tend to occur in the production of the political phenomena which affect the interaction of (S–p) and p. The second principle postulates the necessary existence of an action of (S–p) on p, and of influence in the opposite direction of p on (S–p). The third principle is relevant to the fact that the influence of (S–p) on p, and the reaction of p on (S–p) are not of equal force. The way in which a power p imposes its norms on the whole of social behaviour within (S–p) depends more on the nature of the latter behaviour than this behaviour depends on the activity of p. 'Each sociological factor within the social radical (S–p) tends to depend on the ensemble of other factors which constitute (S–p) *more* than it depends on the power p. The activity of the power p, an the other hand, tends to depend more on the factors contained in (S–p) than on the *sociologically unconditioned element* in the activity of the governing bodies, the *partial independency* of p in relation to (S–p) being able indeed to *limit* the influence exerted by (S–p) on p, but *not* being able to be a substitute for it.' (Our italics.) If we take *the political attitude adopted by the subjects to a decision taken by the power p*, relative to their social situation, this attitude depends to a certain extent on p, but even more on the other sociological factors connected with it in (S–p) e.g. political ideologies, interior norms in the common social behaviour, social positions. (We use Bernard's 'ideologies', though we should prefer 'political culture' or 'political orientation'.) Authority and society are in a constant state of interaction. But society, more often than not, has the upper hand. So, we designate the influence of (S–p) as (capital) A, and that of p as (small) b.

But it is further necessary to show that the nature and intensity of the *reaction* exerted by authority on society are basically dependent on the influence in the other direction by society on authority. The fourth principle (above) implies that in so far as (S–p) conditions the standard activity of its political centres p, the standard *reaction* exerted by p on (S–p) depends itself on the influence exerted by (S–p) on p. To say that A (above) influences b strongly, is tantamount to saying that A conditions strongly the *activity* of b, although there is always part of the activity of the politician which escapes social conditioning, and consequently any sociological predictability. (Which is however, surely not to say that it might not be predicted from our knowledge of the 'sociologically unconditioned elements' in the activity of governing bodies.) To say that b reacts little on A is tantamount to saying, conversely, that the activity of the political centre b conditions to a lesser degree the activity of A. 'The reaction exerted by the political centre b on the social radical A being identified with the activity of b, itself strongly influenced by A, it may be concluded that b only influences basically the society A to the extent that society A confers on its own political centre b the possibility of influencing itself' (with the exception of that part of the governing activity which is not conditioned by A). (This analysis provides for what others have described as the 'limited autonomy of the political system'.) This is what is implied by *social control*. The statement that the leaders of a society exert 'social control' means that society controls itself, the leaders being active as spokesmen. The latter do not exert over society a capacity for unconditional and unlimited control. (We recall the allied point that demands made on the polity are, in fact, demands made on other members of society *through* the polity.)

We add that the above analysis does not enable us to determine the *absolute value of the authority-potential* in any given society at a precise moment; it merely asserts that it is society which regulates the value of this potential, not the leaders. Perhaps it should be pointed out that this is not to credit the community as such with a will distinct from that of the governing bodies, but merely to state that the capacity for decision of such bodies is determined by collective attitudes. The potential of authority may be relatively strong, as in the Stalin regime, or very weak, as in the French Fourth Republic. 'The fourth principle merely teaches us that it is not the prerogative of those invested with a certain authority-potential to modify it arbitrarily.' A corollary of this is that the leaders of a society cannot delegate to themselves the supplementary authority necessary for them to take decisions normally outside their range. To quote Bernard's example, Guy Mollet in the Fourth Republic could take decisions A and B; the existing system did not allow him to take decision C. President de Gaulle in the Fifth Republic can take decisions A, B and C. The present form of French society prevents his taking decision D. The President has a greater scope for decisions than Mollet, but, like the latter, he is 'conditioned' and not in a position to set aside the conditions to delegate to himself an authority-potential greater than that which the present state of affairs —including his personal prestige and grasp of problems— allows him. (It is easy to suggest what C might be—e.g. the conferment of independence on Algeria. It is not so easy to speculate as to a possible D!)

To say that 'the authority-potential of governing bodies depends on the political attitudes of the subjects' would be meaningless if governing bodies could manipulate such attitudes so as arbitrarily to increase their own authority. In the balance of interactions, society takes precedence over authority. 'It is the essence of the political phenemenon that authority depends more on sociological factors which condition its power than these factors depend on the authority itself.' The way in which such conditioning takes place depends on the societies involved and the circumstances of the situation. But it does escape to a great extent the influence of authority. Such limitation of authority is, to Bernard, 'indispensable to the understanding of the mechanism of social conflicts'. Such conflicts are inextricably linked with certain deficiencies in authority; an understanding of the mechanism of conflicts depends largely on discovering whether such deficiences are necessary or accidental.

If we regard the *political system as a complex of variables* it consists of three successive levels of factors, (1) the 'situation' of the groups of subjects, (2) the 'attitudes' of such groups, especially 'assent' and 'opposition' to authority, and (3) the political authority and the force at its disposal. There are two principal relationships, (1) which links political attitudes to the collective situations governing them, and (2) which links capacity for decision and force of governing bodies to political attitudes of assent and opposition. The 'authority-potential of a political system' is a function (1) of collective attitudes and (2) collective situations determining these attitudes.

We consider first the *political attitudes–situation relationship.* It is not necessary to refer in detail to evidence about the connection between social position and voting habits, or to that concerning the influences affecting political attitudes within a social class. But it should be noted that such evidence

233

tells us neither the *relative importance* of different factors of situation nor the mechanism which regulates the *transformation* of political attitudes. Nor do we know why conservatives and partisans of change tend to strike a balance so that democratic electors oppose a political solution which might place them under the control of an absolute majority.

Similar problems appear in non-democratic regimes, e.g. colonial systems. The attitudes of social groups in such systems are also conditioned by this situation. But such attitudes are not normally expressed by votes, and the correlating of attitudes with groups can be ascertained only roughly. On the other hand, such correlation of attitudes with groups is carried out in a far more simple way. Broadly, there is a cleavage in society springing from two dominant attitudes—the anti-colonalism of the subjects and the conservatism of governing bodies, though each group has a fringe which 'crystallises against the stream'.

Whatever the political regime and social milieu may be, the political attitude–situation relationship raises four successive problems. They are (1) the cataloguing of attitudes according to social group, (2) the global correlating of social situations and systems of attitudes derivde from them, (3) the interpretation of these correlations factor by factor, and (4) the 'elucidation of the mechanism of the evolution of these systems of attitudes as a function of considered situations'.

We now turn to the relationship of *authority-force and political attitudes*, which 'leads to the heart of the problems of political science'. Bernard's starting point is Pareto. 'Apart from exceptions which are few in number and short-lived, there is everywhere a minority governing class which retains its authority in part through force, in part with the consent of the governed class which is far more numerous. From the point of view of substance the differences largely reside in the proportions of force and assent; from the point of view of form, in the ways in which the force is exercised and in which assent is obtained'.[9] The only modification needed to this is that our concern is not with the relationship between the elite as a whole and the rest of society, but with that between the true governing bodies and the whole body of subjects. The four variables involved are authority, force, assent, and opposition. *Political authority* is the capacity for bringing subjects, by simple injunction, force, or a combination of both, to do or not to do certain things, express or not express certain emotions, think or not think in a certain way. *Governing force* is a capacity for constraint which rests on the spontaneous or organised obediences of the specialised groups to whom authority entrusts the monopoly of material means at its disposal. *Assent* and *opposition* are political attitudes or predispositions to obey or disobey the injunctions of authority. In fact, subjects are rarely completely assenting or opposed, but both at once. (cf. Almond and Verba: members of a political system may themselves, as individuals, be a mixture of 'subject' and 'participant', though it is not suggested that this is an *exact* parallel.) The key factor is where the attitude lies on the continuum between the extremes of maximum assent—minimum opposition, and maximum opposition—minimum assent.

Bernard then states six propositions 'easily deduced from mere observation of political life'.

1. Political authority is a function of assent ('function' here is used in the mathematical sense); it tends to increase when this assent increases.

2. Political authority is a function of the governing force; it increases when this force increases, and decreases in the opposite case.

3. The governing force is a function of the assent of specialised groups which it sets in motion, and of that of the groups of subjects to which it is applicable and from which the agents are recruited; it increases or diminishes according to the way in which the pair assent–opposition varies in the two sorts of groups.

4. The governing force is a function of authority; in civil as in military affairs it increases or diminishes according to whether the leaders exercise their authority well or badly on the specialised groups which set the force in motion.

5. The assent of the subjects, and of the agents of authority, is, conversely, a function of force. Within certain limits, the recourse to force neutralises the elements of opposition which hinder assent, and stabilises the residual tendencies which accompany the opposition of the subject; this enables it to obtain a greater degree of obedience.

6. Assent is a function of political authority of constant

235

strength; this signifies that the governing bodies are not without means to influence subjects' attitudes, even when subjects reject the reinforcing of existing constraints to bring them to obedience. Information, propaganda, the manipulation of judicial norms, are methods of such influence.

Quite apart from these three pairs of relationships, *political authority still depends on the nature of the regime which exerts it*. It is not the result of a mere numerical composition of attitudes of assent and opposition, for each regime tends to *form* these attitudes. It exaggerates the assent and opposition of certain groups, and underrates those of others. Such aptitude for exaggerating or underrating assent (or, conversely, opposition) is identifiable with what may be called the *structure of authority* of the regime. This determines the relative importance the political system attributes to the various groups, or the sensitivity of political organisations to different groups. In many political phenomena, of course, the structure of the authority may be a constant. In such cases, political authority is a function of a constant (the structure of authority) and two connected variables (assent and force). Bernard now proceeds to a detailed explication of this general approach.

If the potentials for authority and force depended too directly on assent, they would be unable to cope with a loss of their 'consenting reserves'. The drop of assent would require an increase of force which could not be realised. But governing bodies can, on the one hand, *realise a normal authority-potential more than proportional to the assent at their disposal*. Their authority then may decrease less quickly than social assent. This situation is achieved by minimising the influence of the least favoured groups, or those least favourable to the regime. Possible methods available include the paid vote, the plural vote, the allotting of seats more than proportional to the number of valid votes, the recruitment of agents from privileged social groups. Military regimes can push this short of procedure to the limit by excluding whole categories of citizens from the 'political circuit'. On the other hand, governing bodies can try to *establish a force-potential more than proportional to the increase of authority achieved by the preceding devices*, so that their disposition to use force decreases less quickly than this extra authority. This may be done by the establishment of greater authority over agents than over subjects. Possible methods available to this end may include rigid discipline, severe training, recruiting from privileged groups, whose assent will continue to be forthcoming even when all other groups are tempted into opposition.

Despite all these devices, however, beyond a certain point a great drop in assent cannot be compensated for by force. If groups on whose assent force is founded turn to opposition, or if virtually the whole community opposes the police force or the army, the regime may be unable to restore the position. The first kind of situation may arise when a revolutionary opposition to a national regime develops. The second arises, typically, when revolutionary opposition is directed against an occupying power. In either case, 'the relative subordination of force to social attitudes, the fact that force depends more on assent than assent on force, is one of the keys of political science'.

Bernard's further elaboration of this approach leads us into a conceptual framework or theory for a typology of regimes. We summarise this section in some detail, and comparisons may be made with the suggestions for such typology already discussed (above, Chapter 3.) The scheme is based on a consideration of how the *structures of authority* which characterise two broad categories of regimes, those which are democratic and those founded on force, influence the respective authority-potentials in each type.

First, we postulate a *modern democracy* in its 'ideal' conditions for functioning. The assent of more or less all its subjects is the obvious and exclusive source of authority. This assent is also the source of the force at the government's disposal. Such force ensures the conformity of the very few deviants; it also stabilises and consolidates the assent of the huge majority who uphold existing standards. The form of the regime is representative; all social groups participate in the governing power both electorally and through recruitment as agents. Any revolutionary split in such regime would split in the same proportion both the assenting basis of authority and the political organs which are the direct source of the force potential.

Variations in the authority of the regime as a function of

237

the factors considered can be thus expressed: the *authority and governing force* will be at a maximum for a maximum social assent, implying a negligible number of revolutionary opposing elements; they will be zero in the case of division into half of the social assent, half the population opposing revolutionarily the other half, with the political organs also split; they will travel from the maximum to the minimum between these two extremes as the number of revolutionary opponents nears fifty per cent.

Three complementary observations must be made. For a loss of assent to be detrimental to a democratic authority there must be a reassessment of the regime by its opponents, for so long as majority and minority accept the regime, no abnormal problem arises. The loss of assent in a democracy is the more serious because irremediable; such regime cannot reform a weakened assent by authority, because the more assent and force diminish, the less authority the regime has. In a revolutionary division into half, two social groups confront each other within a framework of forces which renders void the political power of the group defending itself and renders valid to the maximum degree that of the opposing group; the former group is operating with a 'paralysed state', while the latter has the capacity to cause the disintegration of the social order.

The situation in a *revolutionary regime* is somewhat different. From the beginning the community is divided into two violently opposed factions. The authority of the regime only progresses by the assent of the social group of which it is the instrument, the opposing group being outside the political system. The restricted but violent assent of the former group is the only possible source of force, and the group may conceivably react against this assent. The first role of the governing force is to deal with an opposing group which is sometimes the most numerous if not the best organised in the community. Its second role is to strengthen the assent of the revolutionary group itself by exerting on it a coercive pressure without limit, as demanded by the political discipline necessary in a civil war. The regime is not representative, both because of its authoritarian form and because the supporting social groups alone participate in power; the instruments of government themselves are predominantly recruited from the same group. Such regime does not demand common consent but only that of the supporting social classes; outside opposition does not affect stability, though passive resistance may constitute a danger.

Despite these differences, however, fluctuations of authority in this type of political system are identical in form to those in the democratic system. Authority still remains a function of social assent and of force. The *authority and force* of the regime will be greatest in the case of the maximum assent of the revolutionary group (leaving aside the question of passive resistance); they will be lowest with a maximum split in the revolutionary group and its instruments of authority; they will decrease as the political division of the revolutionary group increases.

In general, then, both democratic and revolutionary regimes illustrate the *law of political authority*. (This statement softens the rigidity of the dichotomy between the two types of regime and meets the criticisms of those who argue that such dichotomy is of little heuristic, or, indeed, practical value.) But democracy is organised on the basis of a (supposed) general assent, and does all it can to preserve this; it ceases to function normally as assent deteriorates. Military regimes are organised on the basis of consent confined to a group, but they endow the regime with a 'technical' value of general assent by recruiting solely from assenting groups, and excluding opponents from the political circle. If the groups on which the regime relies split, the opposing groups are 'purged'. But this loss of assent must be compensated for by constraint. If this process continues, the assenting foundation is reduced 'to a pinhead', with a 'formidable apparatus of constraint', as, for example, in the Stalin regime.

If authority could only command when subjects agree to obey, 'it would then be only an instrument for their convenience and would lose all sociological standing'. But assent does not exclude opposition; subjects always tend simultaneously to obey and disobey, whether this takes the form of 'obeying' and 'disobeying' individuals or groups, or an 'ambivalence' in each individual or group. 'Authority, considered in its dual state of assent and intimidation, is, in the final analysis, only possible and necessary because each subject is permanently affected with a veritable split in his political personality.' To govern is not to follow subjects, though a weakened power has no alternative. To govern is to rely on social predispositions to obedience, in order to curb tendencies to opposition. 'If authority depends on the assent of each subject, the obedience of each subject depends in turn on the capacity for command and intimidation with which each authority is invested by the whole community.' Political science needs to study two relationships of authority: that which exists between the political power and the whole of society; and that which exists between the political power and each subject. In the former case, society 'commands' the political power; in the latter, the political power 'commands' each subject. But the political power will have more authority over each subject the more it conforms to the needs and aspirations of the community.

In the foregoing account we have inevitably referred to Bernard's consideration of the notion of 'interaction between variables', as well as to his account of 'organic function'. (cf. Robert K. Merton, *Social Theory and Social Structure*, Free Press of Glencoe, 1957, p. 21. 'Normally, the context allows us to see clearly whether the word [function] is to be taken in its mathematical sense; but sociologists often vacillate between this meaning and another, connected but distinct, which also implies the notions of "interdependence", of "reciprocal relationship", or of "variables with mutual dependence". This [second] meaning of the idea is basic for the functional analysis as it is practised in sociology and anthropology. Partly descended from the primitive mathematical meaning of the idea, this way of reasoning is most often explicitly borrowed from the biological sciences.') He concludes that sociology 'vacillates continuously between functionalist reasoning and reasoning by variables . . . They are never combined in practice so as to systematically benefit the study of one particular phenomenon through the particular advantages which are part of them'. He goes on, 'to understand how these two explanatory methods . . . may serve in the study of identical phenomena, it is necessary to consider the relation that exists between the notion of *social structure* (in the sense of relation of part to whole) and the different interpretations of the notion of *function*'.

The concepts of structure and function, he suggests, need to be clearly distingushed. Social systems are firstly, and above all, structures. The two functionalisms (quasi-mathematical and quasi-organic) are only 'explanatory methods which allow for the scientific study of activities which are part of the structures, and developments which affect them'. We do not intend to deal with the detailed discussion which follows this generalisation, but merely to refer to one conclusion.

The social structure may be interpreted either as a complexity of quasi-organic elements fulfilling specific functions within the whole, or as a network of sociological factors in a constant state of dynamic interaction. This ambivalence of social structure suggests two approaches to a study of social systems. Because the social structure appears, in certain respects, in the form of a quasi-organic relationship of parts with the whole, it is permissible to analyse it in terms of *sociological functionalism*. Because it appears in other respects as a complexity of factors linked together as material magnitudes, it is permissible also to analyse it in terms of variables and of quasi-mathematical functions. Bernard suggests that the concept of functionalism is able to be transposed without difficulty into the sphere of interaction between sociological variables. Collective attitudes, political decisions etc., are 'at once' sociological variables and elements fulfilling definite social functions. Moreover, because each of the structural elements of society is quasi-organically linked to all the others, *even in the dimension of the future*, the structural factors which serve as support for the diverse social functions can be assimilated directly and without any change of vocabulary to the variables. Because each social quasi-organ has the possibility of forcing all the others to alter and become linked with it, it is a sociological variable. Any sociological factor tending thus to appear simultaneously as a variable and as the support for a social function, it follows that any relationship of variable to variable will necessarily involve a functionalist aspect. 'It is just as important to find out how the authority of a political regime varies as a function of the variables of attitude and situation which condition it, as to examine how this regime fulfils its "social function" by setting in motion the authority-potential at its disposal to resolve the social problems which are presented to it.' The function of the political organs of society is to resolve certain problems by means of gecisions. But these problems, and the decisions which regulate them, are also variables since their solutions vary as a function of their declarations and these declarations themselves change with the elements of social structure which are embodied in them.

Bernard admits in his concluding paragraph that 'it would be useless to elaborate here on the interest which the *structural-functional* theory can present for the study of the political system. We in no way conceal, therefore, that the proof of the ability of the conception of the political system which has been outlined in this article remains to be seen in its practical application'. (It should be added, however, that Bernard has provided brilliant proof of its applicability in his *Franco-Moroccan Conflict, 1943–1956*, Editions de l'Institut de Sociologies, Parc Leopold, Bruxelles 4, 1963. 3 Vols. Especially Vol. II, 'Contribution a la théorie du système politique'.)

V: STRUCTURAL-FUNCTIONAL ANALYSIS AND BEHAVIOURALISM

From time to time confusion has occurred about the precise distinction and relationship between a 'behavioural' and a 'structural-functional' approach to the analysis of political systems and political activity. It seemed useful, therefore, to conclude with a summary of a brilliant discussion of this problem by Apter.[10]

The *structural approach*, Apter suggests, is an effort to find the general properties of systems that limit the range of action open to individuals. It delimits gross behaviour and is particularly useful for large-scale comparative studies. It seeks qualitative rather than quantitative precision (cf. Easton, above, pp. 221–4), partly out of necessity. The *behavioural school* begins with the individual and his motivations; in so far as individual behaviours and motivations can be aggregated, then general propositions become possible. The structural approach, further, establishes categories whereby action is itself limited and restricted by what Durkheim calls 'social facts'. The behavioural approach emphasises choices and motivations and *infers* structural limitations from the behaviour of individuals, rather than from the properties of collectivities.

The institutionalists, among whom Apter cites Bryce, Barker, Laski, Friedrich, and Finer, began to bring the two approaches, which were not as clearly defined for most of them as they are today, together. They presented 'an encompassing view of politics in which the political process is related to the wider coherence of social institutions'. This led on to furthre consideration of two aspects of the political system. The first was concerned with structure, the relationships in a social system which limit the process of choice, including political choice, to a particular range of alternatives. The second, the behavioural approach, was concerned with the selection process in choice, i.e. deciding between alternatives. We may now pursue the distinction between the two approaches a little further.

First, there is the comparison as regards *theory*. The objectives which are uppermost in the minds of the behaviouralists are to develop firstly the most highly generalised explanatory theories of human behaviour itself, and secondly the most highly particularised, i.e. empirical theories of limited generalisation and great precision. With the structuralists, on the other hand, explanatory theories are less general than in the first case with the behaviouralists. They deal with the propensities of collectivities, and the limitations which these impose on behaviour. But their theories are also less precise and unique to a particular unit.

Next, there is the comparison as regards *method*. Structural concepts tend to be synthetic and less experimental, while behavioural methods commonly employ the input–output model, as with Easton. (Thus Apter, but Mitchell uses this model and claims that his approach is *structural-functional.*) The structuralists use varied methods, but they mostly tend to be tailored to the requirements of macrocosmic units, for example, Weber's 'ideal types'; the emphasis is on comparative studies of large-scale units. The structuralists are concerned with the identification of the relevant aspects of social and political life in their relationship to the unit under analysis. They have gone beyond the notion of ideal types to demarcate a range of possible relevant variables that in their inter-connections cast light on the entire system under discussion.

This approach has led to efforts at comparison in two dimensions. Firstly, there is the analysis of changes over a period of time in a particular system, especially in relation to revolutions, or changes of regime, or similar dramatic instances of events that indicate an alteration in the relationships of variables within the system. Secondly, there is the analysis of different systems in space, comparisons between countries or governments. Here the concern is with the different ways in which the variables arrange themselves from one system to another; an attempt is made to specify those variables which are more significant than others, and also to specify the variables which are unique to each of the cases used for comparison.

To pursue this a little further, there are two other related approaches. The one is to use both structural and functional components so as to indicate those factors which are essential to the maintenance of the unit under analysis, i.e. structural-functional requisite analysis.[11] The other is to examine structures not merely as derived from the observation of a given unit, or comparatively, but rather in terms of their latent propensities for the unit. This is related to the analysis of political change.

As a result of these methods, then, structural theories derive from highly generalised statements about the functional and structural properties of a given class of system. They are more deductive and, *a priori*, they rely more directly on comparison, than behavioural theories. The latter are more inductive, building up general statements through repeated experiments.

As regards *techniques*, as Easton has also emphasised and as regards which Bernard has attempted to suggest remedies, the qualitative concepts in structural analysis are more difficult to quantify. This approach includes 'intuitive skills as well as such tools as chi-squares or factor analysis'. (Though n.b. Bernard's use of 'factors' in his structural functional approach.)

We may summarise the distinction between the two approaches briefly. First, the most important difference is in the realm of theory; action may be explained in the behavioural

244

approach by motivation, in the structural approach by organisational factors. Secondly, there is a difference in the size of the units which are the central concern; the structural approach is concerned with macro-units, large-scale systems. Thirdly, comparative studies are far more characteristic of structural theory than of behavioural analysis. Finally, the theories resulting from behavioural analysis are more highly generalised than those of the structuralists.

Apter next turns his attention to 'closing the gap'. One of his main themes is the 'problem of analysis of specialised mechanisms of government'. The social consequences of political machinery provide one of the core interests of comparative politics. Although Bernard, as we have seen, stresses the predominant influence of society over the political system, the instrumentalities of government should not be regarded as simply a reflection of social factors. Bernard, Binder, and others have all pointed out the 'reaction' of the political system on society, and the relative autonomy of the political system. It is thus necessary to discover what independent role these instrumentalities play, and how best to determine their potentialities in given societies. 'It is the intermeshing of social needs with political machinery that represents the core interest of political science.' This relationship provokes our concern with such things as decision-making, political stability, law and change, political ideals. As to the last, 'if there is no one-to-one correspondence between political mechanisms and political forms, there is at least a close relationship between an ensemble of political mechanisms and political ideals'. (Though as Almond and Verba point out, one task is to ascertain the *degree* of congruence.) We need more adequate theories to explain the complex motivations of people in their relation to government. Symbolic affiliations, identifications of the individual with a wide social group in countries where historic particularisms are powerful, the existence of a complex range of sub-groups in society—all these factors, and many others, may affect the role of government.

Both behavioural and structural approaches have been made to problems such as these. Apter refers, for example, to Nathan Leites's 'Ritual of Liquidation'[12] as an analysis which proceeds from motivation to structure and from perception to action.

'From motivation and perception to role . . . one sees structure emerging from process in the wider context of past events.' Here is a behavioural approach which raises the question as to how individual behaviour is both reflected in the nature of the collectivity and helps to determine it. As this volume is concerned primarily with structural-functional analysis, it is even more interesting to see what Apter has to say of Almond's and Coleman's 'Politics of the Developing Areas'.

> 'A volume which begins with the structural and moves to a few of the interstices of human motivation . . . Advocating a functional and structural point of view, it attempts to delimit the area of the political from other aspects of social behaviour and to show how a functional core of analysis can reveal those differences in mechanisms of government that cannot be derived simply from an examination of the mechanisms themselves. Similarly, in the linkages between government and the individual, such problems as political socialisation and recruitment take on a particular significance.'

Whatever its defects, Apter considers that the structural method attempts with some success to use comparative treatment to exhaust explanation at a more general level before proceeding to a particular one.

We shall not examine in detail Apter's account of two studies which are 'at the intermediate range between the structural on the one hand, and the behavioural on the other'.[13] At this point he turns to a brief examination of the approach through the notion of 'roles', to which we referred in our first chapter. Finally, having examined the 'two extremes' of behaviouralism and structuralism, he summarises the 'contemporary forms of comparative analysis'. It will be seen that in most of these the structural-functional approach which we have stressed in this survey is of relevance.

First, there is the concern with the nature of the functioning of political instrumentalities in different societies. This has been extended to include problems of social change and developing areas; the introduction of sociological methods as a means of determining those social variables which affect the operations of government and shape the nature of the demands made on government; an interest in subjects lying between government and society—political recruitment, social backgrounds of political leaders, elite studies, problems of voting and non-voting, ideologies, political socialisation, inculcation of values, determination of discontinuities in culture and social status, and the effects of such discontinuities on political instrumentalities.

Secondly, there are the attempts to account for the political consequences of economic development and changing technologies; can one find innovations or political practices capable of resolving problems of economic and political development?

Thirdly, between the behavioural and the structural approaches, there is the concern with both economic development and planning on the one hand, and their consequences for the evolution of the political system on the other.

Fourthly, there is the interest in the groups which create roles intermediate between government and society, and their effect on such things as political participation and the maintenance of a pluralistic distribution of power.

Fifthly, there is the comparative study of mass media and social communications.

Finally, there is the reconsideration of such 'large questions' as 'what are the political goals of differing societies, and how do they vary?' Or, 'what political structures are the most suitable for certain given ends?'

Expressed more generally, all this may be summed up as a general concern with the analysis of change and stability, and the 'intellectual mapping' of the varieties of experience represented by changes from one type of system to another, e.g. a comparative study of revolutions; with the place of traditions and traditionalism, and their implications for future change; with the comparative study of political participation; and with an examination of the groups concerned with political socialisation.

It has not been our intention to put forward a general sociological or a specific structural-functional approach as the *only* fruitful one to these and other problems. Such approaches have, however, we believe, on the evidence presented here, a contribution to make to the study of all these fields of interest.

NOTES

[1] cf. Carl G. Hemple, 'The Logic of Functional Analysis' *in* L. Gross ed. *Symposium on Sociological Theory*, 1959.

[2] Kingsley Davis, 'The Myth of Functional Analysis in Sociology and Anthropology', *Am. Soc. Review*, XXIV, 1959.

[3] Easton, *in* Eulau etc. eds., *op. cit.*, pp. 397–404.

[4] cf. further, Easton, *The Political System*, N.Y., 1953 especially Ch. 11.

[5] Stephane Bernard, 'Esquisse d'un théorie structurelle-fonctionnelle du système politique', *Journal de l'Institut de Sociologie de l'Université Libre de Bruxelles*, Jan., 1963, pp. 569–614.

[6] T. Parsons, *The Social System*, Free Press of Glencoe, 1951, pp. 126–127.

[7] Charles Merriam, 'New Aspects of Politics', *in* Eulau etc. eds., *op. cit.*, pp. 24–31.

[8] James G. March, 'An Introduction to the Theory and Measurement of Influence', *in* Eulau etc. eds., *op. cit.*, pp. 385–397.

[9] Vilfredo Pareto, *Traité de sociologie générale*, Pierre Boven, 1919, Vol. II, p. 1438, para. 2244.

[10] 'Past Influences and Future Development' *in* Eulau etc. eds., *op. cit.*, pp. 725–740.

[11] cf. 'The Functional Prerequisites of a Society', D. F. Aberle, A. R. Cohen, A. K. Davis, M. J. Levy Jr. and F. X. Sutton *in Ethics*, Vol. LX, No. 2 (Jan. 1950), and Marion J. Levy Jr., *op. cit.*

[12] N. Leites and E. Bernant, Free Press of Glencoe, 1954.

[13] They are D. Lerner, *Passing of the Traditional Society*, Free Press of Glencoe, 1958, and Duverger, *Political Parties*, Methuen, 1954.

Note:—Two books by David Easton appeared too late for consideration here. They are:—

1. *A Framework for Political Analysis*, Prentice-Hall, 1965.
2. *A Systems Analysis of Political Life*, Wiley, 1965.

Select Bibliography

A SELECT LIST OF BOOKS and articles is provided for each chapter in the book, placed in the order to which reference is made to each in the text. Full details are given on first mention; where a book is referred to again later, it is shown simply by author and title.

1 : SOME GENERAL CONCEPTS

HARRY M. JOHNSON, *Sociology, A Systematic Introduction*, Routledge & Kegan Paul, 1961.

H. C. BREDEMEIER *and* R. M. STEPHENSON, *The Analysis of Social Systems*, Holt, Rinehart, Winston, 1962.

MARION J. LEVY, JR., *The Structure of Society*, Princeton U.P., 1952.

CLIFFORD GEERTZ ed., *Old Societies and New States*, Free Press of Glencoe, 1963, espec. LLOYD FULLER, 'Equality, Modernity and Democracy in the New States'.

LA PALOMBARA ed., *Bureaucracy and Political Development*, Princeton U.P. 1963.

ECKSTEIN *and* APTER eds., *Comparative Politics*, Free Press of Glencoe, 1963.

HYMAN H., *Political Socialisation*, Free Press of Glencoe, 1959.

WILLIAM C. MITCHELL, *The American Polity*, Free Press of Glencoe, 1962.

BURDICK *and* BRODBECK eds., *American Voting Behaviour*, Free Press of Glencoe, 1959, espec. T. PARSONS, 'Voting and the Equilibrium of the American Political System'.

H. SPIRO, *Government by Constitution*, Random House, 1959.

S. LIPSET, *The First New Nation*, Heinemann, 1964.

The following seven works of TALCOTT PARSONS:

The Social System, Tavistock Publications, 1951.

With ED. A. SHILS, *Towards a General Theory of Action*, Cambridge, Massachusetts, 1951.

With ROB. F. BALES *and* ED. A. SHILS, *Working Papers in the Theory of Action*, Free Press of Glencoe, 1953.

249

Select Bibliography

Essays in Sociological Theory, revised ed., Free Press of Glencoe, 1954.
With NEIL J. SMELSER, *Economy and Society*, Routledge & Kegan Paul,
1956.
Structure and Process in Modern Society, Free Press of Glencoe, 1960.
'Pattern-variables revisited', *Am. Soc. Rev.*, 25(1960).

R. K. MERTON, *Social Theory and Social Structure*, revised ed., Free
Press of Glencoe, 1957.
M. BLACK, ed., *The Social Theories of Talcott Parsons*, Prentice-Hall,
1961.
MAX WEBER, *Theory of Social and Economic Organisation*, trans. A. M.
HENDERSON *and* T. PARSONS, O.U.P., 1947.
From Max Weber: Essays in Sociology, trans. and ed. by C. W. MILLS
and HANS GERTH, Routledge & Kegan Paul, 1948.

2: POLITICAL CULTURE

GABRIEL ALMOND, 'Comparative Political Systems,' *Journal of
Politics*, Vol. 18, 1965.
Also *in* EULAU etc., eds., *Political Behaviour*, Free Press, 1956,
pp. 34–42.
and MACRIDIS *and* BROWN, eds., *Comparative Politics*, 1961, pp. 439–454.
S. H. BEER *et. al.*, *Patterns of Government*, Random House, 1958.
SPIRO, *Government by Constitution*.
ALMOND *and* COLEMAN eds., *The Politics of the Developing Areas*,
Princeton U.P., 1960.
LUCIEN PYE, 'The Non-Western Political Process,' *Journal of Politics*,
XX, 1961. Also *in* ECKSTEIN *and* APTER, *Comparative Politics*,
pp. 657–665.
ALMOND *and* VERBA, *The Civic Culture*, Princeton U.P., 1963.
LIPSET, *Political Man*, Heinemann, 1960.
S. E. FINER, *The Man on Horseback*, Pall Mall Press, 1962.
WORSLEY, *The Third World*, Weidenfeld and Nicolson, 1964.

3: TYPOLOGIES OF POLITICAL SYSTEMS

T. B. BOTTOMORE, *Sociology*, Unwin University Books, 1962.
SCHAPERA, *Government and Politics in Tribal Societies*, Watts, 1956.
GINSBERG, *Essays in Sociology*, Vol. III, 1961, 'Evolution and Progress'.
WEBER, *Theory of Social and Economic Organisation*.
JOHNSON, *Sociology, A Systematic Introduction*.
WORSLEY, *The Third World*.
KAHIN, PAUKER, PYE, 'Comparative Politics of Non-Western
Countries', *Am. Pol. Scie. Rev.*, 49, 1955.
SHILS, 'The Intellectuals in the Political Development of the New
States', *World Politics*, 12, 1959–60.

K. J. RATTRAM, 'Charisma and Political Leadership', *Political Studies*, XII, No. 3, 1961.

F. X. SUTTON, 'Social Theory and Comparative Politics', *in Comparative Politics*, ed. Eckstein etc.

FRED. W. RIGGS 'Agraria and Industria': Towards a Typology of Comparative Adminstration' in Siffin, ed., *Towards a Comparative Study of Public Administration*, Indiana U.P., 1957.

RIGGS, *The Ecology of Public Administration*, Asia Publishing House, 1961.

LA PALOMBARA, ed., *Bureaucracy and Political Development*.

S. N. EISENSTADT, *The Political Systems of Empires*, Free Press of Glencoe, 1963.

L. BINDER, *Iran, Political Development in a Changing Society*, Univ. Calif. Press, 1962.

D. LERNER, *The Passing of Traditional Society*, Free Press of Glencoe, 1958.

E. SHILS, *Political Development in the New States*, Mouton, 1962.

M. JANOWITZ, *The Military in the Political Development of New Nations*, Chicago U.P., 1964.

J. H. KAUTSKY, ed., *Political Change in the Under-developed Countries*, Wiley, 1962.

DAVID E. APTER, *The Political Kingdom in Uganda*, Princeton U.P., 1961. *The Gold Coast in Transition*, Princeton U.P., 1955.

ROBERT C. TUCKER, *The Soviet Political Mind*, Praeger Paperback, 1963.

4: THE POLITICAL SYSTEM—I

B. DE. JOUVENEL, *The Pure Theory of Politics*, C.U.P., 1963.

C. E. G. CATLIN, *Systematic Politics*, Allen and Unwin, 1962.

D. EASTON, 'An approach to an analysis of political systems', *World Politics*, Vol. 9, No. 3. April 1957.
Also *in* MACRIDIS and BROWN eds., *Comparative Politics*, 1961, Dorsey Press, pp. 81–94.

W. G. RUNCIMAN, *Social Science and Political Theory*, C.U.P., 1963.

R. E. DAHL, *Modern Political Analysis*, Prentice-Hall, 1963.

JOHNSON, *Sociology, A Systematic Introduction*.

J. D. B. MILLER, *The Nature of Politics*, Duckworth, 1962.

BREDEMEIER *and* STEPHENSON, *The Analysis of Social Systems*.

APTER, 'A comparative method for the study of politics', *Am. Journal Soc.*, LXIV, No. 3, Nov. 1958.
Also *in* EULAU etc. eds., *Political Behaviour*, pp. 82–94.

MITCHELL, *The American Polity*.

Select Bibliography

KARL W. DEUTSCH and WILLIAM J. FOLTZ, eds., Nation-Building, Atherton Press, 1963.
EISENSTADT, The Political Systems of Empires.

5: THE POLITICAL SYSTEM—II

ALMOND and COLEMAN, eds., The Politics of the Developing Areas.
B. HOSELITZ, 'Levels of Economic Performances and Bureaucratic Structures' in La Palombara, ed., Bureaucracy and Political Development.
ALMOND, 'Interest Groups in the Political Process', Am. Pol. Scie. Rev., LII, No. 1, March 1958.
Also in MACRIDIS and BROWN eds., Comparative Politics, pp. 128–156.
JAMES S. COLEMAN and CARL G. ROSBERG JR., eds., Political Parties and National Integration, in Tropical Africa, Univ. of Calif. Press, 1964.
H. LASSWELL, The Future of Political Science, Atherton Press, 1964.
BINDER, Iran, Political Development in a Changing Society.
MERTON, Social Theory and Social Structure.
EASTON, The Political System, Knopf, 1953. See also books on p. 133.
LIPSET, Political Man, Ch. III.

6: ECONOMIC AND SOCIAL DEVELOPMENT AND THE POLITICAL SYSTEM

LIPSET, Political Man, Chapter II.
ALMOND and COLEMAN, eds., The Politics of the Developing Areas.
LA PALOMBARA, ed., Bureaucracy and Political Development.
LERNER, The Passing of Traditional Society.
BINDER, Iran, Political Development in a Changing Society.
KARL DE SCHWEINITZ JR., Industrialisation and Democracy, Free Press of Glencoe, 1964.

7: STRUCTURAL-FUNCTIONAL ANALYSIS

BREDEMEIER and STEPHENSON, The Analysis of Social Systems.
JOHNSON, Sociology, A Systematic Introduction.
BOTTOMORE, Sociology.
RUNCIMAN, Social Science and Political Theory.
EASTON, 'Equilibrium and the Social System', in EULAU etc. eds., Political Behaviour, pp. 397–404.
S. BERNARD, 'Esquisse d'un théorie structurelle-fonctionnelle du système politique', Journal de l'Institut de Sociologie de l'Université Libre de Bruxelles, Jan. 1963, pp. 549–614.
PARSONS, The Social System.
ALMOND and COLEMAN, eds., The Politics of the Developing Areas.

Index

For Product Safety Concerns and Information please contact our EU
representative GPSR@taylorandfrancis.com
Taylor & Francis Verlag GmbH, Kaufingerstraße 24, 80331 München, Germany

www.ingramcontent.com/pod-product-compliance
Lightning Source LLC
Chambersburg PA
CBHW071850270326
41929CB00013B/2176

* 9 7 8 1 0 3 2 7 0 0 3 3 5 *